The Early Modern Englishwoman:
A Facsimile Library of Essential Works

Series II

Printed Writings, 1641–1700: Part 3

Volume 6

Mary Carleton

Advisory Board:

Margaret J.M. Ezell
Texas A & M University

Elaine Hobby
Loughborough University

Suzanne W. Hull
The Huntington Library

Barbara K. Lewalski
Harvard University

Stephen Orgel
Stanford University

Ellen Rosand
Yale University

Mary Beth Rose
University of Illinois, Chicago

Hilda L. Smith
University of Cincinnati

Retha M. Warnicke
Arizona State University

Georgianna Ziegler
The Folger Shakespeare Library

Patrick Cullen: Editor Emeritus

The Early Modern Englishwoman:
A Facsimile Library of Essential Works

Series II

Printed Writings, 1641–1700: Part 3

Volume 6

Mary Carleton

Selected and Introduced by
Mihoko Suzuki

General Editors
Betty S. Travitsky and Anne Lake Prescott

LONDON AND NEW YORK

First published 2006 by Ashgate Publishing

Published 2016 by Routledge
2 Park Square, Milton Park, Abingdon, Oxon OX14 4RN
711 Third Avenue, New York, NY 10017, USA

Routledge is an imprint of the Taylor & Francis Group, an informa business

Copyright © Mihoko Suzuki 2006

All rights reserved. No part of this book may be reprinted or reproduced or utilised in any form or by any electronic, mechanical, or other means, now known or hereafter invented, including photocopying and recording, or in any information storage or retrieval system, without permission in writing from the publishers.

Notice:
Product or corporate names may be trademarks or registered trademarks, and are used only for identification and explanation without intent to infringe.

British Library Cataloguing-in-Publication Data
Carleton, Mary, 1642?–1673
   Mary Carleton. – (The early modern Englishwoman : a
   facsimile library of essential works. Series II Printed
   writings, 1641–1700, Part 3 ; v. 6)
   1.Carleton, Mary, 1642?–1673 2.Carleton, Mary, 1642?–1673 –
   Trials, litigation, etc. 3.Imposters and imposture –
   England – Biography 4.Great Britain – History – Charles II,
   1660–1685 – Biography
   I.Title II.Suzuki, Mihoko, 1953–
   941'.066'092

Library of Congress Cataloging-in-Publication Data
See page vi for complete CIP block

The image reproduced on the title page and on the cover is from the frontispiece portrait in *Poems. By the Most Deservedly Admired Mrs. Katherine Philips* (1667). Reproduced by permission of the Folger Shakespeare Library, Washington DC.

ISBN 13: 978-0-7546-3104-0 (hbk)

CONTENTS

Preface by the General Editors

Introductory Note

Mary Carleton
    The Case of Madam Mary Carleton (1663)

*The Arraignment, Tryal and Examination of Mary Moders, Otherwise
    Stedman, now Carleton* (1663)

John Carleton
    The Replication, Or Certain Vindicatory Depositions (1663)

T.P. [Thomas Porter]
    A Witty Combat: Or, The Female Victor (1663)

F.B.
    *Vercingetorixa: Or, The Germane Princess Reduc'd to An English
    Habit* (1663)

J.G. [John Goodwin]
    The Memoires of Mary Carleton (1673)

Library of Congress Cataloging-in-Publication Data
Mary Carleton / selected and introduced by Mihoko Suzuki.
   p. cm. — (Early modern Englishwoman. Printed writings, 1641–1700, Series 2, Part 3 ; v. 6)
Includes bibliographical references.
ISBN 0-7546-3104-4 (alk. paper)
1. Carleton, Mary, 1642?–1673. 2. Impostors and imposture—Great Britain—Biography. 3. Female offenders—Great Britain—Biography. I. Carleton, Mary, 1642?–1673. Case of Madam Mary Carleton. II. Carleton, John, b. 1645? The Replication, or, Certain vindicatory depositions. III. Porter, T. (Thomas), 1636–1680. Witty combat, or, The female victor. IV. F. B. Vercingetorixa, or, The Germane princess reduc'd to an English habit. V. G. J. Memoires of Mary Carleton, commonly stiled the German princess. VI. Suzuki, Mihoko, 1953– VII. Title: Arraignment, tryal, and examination of Mary Moders, otherwise Stedman, now Carleton. VIII. Series.

HV6248.C178M4 2006
828'.408080351—dc22
                                      2005043541

PREFACE
BY THE GENERAL EDITORS

Until very recently, scholars of the early modern period have assumed that there were no Judith Shakespeares in early modern England. Much of the energy of the current generation of scholars has been devoted to constructing a history of early modern England that takes into account what women actually wrote, what women actually read, and what women actually did. In so doing, contemporary scholars have revised the traditional representation of early modern women as constructed both in their own time and in ours. The study of early modern women has thus become one of the most important – indeed perhaps the most important – means for the rewriting of early modern history.

The Early Modern Englishwoman: A Facsimile Library of Essential Works is one of the developments of this energetic reappraisal of the period. As the names on our advisory board and our list of editors testify, it has been the beneficiary of scholarship in the field, and we hope it will also be an essential part of that scholarship's continuing momentum.

The Early Modern Englishwoman is designed to make available a comprehensive and focused collection of writings in English from 1500 to 1750, both by women and for and about them. The three series of *Printed Writings* (1500–1640, 1641–1700, and 1701–1750) provide a comprehensive if not entirely complete collection of the separately published writings by women. In reprinting these writings we intend to remedy one of the major obstacles to the advancement of feminist criticism of the early modern period, namely the limited availability of the very texts upon which the field is based. The volumes in the facsimile library reproduce carefully chosen copies of these texts, incorporating significant variants (usually in the appendices). Each text is preceded by a short introduction providing an overview of the life and work of a writer along with a survey of important scholarship. These works, we strongly believe, deserve a large readership – of historians, literary critics, feminist critics, and non-specialist readers.

The Early Modern Englishwoman also includes separate facsimile series of *Essential Works for the Study of Early Modern Women* and of *Manuscript Writings*. These facsimile series are complemented by *The Early Modern Englishwoman 1500–1750: Contemporary Editions*. Also under our general editorship, this series includes both old-spelling and modernized editions of works by and about women and gender in early modern England.

New York City
2006

INTRODUCTORY NOTE

[*Although this volume appears in a tranche of single-author volumes, it offers the notorious Mary Carleton as a discursive focus because of her unusual public visibility, and therefore reprints some of the many texts about Carleton that appeared in the early modern period as well as a listing of seventeenth- and eighteenth-century texts concerning her* – General Editors]

Born in 1642 as Mary Moders (though some accounts date her birth in 1634 or 1639), Mary Carleton, commonly known as the German Princess, was a scandalous celebrity in Restoration London. By most accounts the daughter of a Canterbury fiddler, Carleton married first a Canterbury shoemaker, Thomas Steadman, then a Dover surgeon, Thomas Day. Returning from travels on the Continent she assumed the identity of a German aristocrat, Maria de Wolway, and married a lawyer's clerk, John Carleton, who also pretended to be an aristocrat. She gained notoriety as a result of her 1663 trial and acquittal for bigamy, which became the occasion of the publication of *The Case of Madam Mary Carleton*, in which she narrated her version of her life as a 'German Princess', the daughter of the Earl of Cologne. Competing versions of her life appeared in the published accounts of her trial as well as in her husband's pamphlets attacking her as an impostor.

In 1670, Carleton was condemned to be hanged for stealing a silver tankard, but the sentence was commuted, and she was transported to Jamaica in 1671. In 1673, having returned to London from Jamaica, Carleton was again indicted for petty theft (this time, of a piece of plate). Having unsuccessfully pled her belly, she was executed at Tyburn, duly confessing her sins and declaring her repentance as a Roman Catholic. The public's fascination with Carleton is evidenced in the many works on her published in 1673 – for example, the *Memoires* by J. G. [John Goodwin] and Francis Kirkman's *The Counterfeit Lady Unveiled*.

In addition to works that focused on Carleton, a number of texts written in the Restoration and the eighteenth century made reference to her: the diary of Samuel Pepys; Defoe's *Roxana*; and the popular series *Poor Robin's Almanack*, which satirically assigned red-letter days to 'the German Princess' as early as 1675 and as late as 1707. More than a decade after her death a 1684 pamphlet, *The German Princess Revived: Or The London Jilt*, gave an account of Jenney Voss, a cross-dressing thief who was, like Carleton, first transported and then executed for petty theft; the absence of any mention of Carleton in the body of the text indicates that the mere phrase 'the German Princess' remained current as a byword for imposture and thievery. Well into the eighteenth century Carleton's story was included in collections such as Alexander Smith's *A Compleat History of the Lives and Robberies of the most Notorious Highway-Men, Foot-Pads, Shop-Lifts, and Cheats of Both Sexes* (1719) and the anonymous *Lives and Adventures of the German Princess, Mary Read, Anne Bonny, Joan Philips, Madame Churchill, Betty Ireland, and Anne Hereford* (1755).

In her own time, Carleton was the subject of more than twenty-six pamphlets published in 1663 and 1673. Kirkman, a prominent Restoration printer, remarked of her notoriety in *The Counterfeit Lady Unveiled* (1673): 'So great novelty had not been known or seen in our age, nor in any other age as I can read of ... It was the only talk for all the coffeehouses in and near London'.

The proceedings of Carleton's 1663 trial for bigamy, recorded in *The Arraignment, Tryal and Examination of Mary Moders, Otherwise Stedman, now Carleton,* produced its own pamphlet war between Mary Carleton and her husband John, who wrote and published at his own expense an extended attack on Mary as well as a self-defence, *The Replication, Or Certain Vindicatory Depositions* (included here), and a longer *Ultimum Vale*. Her story inspired a play and a mock epic, texts which significantly responded to Carleton's own emphasis on performance and epic romance in fashioning her aristocratic identity. In T. P. [Thomas Porter]'s play *The Witty Combat: Or, the Female Victor,* Carleton acted the part of herself; in the mock epic *Vercingetorixa: Or, The Germane Princess Reduc'd to an English Habit,* by F. B., Carleton becomes a latter-day, if parodic, Spenserian heroine. Finally, *The Memoires of Mary Carleton* by J. G. [John Goodwin], which gives an account of Carleton's life, including her conviction for theft and execution in 1673, casts the whole affair in the literary framework of satire as well as of the romance epic of Ariosto and the proto-novelistic *Don Quixote* of Cervantes. Space does not permit the inclusion here of all the pamphlet literature, but this volume reprints Carleton's own *The Case of Madam Mary Carleton* along with representative selections from pamphlets written about her; a list of seventeenth- and eighteenth-century texts concerning Carleton is appended to the references section.

The Case of Madam Mary Carleton

Earlier male scholars, such as Ernest Bernbaum and C.F. Main, considered *The Case of Madam Mary Carleton, Lately stiled The German Princess, Truly Stated* to have been ghost-written by a male hack, but Elaine Hobby argued for, and recent feminist scholars have assumed, Carleton's authorship of the work. *The Case* expands upon her much shorter *Historicall Narrative of the German Princess*, published earlier in the same year (1663). In the first preface to *The Case*, Carleton buttresses her claim to be a 'German Princess', the daughter of an earl of Cologne, by appealing to Prince Rupert, Count Palatine of the Rhine, the grandson of James I and a royalist general during the Civil War who became privy counsellor to Charles II after the Restoration. By juxtaposing her own portrait to that of Rupert, she seeks visually to further her association with him. In her first prefatory letter, she protests the injustice of the 'Laws of this Kingdom made against *Femes Covert*' (A3), and in her text, she styles herself a princess in her own right, 'entirely possesst of [her father's] estate, without any Guardian or Trustees' (12–13). In the second preface, addressed 'To The Noble Ladies and Gentlewomen, of England', she takes care to deny the rumours of 'leudness, baseness or meanness' (A7) while seeking her reader's sympathy for an unhappy marriage. Placed early in a nunnery, she writes of her desire to escape women's allotted position of confinement: 'I blindly wished I were (what my Inclinations prompted me to) a man' (16); she further characterizes her experiences as recounted in her narrative as a 'prosecution of my masculine conceptions' (19), such as acquiring an education, learning a number of languages and reading history. Referring to literary genres such as romance and travel narrative, Carleton fittingly usurps the role of the male knight or explorer. In the transcript of the proceedings of the trial from which she emerged victorious, she calls attention to her familiarity with the legal system and its terminology, thereby challenging the gender hierarchy that closed the legal profession to women.

The copy reproduced here, chosen for its legibility and availability, is housed at the Newberry Library.

The Arraignment, Tryal and Examination of Mary Moders, Otherwise Stedman, now Carleton

The Arraignment, Tryal and Examination of Mary Moders, Otherwise Stedman, now Carleton, (Stiled, The German Princess) was considered an official and impartial account of the 1663 trial and was included in the *Collection of State Trials* by Thomas Bayly Howell and William Cobbett. It gives in full the indictment read to Carleton and then reports the dialogue between the clerk of the peace and Carleton as if it were a play. The pamphlet describes in detail the cross-examination of the witnesses and accused and gives Carleton's lengthy and eloquent speech in her own defence: she calls attention to her father-in-law's malice, to his vindictive determination to convict her, and to her accuser's failure to produce a marriage certificate or registration; she claims that her enemies bribed witnesses, adducing the inability of her supposed schoolmates from Canterbury to identify her. The judge instructs the jury to decide the case solely on whether Carleton had in fact been legally married before, a question that depends on one witness, and reminds the jury of the gravity of a guilty verdict and the unavailability to women of the 'benefit of clergy', a literacy test that would have allowed Carleton to escape execution. After a short deliberation, the jury returned a verdict of not guilty: the judge and the jury evidently concluded either that there was insufficient evidence to convict Carleton or that the inevitable punishment exceeded her offence. Despite her dramatic victory – a great number of people in the court hissed and clapped – her acquittal from the capital crime of bigamy reaffirmed her marriage to John Carleton; when she asked for her jewels and clothes to be returned, the court pronounced that they belonged to her husband.

The copy reproduced here, chosen for its legibility and availability, is owned by The Huntington Library.

John Carleton, *The Replication, Or Certain Vindicatory Depositions*

John Carleton wrote and had published *The Replication, Or Certain Vindicatory Depositions* in order to refute the accusation by the 'scurrilous scribbler', who claimed to 'demonstrate a great Friendship to that distressed Lady' (4), that he and his family had designs on Mary. Rather, his account of their first meeting emphasizes Mary's great charm, seductiveness, and wit, so that 'she left no room for suspition' and not only John, who boasts of being 'the most Critical person in the World', but also others 'of great Wisdom, Gravity, and Quality' were persuaded (4). Although John identifies himself as 'Gentleman of the Middle Temple' and quotes from Cicero and Ovid in Latin, his work indicates that he is no match for Mary. His likening of her to a Medusa's head which turned him into stone and of his marriage to that of Menelaus and Helen of Troy as well as to that of Adam and Eve suggests that his encounter with Mary has left him overpowered by her superior abilities and feeling emasculated. This is a theme that will run through his later and lengthier complaint, *Ultimum Vale*.

The copy reproduced here, chosen for its legibility and availability, is housed at the Newberry Library.

T. P., *A Witty Combat: Or, The Female Victor*

In *An Account of the English Dramatick Poets* (1691), Gerard Langbaine includes T. P. [commonly identified as Thomas Porter] as the author of *The French Conjurer*, a comedy 'founded on two Stories in the Romance of Guzman,* the *Spanish* Rogue' (520); and *A Witty Combat: Or, The Female Victor. A Trage-Comedy*. Pepys records his attendance at a performance of

The Witty Combat on 15 April 1664. This play about Mary Carleton emphasizes throughout the performative nature of class: Mary Moders (as she is here called) self-consciously sets out to fashion her identity, proud of the 'Education' and 'Wit' (D) that allow her to play the role of an aristocrat, deploying props such as a letter she intends to be intercepted and class-appropriate deportment such as generosity to servants. In a soliloquy she ponders alternative theatrical identities for herself, settling on that of a noblewoman in exile, modelling herself on Christina, the '*Sweedish* Queen' (Dv). John Carleton, the brother of the keeper of the inn where she lodges, though insulted by the cellarman as a 'Scriveners Boy' and a 'Rump of a Lawyer' (C3), also seeks to perform the part of a Lord by hiring a coach and footboys. Although the characters are initially taken in by Moders's performance as a 'person of Quality' (D2v), she is unmasked immediately after her marriage to John, and excoriated by his father as a 'base imposture' and 'Strumpet' (F2). At the conclusion of the play, a discussion among several 'Gentlemen' concerning her deportment at the trial and the prospective verdict is followed by the heroine's declaration to the audience that it has no grounds to judge her because 'The Worlds a Cheat, and we that move in it / In our degrees do exercise our Wit' (F2v). The play thus allows her the final word, spoken on stage by Carleton herself.

The copy reproduced here, chosen for its legibility and availability, is owned by the Folger Shakespeare Library.

F. B., *Vercingetorixa: Or, The Germane Princess Reduc'd to An English Habit*

Vercingetorixa: Or, The Germane Princess Reduc'd to An English Habit, a mock-epic in heroic couplets, derives its title from the feminine form of *Vercingetorix*, a famous leader of the Gauls in Caesar's *Bellum Gallicum* (*The Gallic Wars*) – familiar to those with basic education, because Caesar was taught in the schools. Following the example of the *Faerie Queene* and *Paradise Lost*, the poem is prefaced with multiple commendatory verses addressed to the poet. Styling its protagonists as Princess and Knight, it parodies Spenser by having Carleton, like Britomart before her, look into a mirror to see the image of her beloved, and a 'wise Magician' (5) – recalling Spenser's Merlin – designate him as her proper mate. The poem also makes clear its royalist allegiance by making repeated disparaging references to '*Oliver*' [i.e., Cromwell] (16), the execution of Charles, and the '*Rump-Parliament*' (31). In general, the poem is not unfavourable to Carleton, for example admiring her 'Pleading her Cause like fluent *Cato*' (41). It concludes by promising a second 'Canto', an account of Carleton's confinement, trial, and acquittal.

The copy reproduced here, chosen for its legibility and availability, is owned by The Huntington Library.

J. G., *The Memoires of Mary Carleton*

J. G. [John Goodwin]'s *The Memoires of Mary Carleton: Commonly stiled, the German Princess. Being A Narrative Of Her Life and Death* was one of three biographies produced after Carleton's trial and execution in 1673. The opening account of her life before she became entangled with the Carletons is a contradictory mixture of admiration for her 'very quick Apprehension' and her 'being Mistris of as many Languages as there are Liberal Arts' (4), and of debunking, at times misogynist and vulgar, satire: 'as common as a Barber's Chair, no sooner one was out, but another was in ... as much addicted to dissimulation as any of that sex' (6). The author directs his satire towards John Carleton (whom he mocks as an 'Irishman' [21]) and towards his family as much as toward Mary herself, finding the '*English* Lord and the *German* Princess' (26) equally guilty: 'to deceive the deceiver is no deceit' (24). In fact the author appears more sympathetic to Mary than to John, whose writings he characterizes as 'abusive Scribble' (38) while he approvingly describes Mary's 'nimble ... Reparties' (44) and equanimity at her trial. Although the account of the years after her acquittal is sketchy (he does assess her performance on stage as coming short of her performances in life), the narrative becomes more detailed after her return from Jamaica, a shift due primarily to the author's access to the testimony of the victims of her thefts. While emphasizing her hybrid or 'piebal'd' nature as 'English–German' and 'Protestant–Papist' (67) as well as her crossing the boundaries of gender, the author appears interested in understanding the essential constancy of Carleton's character throughout her life and in different places: 'Change of Aire works no change on the Affections of the Mind' (54). The essential quality for Carleton is her energetic intelligence: he calls her an 'active Woman ... Machivilianess, whose restless spirit was always plotting new mischiefs; her wits were always at work to find out new adventures' (75–6). Despite the clever pun on 'Machivilianess', the author's predominant judgement of Carleton is positive. Throughout, he places Carleton in literary contexts, comparing her to '*Guzman, Quixot, or Lazarillo*' (8), calling her a 'Lady Errant', mockingly praising her as a 'Brave bold *Virago!* Fit to be Queen of the *Amazons*' (90); while admiring Carleton's fluency in languages, including French, the author himself quotes from Virgil, Cicero, Ovid and other Latin authors, as well as from Ariosto's *Orlando Furioso*.

The copy reproduced here, chosen for its legibility and availability, is housed at The Huntington Library.

Twentieth-Century Scholarship and Criticism about Carleton

In 1914, Ernest Bernbaum's monograph treated the narratives about Mary Carleton as forerunners of the eighteenth-century English novel, and in 1956 C.F. Main wrote a bibliographic essay on Carleton with the aim of updating Bernbaum. Although Main located a number of pamphlets that Bernbaum considered to have been lost (including *The Case*), additional pamphlets that Main considered lost have now come to light, as well as some others of which neither had been aware. In 1961, Spiro Peterson included Kirkman's *The Counterfeit Lady Unveiled* in a collection of seventeenth-century English criminal fiction. In the 1980s, Carleton's *Case* received attention from critics interested in the new scholarship on gender and class: Janet Todd initiated the feminist re-examination of Carleton by discussing *The Case* as an example of 'growth in the power of female self-selling'; Michael McKeon extended Bernbaum's project from a Marxist perspective by treating *The Case* as an example of 'progressive' fiction of social mobility in his *Origins of the English Novel*. In the 1990s, the flourishing of feminist scholarship and the concomitant interest in recovering and re-examining women's writings refocused work on Carleton: Janet Todd and Elizabeth Spearing edited *The Case* along with *The Life of Mary Frith,* and Hero Chalmers and I examined Carleton's narrative as an exemplary representation of the female subject in seventeenth-century England. *Her Own Life*, an anthology of seventeenth-century women's autobiographies, included excerpts from *The Case*, making the text available for use in the classroom; in a separate essay, Helen Wilcox, one of the editors of the anthology, discussed *The Case* along with other autobiographies by Anne Clifford and Anne Wentworth. More recently, a selection from the same work was included in *The Longman Anthology of British Literature* (along with selections from Pepys and John Evelyn), exemplifying the rethinking of the canon of British literature in order to include more women writers, especially those not of the elite classes, as well as reflecting the renewed scholarly interest in Carleton. Similarly, Betty S. Travitsky and Anne Lake Prescott's anthology of paired writings from early modern England by both men and women included an excerpt from Carleton's *Arraignment* as a text that illuminates women's status under early modern law. In 2004, almost a century after Bernbaum's book, another monograph on Carleton was published by Mary Jo Kietzman, this time as an example of 'the self-fashioning of an early modern Englishwoman', as well as a new *DNB* article by Todd and an article by Valerie Wayne on Carleton's successful performance of class in the context of plays by Thomas Middleton and Aphra Behn.

Acknowledgements

I thank first and foremost the general editors of the series, Betty S. Travitsky and Anne Lake Prescott, for their invaluable help and patience throughout the process of editing this volume. The University of Miami Research Council funded my travel to libraries. The librarians at the Folger, Huntington, and Newberry libraries provided essential assistance in securing texts and obtaining permissions. Thanks are due also to my research assistant Jennifer Rodriguez and to Dymphna Evans, Jane Fielding and Ellen Keeling at Ashgate. As always, Frank Palmeri offered editorial and other much needed support.

References

Wing C586A [M. Carleton], Wing A3764 [*Arraignment*], Wing C585A [J. Carleton], Wing P2998 [T. P.], Wing B65 [F. B.], Wing G35B [J. G.]

Bernbaum, Ernest (1914), *The Mary Carleton Narratives, 1663–1673: A Missing Chapter in the History of the English Novel*, Cambridge, MA: Harvard University Press

Chalmers, Hero (1992), '"The Person I am, or What They Made Me to Be": The Construction of the Feminine Subject in the Autobiographies of Mary Carleton', in Clare Brant and Diane Purkiss (eds), *Women, Texts and Histories, 1575–1760*, London and New York: Routledge, 164–94

Damrosch, David, and Stuart Sherman (eds) (1999, 2003), *The Longman Anthology of British Literature*, vol 1, 'c: The Restoration and the Eighteenth Century', New York: Longman

Graham, Elspeth, Hilary Hinds, Elaine Hobby and Helen Wilcox (eds) (1989), *Her Own Life: Autobiographical Writings by Seventeenth-Century Englishwomen*, London and New York: Routledge, 131–46

Hobby, Elaine (1989), *Virtue of Necessity: English Women's Writing, 1646–1688*, Ann Arbor: University of Michigan Press

Kietzman, Mary Jo (2004), *The Self-Fashioning of an Early Modern Englishwoman: Mary Carleton's Lives*, Aldershot: Ashgate

Langbaine, Gerard (1691), *An Account of the English Dramatick Poets*, Oxford

McKeon, Michael (1998), *The Origins of the English Novel, 1600–1740*, Baltimore: Johns Hopkins University Press

Main, C.F. (1956), 'The German Princess; or Mary Carleton in Fact and Fiction', *Harvard Library Bulletin* 10 (1956): 166–85

Pepys, Samuel (1974), *The Diary of Samuel Pepys*, vol. 5, ed. Robert Latham and William Matthews, Berkeley: University of California Press

Peterson, Spiro (ed.) (1961), *The Counterfeit Lady Unveiled and Other Criminal Fiction of Seventeenth-Century England*, Garden City, NY: Doubleday Anchor

Suzuki, Mihoko (1993), 'The Case of Mary Carleton: Representing the Female Subject, 1663–1673', *Tulsa Studies in Women's Literature*, 12.1 (Spring): 61–83

Todd, Janet (1983), 'Marketing the Self: Mary Carleton, Miss F and Susannah Gunning', *Studies in Voltaire and the Eighteenth Century*, 217: 95–106, rpt. 1993, *Gender, Art and Death*, New York: Continuum, 81–95

―――― (1989), *The Sign of Angellica: Women, Writing and Fiction 1660–1800*, New York: Columbia University Press
―――― (1999), 'The German Princess: Criminalities of Gender and Class', in Rosamaria Locatelli and Robert De Romanis (eds), *Narrating Transgression: Representations of the Criminal in Early Modern England*, Frankfurt: Lang, 103–112
―――― (2004), 'Carleton, Mary (1634x42–1673)', *Oxford Dictionary of National Biography*, Oxford: Oxford University Press
Todd, Janet, and Elizabeth Spearing (eds) (1994), *Counterfeit Ladies: The Life and Death of Mary Frith / The Case of Mary Carleton*, New York: New York University Press
Travitsky, Betty S. and Anne Lake Prescott (eds) (2000), *Female and Male Voices in Early Modern England: An Anthology of Renaissance Writing*, New York: Columbia University Press
Wayne, Valerie (2004), 'Assuming Gentility: Thomas Middleton, Mary Carleton and Aphra Behn', in James Daybell (ed.), *Women and Politics in Early Modern England, 1450–1700*, Aldershot: Ashgate, 243–56
Wilcox, Helen (2000), 'Her Own Life, Her Own Living?: Text and Materiality in Seventeenth-Century Englishwomen's Autobiographical Writings', in Frank Dragstra, Sheila Ottway, and Helen Wilcox (eds), *Betraying Our Selves: Forms of Self-Representation in Early Modern English Texts*, Basingstoke: Macmillan; New York: St. Martin's Press, 105–119

Seventeenth-Century Texts concerning Carleton

1663
The Arraignment, Tryal and Examination of Mary Moders, Otherwise Stedman, now Carleton, (Stiled, the German Princess), Wing A3764
The Articles and Charges of Impeachment against the German Lady, Prisoner in the Gate-House, to Be Exhibited According to the Records of the City of Canterbury, in Order to Her Trial at the Sessions-House in the Old Bailey. With the Confession of the Witnesses and Her Father in Law, Touching Her Strange Pranks and Unheard of Designs. As Also a True Narrative of Her Proceedings since the 25th Day of March Last, to the Time of the Contract of Marriage, betwixt This Rare Inchantress, and That Worthy Gentleman Mr. Carlton, Wing A3805
B., F., *Vercingetorixa: Or, The Germane Princesse Reduc'd to an English Habit*, Wing B65
Carleton, John, *The Replication, Or Certain Vindicatory Depositions*, Wing C585A
―――― , *The Ultimum Vale of John Carleton, of the Middle Temple, London, Gent. Being A true Description of the Passages of that Grand Imposter, Late a Pretended Germane-Lady*, Wing C586
Carleton, Mary, *An Historical Narrative of the German Princess, containing All material Passages, from her first Arrivall at Graves-end, the 30th of March last past, untill she was discharged from her Imprisonment, June the Sixth instant. Wherein also is mentioned, Sundry private Matters, between Mr. John Carlton, and others, and the said Princess: Not yet Published. Together with a brief and notable Story of Billing the Brick-Layer, one of her pretended Husbands, coming to New-Gate, and demanding of the Keeper her Deliverance, on Monday the Eighth instant*, Wing H2106
―――― , *The Case of Madam Mary Carleton, Lately stiled The German Princess, Truly Stated*, Wing C586A

The Female Hector, or, The Germane Lady turn'd Mounsieur: With the manner of her comming to the White-Hart Tavern in Smithfield like a young lord in Mans Apparel, with a perriwig down to her shoulders, a rich belt, and a rapier by her side. How she deceiv'd the gentry at Amsterdam under the notion of the distressed lady of a banished lord, and being after discovered by a gentleman that came thither from London, was by order of the governour stript of her rich apparel, and banish'd the city in her own old weeds. How she deceiv'd an inn-keeper at Sandwitch in Kent, who pawnd all his plate, debursed his mony, and pass'd his word for her, till that he was forc'd to fly beyond sea, not daring to go home after she had given him the slip at Billingsgate, where she promis'd to pay him all out of a great treasure she told him she had there. How she made her escape from the Kings-bench, to the cost of the turn-key 100 pound thick, with all the rest of her notable pranks and cuning deceits from her birth to this present, that have not been yet publish'd, Wing F667

The Great Tryall and Arraignment of the late Distressed Lady, otherwise called the late Germain Princess. Being brought to her Tryal in the Old Bayley, on Thursday last the 4th Instant of this month of June, before the Right Honourable, the Lord Mayor, the Lord Chief Justice of Common Pleas, the Right Worshipfull, the Court of Aldermen, and All the rest belonging to that Most Honourable bench. The tenure of her indictment, of having two husbands and her answer to the same. Also the several witnesses which came in against her, with her absolute confutation upon each of their evidences by her acute wit and impregnable reasons, Whereby she was acquitted by publique proclamation, Wing G1758

The Lawyer's Clarke Trapann'd by the Crafty Whore of Canterbury, or, A True Relation of the whole Life of Mary Mauders, the Daughter of Thomas Mauders, a Fidler in Canterbury, Wing L739F

P., T. [Thomas Porter], *A Witty Combat: Or, The Female Victor*, Wing P2998

A True Account of the Tryal of Mrs. Mary Carlton, at the Sessions in the Old-Bayly, Thursday the 4th of June, 1663. She being Indicted by the Name of Mary Mauders alias Stedman. Published for Her Vindication, at Her Own Request, Wing T2406A

A Vindication of a Distressed Lady in Answer to a pernitious, scandalous, libellous Pamphlet; Intituled, The Lawyers Clarke Trappan'd by the Crafy Whore of Canterbury, Wing V463B

The Westminster Wedding; or Carlton's Epithalamium, Wing W1472

1671

News from Jamaica in a letter from Port Royal written by the German Princess to her fellow collegiates and friends in New-Gate, Wing 976B

1672

The Deportment and Carriage of the German Princess, Immediately before her Execution: and Her last Speech at Tyburn: Being on Wednesday the 22th of January, 1672, Wing D1077A

An Exact and True Relation of the Examination, Tryal, and Condemnation of the German Princesse, otherwise cal'd, Mary Carleton, at Justice-Hall in the Old Bailey, January 17: 1672. Also, An account of the pretended Treachery which she was to discover to the Bench; and the reason of her return from Jamaica, Wing E3619

1673

An Elegie on the Famous and Renowned Lady, for Eloquence and Wit, Madam Mary Carleton. Otherwise styled, the German Princess, Wing E417

G., J. [Goodwin, John], *The Memoires of Mary Carleton: Commonly stiled, the German Princess. Being a Narrative of her Life and Death*, Wing G35B

K., F. [Kirkman, Francis], *The Counterfeit Lady Unveiled. Being a full Account of the Birth, Life, most remarkable Actions, and untimely Death of Mary Carleton, Known by the Name of the German Princess*, Wing K630A [second edition corrected, 1679]

The Memoirs of the Life and Death of the Famous Madam Charlton; Commonly Stiled the German Princess. Setting forth the whole series of her Actions, with all their Intrigues, and subtile Contrivances from her Cradle to the fatal period of her Raign at Tiburn. Being an account of her Penitent behaviour, in her absteining from food and rest, in the Prison of Newgate, from the time of her Condemnation, to her Execution, January 23, 1672. Taken from her own Relation, whilst she was Prisoner in the Marshalsea, and other certain information. With her Nativity Astrologically handled, and an Epitaph on her Tomb, Wing M 1670

Memories of the Life of the Famous Madam Charlton; Commonly Stiled the German Princess, Wing M1700 [identical to Wing M1670 except for slight variations in title]

Some Luck Some Wit, Being a Sonnet upon the merry life and untimely death of Mistriss Mary Carlton, commonly called the German Princess, Wing S4515

1678

The Life and character of Mrs. Mary Moders, alias Mary Stedman, alias Mary Carleton, alias Mary —— the famous German princess. Being an historical relation of her birth, and fortunes, with the havock and spoil she committed upon the publick in the reign of King Charles the second. Together with her tragical fall at Tyburn, on the 22d of January 1678, added by way of appendix ('the second edition'), Wing L1990 [another edition in 1732]

Eighteenth-Century texts concerning Carleton

Caulfield, James (1793?), *Blackguardiana: or, a Dictionary of Rogues, Bawds, Pimps, Whores, Pickpockets, Shoftlifters, Mail-robbers, Coiners, House-breakers, Murderers, Pirates, Gipsies, Mountebanks, &c. &c.*, ESTC T95154

—————— (1794–95), *Portraits, Memoirs, and Characters of Remarkable Persons, from the Reign of Edward the Third, to the Revolution*, 2 vols, ESTC T139234

A Complete Collection of State-trials, and Proceedings for High Treason, and other Crimes and Misdemeanours; From the Reign of King Richard II to the End of the Reign of King George I (1730), second edition, 6 vols, ESTC T108500

A Complete Collection of State-Trials, and Proceedings for High Treason, and other Crimes and Misdemeanours; From the reign of King Richard II to the reign of King George II (1742), third edition, 6 vols, ESTC T148933

A Compleat Collection of State-Tryals, and Proceedings upon Impeachments for High Treason, and other Crimes and Misdemeanours; From the Reign of King Henry the Fourth, to the End of the Reign of Queen Anne (1719), 4 vols, ESTC T108672

A Complete Collection of State-Trials, and Proceedings for High-Treason, and other Crimes and Misdemeanours; Commencing with the Eleventh Year of the Reign of

King Richard II and Ending with the Sixteenth year of the Reign of King George III (1776–81), fourth edition, 11 vols, ESTC T112654

Granger, James (1775), *A Biographical History of England, from Egbert the Great to the Revolution*, second edition, 4 vols, ESTC T27645

Johnson, Charles (1734), *A General History of the Lives and Adventures of the Most Famous Highwaymen, Murderers, Street-robbers, &c.*, ESTC T112552.

The Life and character of Mrs. Mary Moders, alias Mary Stedman, alias Mary Carleton, alias Mary —— the famous German princess. Being an historical relation of her birth, and fortunes, with the havock and spoil she committed upon the publick in the reign of King Charles the second. Together with her tragical fall at Tyburn, on the 22d of January 1678, added by way of appendix (1732) [reissue of Wing L1990], ESTC T106293

The Lives and Adventures of the German Princess, Mary Read, Anne Bonny, Joan Philips, Madame Churchill, Betty Ireland, and Anne Hereford (1755), ESTC T118670

Salmon, Thomas (1735), *A Critical Review of the State Trials. Containing, I. The Substance of the Indictment... II. The Evidence. III. The Prisoner's Defence ...*, ESTC T151093

—— (1737), *A New Abridgement and Critical Review of the State Trials.* 2 vols, ESTC T106465

Smith, Alexander (1719), *A Compleat History of the Lives and Robberies of the most Notorious Highway-Men, Foot-Pads, Shop-Lifts, and Cheats of Both Sexes, in and about London and Westminster, and all Parts of Great Britain, for above an Hundred Years past, continu'ed to the present Time. Wherein their most Secret and Barbarous Murders, Unparalell'd Robberies, Notorious Thefts and Unheard of Cheats, are set in a true Light, and expos'd to publick View, for the common Benefit of Mankind,* fifth edition, 3 vols, ESTC T97129

MIHOKO SUZUKI

The Case of Madam Mary Carleton (Wing C586A) is reproduced by permission of the Newberry Library. The text block measures 109–111.5 × 57 mm.

The following pages are mis-numbered in the original: 46 for 38; 47 for 39; 43 for 42; 42 for 43; 38 for 46; 39 for 47; 73–139 for 85–151.

The illustration preceding signature B is a reduction of an oversize tipped-in fold-in in the original.

Hard-to-read words in the original:
Av: as in the loudest and clamorous noise of the War
A7v: I will not

Behold my innocence after such disgrace
Dares show an honest and a noble Face
Henceforth there needs no mark of me be known
For the right Counterfeit is herein shown

Ætatis meæ proximo 22 Ianuar: stilo novo vicesimo primo 1663 :

Io: Ch: sculp: M. G.

THE
CASE
OF
Madam MARY CARLETON
Lately ſtiled
The German Princeſs,
Truely Stated:

With an
HISTORICAL RELATION
OF HER
Birth, Education, and Fortunes;
IN AN
APPEAL
TO
His Illuſtrious Highneſs
PRINCE RUPERT.

By the ſaid MARY CARLETON.

Sic-ſic juvat ire ſub umbra------

London, Printed for *Sam: Speed* at the Rainbow in Fleetſtreet, and *Hen: Marſh* at the Princes Arms in Chancery-lane. MDCLXIII.

TO HIS
Most Illustrious Highness
PRINCE
RUPERT,
Count Palatine of the Rhine,
AND
Duke of Cumberland, &c.

Great Prince,

TO whom should the injured innocence of a Forain & desolate woman address it self but to your Noble and Merciful Protection, who with the *Maje-*

The Epistle
stical Glories of your Relation to this *Crown*, have most *condescending compassions* to the distressed and low *estate* of the *afflicted*.

For when I considered the general report of this your Generosity and Clemencie even in the greatest incitements of passion, amidst the victorious progress of your Arms; I could not but presume Your Highness would open Your ears to the Complaints of an abused Woman, in a Case wherein the Laws are altogether as silent, as in the loudest and clamorous noise of the War. Be-

Dedicatory.

Besides, the different necessity of my Cause, and the vindication of it, did inevitablie put me upon your Highnesses Patronage, I am traduced and calumniated as an Impostor (and the scandal continues after all the umbrages of it are vanished) and that *I* am not a *German*, nor so well descended there as I have alledged, and do and will maintain: Therefore to your Highness as the sacred and fittest Sanctarie of this truth I have betook my self; whose excellent purity I do so revere and honour, that I would not soil it with the

least

The Epistle

least tincture of a pretence, or paint of falshood for a world.

Your Highnefs drew your firſt Princely Breath, which hath ſince filled the Trump of Fame, within the limits of that circle of the *Rhine*, where I was born: and within the Confines of your paternal Dominions, my Infant cries were to be heard; and therefore with all alacrity I ſubmit my cauſe, and my *ſtronger cries for Juſtice* to your Highnefs, who partakes equallie of this and my Countrie.

Notwithſtanding I ſhould
not

Dedicatory.

not have been so bold as to have given your Highness this trouble, but that I have been informed you have been graciouslie pleased to pity my ruines, and to express your resentment of those incivilities I have suffered: And indeed that with the just indignation of other Noble persons, who are pleased to honour my desertion and privacy with their company, is the only support I have against those miseries I indure, the more unsupportable because irremediable by the Laws of this Kingdom made against *Femes Covert.*

The Epistle Dedicatory.

I take not upon me to dispute the equity thereof, but in all submiss obedience do cast my self and my cause at your Highnesses feet, most humbly requesting and beseeching your Grace and Favour in some extraordinary redress to be vouchsafed to

Your *Highnesses* most

Obedient and most Devoted Servant,

MARY CARLETON.

TO

Mary Carlton.

TO THE
Noble Ladies
AND
Gentlewomen,
OF
ENGLAND

Madams,

E *pleased to lay aside that severity of your judgement, by which you examine and castigate the licitness and conveni-*
ence

To the Ladies.

ence of every of your actions or passages of moment, and therefore seldom run into the misgovernment of Fortune, and cast a favourable eye upon these Novels of my life, not much unlike those of Boccace, but that they are more serious and tragical.

The breach that is made in my Credit and reputation, I do feel and understand to be very wide, and past

To the Ladies.

past my repayring, whatever materials of defence, excuse, and purgation I can bring to the scrutiny of men, who are not sensible to what sudden changes our natures are subjected, and that from ayry thoughts and motions, things of great influence, sometimes good, somtimes bad, have been exhibited to the world, equal to the most sober and firm resolution,

To the Ladies.

lutions of the valiant and the wise.

It hath been my mishap for one among many others to miscarry in an affayr, to which there are more intrigues and perplexities of kin and alliance, and necessary dependance, then to any other thing in the world, i.e. marriage: (Hymen *is as* blind *as* Fortune and gives her favours by guess) the mistaken advantages

To the Ladies.

tages whereof, have turned to my real damage: so that when I might have bin happy in my self, I must needs transplant my content into a sterile ungrateful soil, and be miserable by another. Yet have I done nothing dishonourable to your better beloved Sex, there is nothing of leudness, baseness or meanness in the whole carriage of this noised story, nor which

To the Ladies:

I will not, cannot justifie, as the actions of a Gentlewoman, with the account of which, from the beginning of my life, I here present you.

My Fortune not being competent to my mind, though proportionable to any gentile degree, hath frowardly shrunk into nothing, but I doubt not to buoy both my honor & estate up together, when these envious clouds are dispelled that obscure my brightness; The shadows are at the longest, and my fame shall speedily rise in its due lusture, till then, and ever I am,

Ladies, your devoted Hand-Maid,

MARY CARLETON.

THE

Mary Carlton.

The German Princess *with her Suppos'd* Husband *and* Lawyer.

THE
CASE
OF
Madam *Mary Carleton*
The Wife of
Mr. *John Carleton*,
Formerly ftiled
A German Princefs.

I Am fo much the the more beholden to my Innocence then to my Fortune, that I dare more confidently appear to the *Vindi-*
cation

cation of the one, then (through the malign deceit and injury of my Adversaries) to the *vendication* of the other; And *challenge* my enemies, and the *Spoils* they have made of me though I dare not *lay claim* to my *Friends*, my *Honour* and my *Estate*, which I shall keep concealed and inviolable from such rude and mischeivous hands as my *Person* hath been betrayed to. And yet the suspicious, noxious world doth very hardly conceive of me other then a Malefactor, and prefer my Wit and Artful Carriage to my Honesty, and take this untoward passage of my life for some festivous and merry accident of the times, and look upon me as a notorious (nay even among the more ingenious, but as a) notable person.

I can give no other reason for this, but the diligent and forestalling slanders of my accusers, who by lewd and most false suggestions have precluded all ways to my justification and defence; and my own unwearied patience in suffering those calumnies to pass unrefuted, further then by a legal Trial; not willing to cast any dirt upon those by way of regesting those foul-mouthed and libellous scandals by personal reflections; for I concluded that time, and the justice of my Cause and the Laws of the Kingdom would clearly absolve me, and that therefore such exasperations on my part would widen that breach, which the fraudulent covetousness of some Relations had made between my Husband and my self, and render it irreconciliable, when as I had resolved to redintegrate that affection, we were mutually bound to have for each other.

But since I have perceived, and have been fully satisfied and informed of their insatiable and implacable malice against me, not onely in prosecuting me with fresh Indictments after the Jury had acquitted me of the former, (though the grand Jury were so fully sensible of the Injustice and maliciousness thereof, that they would not receive any more) to say nothing also of the Witnesses brought against me, the blind and the lame (as to their tales and stories) procured by most wicked and detestable practises, (whom God forgive) but by advising my Husband after

ter my acquittal to forsake me, and renounce my bed, and so defeating me of my Jewels and other things of value of mine own, and leaving and exposing me destitute to the World, and to the pity or scorn of people, as my condition shall weigh with them: These unsufferable mischeifs have now at last extorted this Narrative from me, which I request the courteous Reader to give Credit to, and equally and seriously consider my Case.

It hath already made a great noyse in the World, sutable to that bluster my Husbands Friends had raised my Fortune and Qualitie to; but those High winds being laid by their weeping showers, I will secretly and clearly tell the World the naked truth of all this story, having premised a short Apology for my self, and given some account of this my (Errant-like) Adventure and Peregrination from the place of my native Country.

I was born at *Collen* in *Germany*, though incredulous people do take that for a pretence, and better concealment from any research that can be made after me; but as I have declared it before that Honourable Judicature in the *Old Bayly*, whose grave and reverend Authority, I hate to prophane and abuse with a lye ; so I do again assure the World by the greatest pledges of a Christian, that I am a Native of that place, and did continue in it, or thereabouts, the most part of my life hitherto. They that know it, know

know it to be one of the Miftreffes and compleateft Cities in that Empire, not onely famed for the birth of very Illuftrious perfons of Ancient Times, and the Honour it hath received from them (as I could largely inftance, efpecially from its Latine adject of *Agrippina*.) but for that modern glory it received by the entertainment of the King of Great *Brittain*, who was moft Hofpitably and Cordially, and with all imaginable refpect and Honour treated Here, when by vertue of *Cromwels* League with *France*, he departed that Kingdom.

I mention this at large, becaufe hence I took up thofe Refolutions, which fince, with fo much misfortune I have put in Execution. I obferved here the

the courteous civility, and affable good temper of the Englifh Nation, for by thofe Gentlemen that then attended the King I meafured his Kingdom. Thofe were perfons of fuch winning and obliging carriage, of fo eafie and familiar addrefs, and yet of that generofe and regardful demeanour, that I was hugely taken with fuch fweet Conditions, and being then young, by their frequent converfe in the Town, which was conftantly in my eares, came to fuch an acceptable knowledge of their manners, that I then thought of paffing over to that Country, for a fuller fatisfaction and delight I had promifed my felf among fuch a people.

As to my Parents, who by *Pythagoras* his fancyful Phylofophy,

phy, or rather envious Witchcraft, have been tranfmigrated into I know not what filthy and vile perfons, of the moft perdite and abhominable fort of men; I do defire pardon of their Ghofts, and fhall fprinkle their afhes with my tears, that I have by my unadvifed and ungoverned Refolution, raifed them from their quiet and Honourable Graves, to be the fufpicious and leud difcourfe of every malevolent and bufie tongue. But let fuch know, that my Fathers name was, *Henry Van Wolway*, A Licentiat and Doctor of the Civil Law, and Lord of *Holmftein*, a man efteemed for his fervices done to this City of *Colen*, in mediating their Peace and Security and Neutrality, in the *Swedifh* and *Ger-*

man War, and for other effects of his Counsels and Endeavours to our Ecclesiastical *Prince Elector*, and the House of *Lorrain*, in all those turmoyls of that Country, in the first rupture of the *Spanish* and *French* War.

I instance these remarques, because having been so long dead some nineteen years, I cannot better describe or Characterize him to strangers, though he were known in his own Country by other great and Noble actions, as well as for his long and ancient descent from an honourable Family of that name: which whosoever shall give himself the trouble of curiosity in Enquiring, may yet find preserved from the ruines of a destructive, and but just composed conflagration.

It

It will seem foolish and sottish flattery in me, to adorn His Monument with any more Elogy, to a strange and perhaps unbeleiving Nation, who have no faith for any thing they see not, or not have heard from plain and undenyable testimony. And if I be taken for uncharitable in this rigid imputation, let the practices of those, who have made their unreasonable incredulity, a pretence to their more barbarous cruelty, be my excuse to the World.

I shall not need therefore to particularize any more of him, for places and circumstances, and the like accidents, will be of no greater demonstration, or convincing verity, then those punctual relations of Sir *John Mandevile*, concerning things that

that were impossible to be in humanity and nature; and I will not so much as seem to impose upon the reader, with those nearer artifices of a Lye. I am capable of doing my self right, (which I suppose will be too readily interpreted to my disadvantage) by any means, within the compass of a womans understanding, and therefore if I thought I should need more ordinary ways, I would have applyed my self thereunto.

And so I will proceed to a further Narrative of my life, having acquainted the Reader, that it pleased God to take away both my Father and Mother before I was full three years old, but my Father died last suddenly, and left me entirely possest of his estate, without

out any Guardian or Trustees; the expectation of many people who had long designs both upon it and me.

Being thus an Orphan, and destitute of a Procurator, as we call it in our Law, the Church as next a Kin to such estates (and claims the right and disposal of the Ward) secured me, and what I had, in their hands, until such time as I should be of age and understanding to determine of my self and my Fortunes, which they hoped by so early a matriculation, and induction of me into the profession of the Religious, to grasp finally into their hands.

By them I was put into the Monastery or Nunnery of *Sancta Clara*, at this Infant age, and educated in all such breeding as was

was fit for one devoted to the service of God and his Church, wherein, if ignorance and innocence might render devotion acceptable, my young probation-years I may be confident were not offensive. But growing up to some capable years, and my active busie soul exerting it self, and biting as it were the bit of this restraint and confinement; the hours and days of this solitude and retirement, in which I was as it were buried as soon as I was born, grew most irksome and tedious to me, though I was not yet acquainted with the World. I felt some such strong impulses and natural instincts to be ranging abroad, and in action, as the first finders of *Terra Incognita*, were urged with, to the discovery of those Regions

Regions, of whofe Exiftence they had no further affurance then their own hopeful bodings and divinations.

The Difcipline alfo, began now to aggrieve me, and the more my thoughts wandred and ftrayed after my roaming and ftrange fancy of the worlds bravery (which I began now to take notice of, from the gallant appearance of perfons of quality, who frequented our Chappel) the more did the orders of the place ftreighten and fret me. I began to be weary of my Company, and the poverty of thofe *Votaries*, called in derifion, as it were the *Barefooted Clares*; and though I fuffered none of thefe hardfhips, nor underwent any of thofe nice penances and mortifications

ons, as having no inordinacies of youth to quell and subdue, yet the customary severity of such dealing with that sweetness and tenderness of our Sex, did much grate me; and I blindly wished I were (what my inclinations prompted me to.) a man, and exempt from that tedious life, which yet was so much the worse, because it was altogether passive and sedentary.

Nor could I find when more matured, but that Religion when imposed as a Task, and made an employment, was one of the greatest burdens I could endure; (though I have learned better things by practise and the troubles of the World, and could wish my self safe in such a retreat from the cares of of the future, and the doleful thoughts of my paſt time, and have a zeal for my Religion, the obligations and conduct whereof I have to my ſorrow ſo much in my late unadviſed reſolutions, abdicated and neglected.) I lookt upon it more as conſtraint, and not a voluntary act, wherein I had no manner of election; and my Libertine ſpirit which miſtook bold Humanity, and the dictates of a generous nature, for ſimple and genuine adoration, confirmed me in this opinion, and finally perſwaded me and prevailed with my Reaſon, which grew not up equall with my paſſion, to abandon this ſerene and bliſsful manſion, and venture upon the Worlds alluring, promiſing vanities.

I was arrived at that age wherein

wherein I was capable of being admitted, and professing my self a Nun, and to take upon me the Vows of the Order of perpetual Virginity, and the like requisites of that Monastical life, and therefore the Fathers and Confessors willing to make me a Proselyte, were very urgent that I would take the Habit and devote my self to a religious life, setting before me the many examples of some excellent Ladies and Gentlewomen then in the Cloyster (though it be one of the poorest Convents of all) who had great and noble friends, and great Estates (some of them) and had notwithstanding with all readiness of mind separated and estranged themselves from all worldly things, and consecrated themselves to God.

God. But my refolutions of forfaking that melancholy and filent abode, were fo far advanced, and fo obftinated in me to the profecution of my mafculine conceptions that I obtained my difcharge at the fame time, as I have partly hinted before, that his Majefty was in *Colen*, whom, with the reft of the defirous world I longed to fee: accompanied therefore with my maid who had attended me in the religious houfe, and a man-fervant who was my Steward or Bayliff abroad, and had prepared all things for my fecular eftate, I went to his Palace, were to pafs other rencounters, I met with a civil perfon, one Mrs. *Margaret Hammond*, the Daughter of Sir *Richard Hammond*, living fomewhere then in the North

North of *England*, a very accomplisht woman, who for her Religion had left *England*, intending to have betaken her self to the English Nunnery at *Lovain*; but some difficulties happening therein, she had journied up hither upon the same account, and perceiving me a stranger, did me the civility with her Countrimen, as to procure me the satisfactory view of the King and his Court, which could do no less then oblige me to invite her home, and to desire her while she staid at *Colen* to make use of my house, and what entertainment she found.

She was pleased to accept of this offer, and hereupon my curiosity having attained some part of its wish, we began to be be familiar, and I for my part to enquire into her condition, the reafon of her travail, and the news of the world, of all which fhe gave me fo delightful an account, infinuating the neceffity of her condition, with the perfection of her Endowments; that I told her if fhe could think it anfwerable to her content, to ftay with me, and be my Governefs, fhe fhould plentifully partake of my fortunes.

We agreed: but not to weary the Reader with thofe Inftructions and fundamentals of Education fhe laid, as fhe was a rare and abfolute Miftrefs of all thofe Arts, it will be fufficient to declare, that feeing fo much vertue in her, my greedinefs of communicating with it more freely

freely and clearly, put me upon giving her the trouble of teaching me the Englifh tongue, the lockt repofitory of fo many Excellencies.

This by a fond and moft pleafing diligence, I pretty well attained in a years time, having my Governefs always in my company, whither abroad, as I I ufed to ride fome miles, by Coach, or elfe pafs in a Pleafure-boat in the Summer, to acquaint my felf firft with my own Country; the tendernefs of my years, offering no man the occafion or thoughts of Love or Marriage, by which means I paffed free and unobserved, and then returned again to my Country retirement neer the City.

I now addicted my felf to the reading of Hiftory, and then to take off the gravity and ferioufnefs of that ftudy, to more facile paftimes of literature; Romances, and other Heroical Adblandiments, which being written for the moft and beft part in *French*, I made that my next bufinefs, though of leffer difficulty, to gain a knowledge in that Tongue, which being counterminous to ours, and fpoke promifcuoufly in the adjacent provinces of the *Walloon* Country, rendred it felf at my devotion.

The felicity of thefe two put me upon a defire of attaquing the reft of the European Languages, wherein without a *¿*legance, and as many can teftifie, I have more then a Smattering, and

and here was lately an *Italian* (as I have since been told upon discourse and some wonder of my readiness in them) who was one of my Masters; and who might have justified the truth of this and the rest of my story; his name was *Giacomo Della Riva*, well known to many Gentlemen in this Town.

In those and the like Studies, and other befitting Exercises of my sex, I past away the age of nineteen years, when I thought it high time to put all this Speculation and Theory into practice, and being furnished with such a fraught, and store of all Forraign necessaries, to lanch into the World, and see what returnes I could make of this stock, but in the interim of such meditations, an unhappy

happy accident, (at my being at the *Spaw* the laſt Summer, to drink thoſe medicinal waters) diſcovered me, and invited two ſtrange Gentlemen, which that place always is furniſhed with, to enquire further what I was: who having obtained my Country, and ſome inckling of my quality, made claym to be my ſervants. I could not in that place, the Mart of good manners, and where there is no nicety of converſe, but all perſons uſe their frankeſt liberty of viſit and diſcourſe, refuſe their Addreſſes, but ſeeing both of them ſo importunate, and both ſo diſparately and unſociably qualified for my choyce or approbation, I privately withdrew home, but could not ſo be rid of my odd payre of Gallants, who quick-

quickly haunted me and my House.

I was thus of a suden encompassed with two evils, of so indifferent a choyce, that I could not tell which was worse: one was an old Gentleman that had fair demeasnes about *Leige* or *Luyck* not many miles distant from *Colen*; a man of serious gravity and venerable aspect for his gray hayrs, but disfigured with some scars his youthful luxury had given him, which were repayred and supplemented by Art, but so that he plainly spoke his infirmity through the ruined Arches of his voyce. He accosted me the rude military way, for he had been a *Soldado*, and had caught as he said, that rotten hoarse cold, and snuffling in the Trenches of *Breda*, in the

the Brigade of Count *Henry* o *Naſſaw* in *Spinolas* Army, and had afterwards ſerved Mounſieur *Tilly* againſt the King of *Sweden*, whom he had ſeen fall at *Lutzen*, and therefore by no means muſt be ſaid no, or denyed his ſuit, ſince he had never known what a repulſe meant in his life.

The other was a young and pale Student in the Mathematicks, Chymiſtry, and Magick, like a fellow here that pretends to be Secretary to God and Nature,, and had exhauſted a plentiful eſtate, and was like to be a ſecond Dr. *Fauſtus*, and like my Lord, threatned either a contract with me, or with the Devil: for having loſt his Projection of the Philoſophers Stone, and decocted all his money

money and estate, his magical Glass shewed him me, who should by my fortune make him up again. In short, the one said he would storm and force me, and the other would make me yeild or else he would set *Archimedes* his unexperimented Engine at work, to remove me with him into some unknown World, to which he added the efficacy of his Spels and Conjurations.

I had by my Servants and some distant friends account of such a design as carrying me away, and forcing my consent by the **Gouty Cavalier**, who had some **Castellanes** and **Governours** in *Alsatia* his friends, and there was no less danger from my *M*agical Sweet-heart, but the open violence of the one, and the

the secret mines of the other were in prudence to be prevented by my absence, which I now concluded on by my self.

I shall not be obliged to give you any further account of my parentage or condion, for by such means my disaster here, may reach the ears of some Friends and Acquaintance, from whose knowledge my purpose is yet to estrange my self, (and to general enquiries *Collen* is too spacious and populous to afford any discovery) It will suffice, that I was liberally and honourably educated, and such principles laid, that I wonder at the superstructure of my fortune. I knew not what belonged to vulgar and Plebeian customes or conditions, and they that idlely tax my discourses and behaviour with mimick pedantry, know not the generous emanations of a right born soul. And so, that which probably makes me obnoxious to the censures of the multitude, as it hath to the hatred of my new Relations, is the low spiritedness, and pityful ignorance of such Mechanick and base people.

I would not be thought to boast of any accomplishments, which some persons (who favour my distrest estate, and they are of honour also) do please to acknowledge in me, all the use I can make of them, shall serve onely for an Argument against that vile and impertinent falshood, that I am of a most sordid and base extraction in this Kingdom, no bet-

better then the Daughter of a Fidler at *Canterbury*.

That Blasphemous lye was first broached in an Anonymous Libel, Entituled the *Lawyers Clark trappanned by the crafty Whore of* Canterbury, but at whose instigation I could never tell, nor did I make enquiry, but at last spontaneously the Roguery discovered it self at my being in custody neer *Newgate*, where I understood the Devil and necessity with the Writer, and undertaker, were as instrumental as the Devil and Covetousness, in the Occasioner of that report; but that fellow is of so leud and miserable an infamy, for such defamatory Pamphlets, that his name will poyson the eyes of the Reader, and fester even my charity in for-

forgiving him, to proceed.

 The time of my deliberated departure being come, and other intervening accidents having confirmed me to the pursuance of that journey, some pece-meal rumours whereof have been scattered up and down, not far distant from the truth, namely Constraint and awe of an unliked and unsutable match, which the freedom of my soul most highly abhominated and resented) I privately by night withdrew from my Governess, and by the way of *Utrecht*, where I stayed a while incognito, thence passed to *Amsterdam*, and so to *Rotterdam*, I came to the *Brill*, and there took Shipping for *England*, the *Elyzium* of my wishes and expectations being in hope to find it a Land of Angels, but I perceive it now to be, as to me, a place of Torments.

I am not single, or the firſt woman, that hath put her ſelf upon ſuch hazards, or pilgrimages, the ſtories of all times abound with ſuch Examples, enough to make up a volume. I might as well have given luſtre to a Romance as any any any of thoſe ſuppoſed *Heroina's*: and ſince it is the method of thoſe peices, and the Art of that way of writing to perplex and intricate the commencement and progreſs of ſuch adventures, with unexpected and various difficulties and troubles, and at laſt bring them to the long deſired fruition of their dear bought content, I am not

not altogether out of heart, but that Providence may have some tender and more courteous consideration of me; for I protest I know not what crime, offence or demerit of mine hath rendred her so averse and intractable as she hath proved to my designs.

Nor do the Modern and very late Times want Examples of the like adventures. I could mention a Princess, and great Personage out of the North, who not long since came into my Country, and hath passed two or three times between *Italy and France*, and keeps her design yet undiscovered, and is the onely Lady Errant in the World. I could mention another of a far worse consequence in this Country, a She-General, who

who followed the Camp to the other World in *America*, &c. and was the occasion of the loss of the designe. Mine compared with those are meer puny stories, and inconsiderable, I neither concerned my travail in negotiatiog peace, or carrying war, but was meerly my own free *Agent*.

Nor can I be blamed for this course, for besides the necessity and enforcements of forsaking my Country, without running into a more unsupportable condition of Marriage then this I am now in, (for my patience and suffering, and Continence I have, I trust in my own power, and shall endeavour to keep them undisturbed and uncorrupted, what ever temptations or occasions, by reason of this unjuſt ſeparation, now are, or ſhall be put upon me hereafter; but my life is not in my diſpoſal or preſervation, which I had certainly endangered at home, if I had been bedded to him whom my heart abhorred:) and beſides other reaſons, which I cannot in prudence yet render to the World, the very civility and purity of my deſign, without any luſtful or vicious appurtenant, would fairly excuſe me.

What harme have I done in pretending to great Titles? Ambition and Affection of Greatneſs to good and juſt purpoſes was always eſteemed and accounted laudable and praiſeworthy, and the ſign and character of a vertuous mind, nor do I think it an unjuſt purpoſe

pose in me to contrive my own advancement by such illustrious pretences as they say I made use of, to grant the Question, that I am not so honourably descended as I insinuated to the Catchdolt my Father in Law, (which yet by their favour they shall first better and more evidently disprove then as yet they have done, before I relinquish my just claym to my Honour) I think I do rather deserve commendation then reproach; if the best *things are to be imitated*, I had a good precept and warrant for my assumption of such a personage as they were willing to beleive me to be; If indeed by any misbecoming act unhandsome and unbefitting such a person, I had prophaned that quality, and bewrayed and
dis-

discovered any inconsistent meanness therewith (as it was very difficult to personate greatness for so long a time without slips or mistakes) I had deserved to be severely punished and abhominated by all Geetlemen; whereas after all these loads of imputations which my enemies have heaped upon me, I do with my acknowledgements to them for it) enjoy, and am happy in many of their loves and good estimation.

And I will yet continue the same respects, and make the World to know that there is no possibility of such perfections, without a more intent care and elegancy of learning, to which I have by great labour and industry attained.

I

I need not therefore engage further in this preluminary part of my defence, onely as an irrefragable confutation of the poorneſs of my birth, and in this Kingdom, I would have my Adverſaries know, as ſome of them do, though they don't well underſtand, that the ſeverall languages I have ready and at my command, as the *Greek*, *Latine*, *French*, *Italian*, *Spaniſh*, *Engliſh*, and ſomething of the Oriental Tongues, all which I pronounce with a Dutch Dialect and Idiome, are not common and ordinary endowments of an Engliſh Spinſter, no not of the beſt rank of the City. And ſince I muſt praiſe my ſelf, in ſhort, I came not here to learn any thing for uſe or ornament of of a woman, but onely the ways to a better fortune.

I come now to the matter of fact, the first place I touched at was *Gravesend*, where I arrived towards the end of *March*, and without any stay took a Tide-boat came to *London* in company with a Parson or Minister, who officiously, but I suppose out of design, gave me the trouble of his service and attendance to the *Exchange-Tavern* right against the *Stocke*, betwixt the *Poultry* and *Cornhil*, the house of one Mr. *King*, not having any knowledge of the Master or his acquaintance, and free, God knows from any design, for I would have entred any other house if I had found the doors open, or could have raised the folks nearer to my landing

landing, for I was diftempered with the nights paffage; but it was fo early in the morning, five a clock, that there was no body ftirring elfewhere, onely here by mifhap *Mr. King* himfelf was up and ftanding at the Bar, telling of brafs farthings, whom the Parfon defired to fill a pint of wine, which he readily performed, and brought to a room behinde the Bar. while the wine was a drinking, (which was Rhenifh wine, the complement being put upon me by the Parfon as the fruit of my own happy Country) Sir *John* very rudely began to accoft me, and to offer fome incivilities to me, which I found no other way to avoid, then by pretending want of reft to the *M*after of the houfe, and
acquaint

acquainting him with my charge of Jewels, and that I was as I do juftifie my felf to be a perfon of Quality. Hereupon a room was provided for me to repofe my felf in, and the Clergyman took his leave with a troublefome promife of waiting upon me another day to give me a vifit, which I was forced to admit, & to tell him, I would leave word where-ever I went; but he confidering as I fuppofe of the unfeafiblenefs of his defires, and the publiquenefs of the place, neglected his promife and troubled me no more.

He being gone, *Mr. King* began to queftion me, what Country woman I was, and of what Religion, I frankly told him; and acquainted him withall

all what charge *I* had about me, which to secure from the danger of the Town, that was full of cozenage and villany, he advised me to stay with him till I could better provide for my self.

I rested my self here till eleven a clock at noon: when *I* arose, and was very civilly treated by *Mr. King*, who well knowing *I* was a stranger and well furnished with money, omitted no manner of respect to me, nor did *I* spend parcimoniously, and at an ordinary rate, but answerable to the quality and account, at their fetching and itching questions, *I* gave of my self.

This invited him earneſtly, with all ſubmiſs addreſs to requeſt my ſtaying with them till I had diſpatched, and had provided all things for my publique appearance, for the better furniſhing and equiping whereof, I acquainted Him I would ſend by Poſt to my Steward, for the return of ſome moneys to defray the expences thereof, which Letters he viewed, and conceived ſuch imaginations in his Head thereupon, that it never left working till it had wrought the effect of his finely begun, and hopefully continued Enterpriſe.

Theſe Letters he himſelf delivered at my deſire, to have them carefully put into the Male, to the Poſt-Houſe; and thereafter obſerved me with moſt

most manifest respects. In the *Interim* of the return of these moneys, I was flightly, and as it were by the by, upon discourse of my Country (wherein they took occasion to be liberally copious) engaged into some discovery of my self, my estate and quality, and the nature of both, the causes of my coming hither, &c. but I did it so unconcernedly, and negligently, as a matter of no moment or disturbance to me, though I had hinted at the discontent of my match, that this did assure them that all was real, and therefore it was time to secure my estate to them by a speedy and secret marriage.

Let the World now judge, whither being prompted by such plain and publique signes of a design

design upon me, to counterplot them, I have done any more then what the Rule, and a received principle of Justice directs: *to deceive the deceiver, is no deceit.*

I knew not neverthelefs, which way their Artifices tended, till Master *King*, brought into my acquaintance old Mr. *Carleton* his Father in Law, and foon after Mr. *John Carleton* his Son: it feems it had been confulted, to have preferred *George* the Elder Brother: He troubled with a fimple modefty, and a mind no way competent to fo much greatnefs, was laid afide, and the younger flufht and encouraged to fet upon me. By this time they had obtained my Name from me, *viz. Maria de Wolway*, which paffage alfo hath

hath suffered by another leuder Imposture, and allusory sound of *De Vulva*: in the language of which I am better versed, then to pick out no civiller and eleganter impress.

To the Addresses of Mr. *John Carleton*, I carried my self with so much indifference, not superciliously refusing his visits, or readily admitting his suit, not disheartening him with a severe retiredness, or challenges of his imparity, nor encouraging him with a freedom or openness of Heart, or arrogance of my own condition, that he and his friends were upon the spur to consummate the match, which yet I delayed and dissembled with convenient pretences, but herein I will be more particular in the ensuing Pages.

In the mean while, to prevent all notice of me, and the difturbance of their proceedings, that might be occafioned thereby, they kept me clofe in the nature of a Prifoner, which though I perceived, yet I made no femblance thereof at all, but colluded with them in their own arts, and pretended fome averfnefs to all company, but onely my enamourate, Mr. *Carleton:* nor was any body elfe fuffered to come near me, or to fpeak with me; Infomuch, as I have bin informed, that they promifed 209*l.* to one *Sackvil,* whom for his advice, they had too forwardly, as they thought imparted the bufinefs, the fum of 200*l.* to be filent, left that it fhould be heard at Court, and fo the Eftate and Honour which they had

had already swallowed, would be lost from their Son, and seized by some Courtier, who should next come to hear of this great Lady.

After many visits passed betwixt Mr. *Carleton* and my self, Old Mr. *Carleton* and Mr. *King* came to me, and very earnestly pressed the dispatch of the Marriage, and that I would be pleased to give my Assent, setting forth with all the qualities and great sufficiencies of that Noble person, as they pleased to stile him. I knew what made them so urgent, for they had now seen the answers I had received by the Post, by which I was certified of the receipt of mine, and that accordingly some thousands of Crowns should be remitted instantly to *London*, and

Coach and Horses sent by the next Shipping, with other things I had sent for, and to reinforce this their *commendamus* the more effectually, they acquainted me, that if I did not presently grant the suit, and their request, Mr. *Carleton* was so far in love with me, that he would make away with himself, or presently travail beyond Sea, and see *England* no more.

I cannot deny, but that I could hardly forbear smiling, to see how serious these *Elders* and *Brokers* were in this *Love-killing* story, but keeping to my business, after some demurs and demands, I seemed not to consent, and then they began passionately, urging me with other stories, some of which long repetition I will now insert:

Wednesday

Wednesday the first of *April*, Mrs. *King* made a great Feast, where were divers persons of quality, as she said, amongst the rest, her Brother Mr. *John Carleton*. At which entertainment Mrs. *King* did advise me to call her Cozen, the which I did. *Thursday* the second of *April*, Mr. *John Carleton* came in his Coach, with two Footmen attending on him, calling him my *Lord*, and Mrs. *King* did also call him my *Lord*. With that I asked Mrs. *King*, if it was not the same person that dined with us yesterday; she said, True, it was so, but he was in a Disguise then, and withal, that in a humour he would often do so: *But*, saith she, *I do assure you he is a Lord.* Upon that I replied, *Then his father must be an Earl, if living.* She affirmed, that he was a person of great honour. The same time my Lord presented me with a rich box of Sweetmeats: I could do no less then thankfully accept thereof.

My Lord came every day to *Mr. Kings,* and by his importunity would carry me abroad in a Coach to *Holloway* and *Islington.* *Mrs. King* would often ask me, what my Lord did say to me; I told her, *nothing that I observed, but his Lordship abounded in civility, mixt with complements.* How; said she, *Madam, He loves you.* Loves me, for what *Mistris King?* I replied. She said, *For your great parts and Endowments.* I asked her, *How my Lord could tell that I had either.* She said, *My Lord must have very good eyes if he could see within*

within me, or else I must be very transparent.

After which, I did order the matter so, that his access to me was not so easie: Mistris *King* importuneth me to admit my Lord to visit me; I told her plainly, *That I did not understand his Lordships meaning.* He provided me a great Banquet, at which his Lordships mother was very fine drest, who questioned what I was. I told my Lord, *That I had received civilities from him, and he had the like from me, and that I had no necessity to give any account to any person what I was, for any thing that I intended; and that if any design or affair of his required any such thing out of convenience, or otherwise he might forbear it.* His Lordship excused his mothers inquifition, by faying, *She was his Mother, and that Parents did think themfelves concerned, in looking after the good of their Children.* But (faid he) *Madam, Wave all this, however I will marry you to morrow.* What (faid I) *my Lord, without my confent*: my Lord, *I defire your Lordfhip not to come near me any more, I will not lye under fuch queftioning and fcrutiny: Your Lordfhip will be fafe in following my advice, in not coming at me any more.* Upon this his Lordfhip wept bitterly: I with-drew my felf from his prefence: He writ a Letter of high Complements to me (the which Letter was loft in that violent furprize of me and my things, by the force of *Mr. George Carleton*, my Husbands Father

Father.) At the same time I had a Gown making upon my own account, by *Mrs. Kings* Taylor in the *Strand*, I took a Coach and went thither; all this while the young Lord not knowing where I was, remained impatient until my return, where I found him standing at the Bar (in a very pensive and melancholy manner, as if he had been arraigned for not paying his reckoning) at the *Exchange-Tavern*, and suddenly claspt about my middle, and violently carryed me to my Chamber. I asked his meaning: He answered, *That I had forbid him my presence; that it had almost made him mad; that he desired nothing more of me, then but to let him look upon me.* Upon that he did, with a very strange gesture, fix his eyes upon

upon me: In compassion to him, I askt him what his Lordship meant, and intended; he replied in a kind of discomposed manner, *I would have you to be my Wife*. I answered him, *My Lord, I rather think you have courted me for a Mistress, then for a Wife: I assure you, that I will never be a Mistris to the greatest of Princes, I will rather chuse to be a Wife to the meanest of men.*

Upon which, he uttered divers asseverations in confirmation of the realty of his intentions, and earnest desire of the Honour in making me his Wife, without any respect to what I had.

After my Lord had insinuated his affections so far, that I began to understand him, and did mix and scatter some such like accep-

acceptable words, which put him into some confidence of obtaining me; he began like other Lovers to set forth the amplitude of his Fortunes, and those brave things he would do if I would finish his suit; among many other finenesses and Grandures he would bestow on me, I well remember, he told me that he had given order for a great Glass Coach of the new fashion to be presently made, against our wedding was over, where eleven or twelve might conveniently sit, and that he would sute it with a set of Lacquies and Pages, the neatest and handsomest of the Town for their Liveries and persons. That I might see I had married a person that not onely dearly loved me, but would also highly honour

nour me, with the most splendid accomodations that *England* yeilded.

At the very same time, he had changed as he told me (and part of it I saw) two hundred pound of silver, into two hundred peices of Gold, for the better portableness thereof, that his Princess might see nothing of meanness belonging to him, and that as soon as the Coach was made and all things fitted to it, he would presently go to Court, and carry me with him, and introduce me to the King and Queen: his further intention being, which as yet he concealed to me, to get a *Knight-hood*, and have something of honour to oppose the envy of men, that so great an Estate was conferred on a private person.

And

And now my Lord spoke nothing but Rodomantadoes of the greatness of his Family, of the delights and stateliness of his Lands and houses, the game of his Parks, the largeness of his stables, and convenience of Fish and Foul, for furnishing his liberal and open House-keeping, that I should see *England afforded more pleasure then any place in the World*, but they were (without the Host) reckoned and charged before-hand to my account, and to be purchased with my estate, which was his, by a figure of anticipation, when we two should be all one, and therefore he lyed not, but onely equivocated a little.

But

But he did not in the least mention any such thing to me, nor made any offer of enquiry what I was, no not the least semblance or shadow of it; he seemed to take no notice of my fortunes, it was my person he onely courted, which having so happily and accidentally seen, he could not live, if I cherisht not his affections. Nor did I think it then convenient or civil to question the credit of his words, and the report given me of him. His demeanour I confess was light, but I imputed that to his youth, and the vanity of a Gallant, as necessary a quality, and as much admired as wit in a Woman.

The last day of my virgin state, *Easter* Eve, the Taylor brought me my Gown to my Lodging, I being drest and adorned with my Jewels, he again renewed his suit to me; with all importunity imaginable: His courteous Mother was also now most forward, pressing me to consent, by telling me, that *she should lose her Son, and his wits*, he being already impatient with denyals and delays, adding withal, that he was a person hopeful, and might deserve my condiscention: I withstood all their sollicitation, although they continued it until twelve of the Clock that night. The young Lord at his taking his leave of me, told me he would attend me betimes the next morning, and carry me to St. *Pauls* Church

Church, to hear the Organs, saying, that there would be very excellent Anthems performed by rare voices, the morrow being Sunday, the 19. of *April* last: in the morning betimes, the young Lord cometh to my Chamber-door, desiring admittance, which I refused, in regard I was not ready; yet so soon as my head was dressed, I let him have access: he hastned me, and told me his Coach was ready at the door, in which he carried me to his Mothers in the *Grey-fryers*, *London*, where I was assaulted by the young Lords tears, and others to give my consent to marry him, telling me that they had a Parson and a *License* ready, which was a meer falshood, and temporary falacy to secure the match.

So

So on *Easter* morning, with three Coaches, in which with the Bride and Bridegroom were all the kindred that were privy to the businefs, and pretended a Licence, they carried me to *Clothfair* by *Smithfield*, and in the Church of Great St. *Bartholomews*, Married me by one Mr. *Smith*, who was well paid for his paynes: and now they thought themfelves poffeffed of their hopes, but becaufe they would prevent the noife and fame, of their good fortune from publique difcourfe, that no finifter accident might intervene, before Mr. *Carleton* had bedded me, offence being likely to be taken at Court, (as they whifpered to themfelves) that a Private Subject had Married a Forraign Princefs, they had before

before determined to go to *Bar-net*, and thither immediately after the celebration of the Marriage we were Driven in the Coaches, where we had a handsome treatment, and there we staid Sunday and Munday, both which nights Mr. *Carleton* lay with me, and on Tuesday morning we were Married again, a Licenfe being then obtained to make the match more faſt and ſure, at their inſtance with me to conſent to it.

This being done, and their fears over, they reſolved to put me in a garb befitting the Eſtate and dignity they fancied I had; and they were ſo far poſſeſſed with a beleif of it, that they gave out, I was worth no leſs then 80000 *li. per annum*, and my Husband, as I muſt now ſtile him

him, publifhed fo much in a Coffee-houfe; adding withal, to the extolling of his good hap, that there was a further Eftate but that it was my modefty or defign to conceal it: And that he could not attribute his great fortune to any thing but the Fates, for he had not any thing to ballance with the leaft of my Eftate and Merits: So do conceited heighths of fudden profperity and greatnefs dazzle the eyes and judgement of the moft, nor could this young man be much blamed for his vainglorious miftake.

My Cloaths being made at the charge of my Father in Law, and other fineries of the mode & fafhion fent me by fome of his Kindred and friends (who prided themfelves in this happy affinity,

finity, and who had an eye upon some advantages also, and therefore gave me this early bribe, as testimonies of their early respect, & as for Jewels I had of mine own of all sorts, for Necklaces, Pendants and Bracelets, of admirable splendor and brightness. I was in a Princelike attire, and a splendid equipage and retinue, accoutred for publique view among all the great Ladies of the Court and the Town on *May* day ensuing. At which time in my Lady *Bludworths* Coach, which the same friends procured for my greater accommodation, and accompanied with the same Lady with Footmen and Pages, I rode to Hide-Park, in open view of that celebrious Cavalcade and Assembly, much gazed upon by them

them all, the eximiousness of my fortune drawing their eyes upon me; particularly that noble Lady gave me precedence, and the right hand, and a neat Treatment after our divertisement of turning up and down the park.

I was altogether ignorant of what estate my Husband was, and therefore made no nicety to take those places his friends gave me, and if I be taxed for incivility herein, it was his fault that he instructed me no better in my quality, for I conceited still that he was some landed, honorable and wealthy man.

Things yet went fairly on, the same observances and distances continued, and lodgings befitting a person of Quality taken for me in *Durham Yard*,

at

at one mr. *Greens*, where my husband and I enjoyed one another with mutual complacency, till the return of the moneys out of *Germany* failing the day and their rich hopes, old Mr. *Carleton* began to suspect he was deceived in his expectation, and that all was not gold that glistered: but to remove such a prejudice from himself, as if he were the Authour of those scandals that were now prepared against my innocence, a Letter is produced, and sent from some then unknown hand, which reflected much upon my Honour and Reputation; and thereupon on the fifth or sixth of *May* ensuing, *I* was by a Warrant dragged forth of my new Lodgings, with all the disgrace and contumely that could be be caſt upon the vileſt offender in the World, at the inſtigation of old Mr. *Carleton*, who was the Proſecutor, and by him and his Agents deveſted and ſtript of all my cloaths, and plundred of all my jewels, and my money, my very bodyes, and a payr of ſilk Stockings, being alſo pulled from me, and in a ſtrange array carried before a Juſtice.

But becauſe this ſtory hath not yet been fully diſcovered, I will more manifeſtly here declare it; That Letter abovefaid, came from one Mr. *John Clay*, the younger Son of Mr. *Clay* a Drugſter at the Bear and Mortar in *Lumber-ſtreet*, a Servant and Admirer of Mrs. *King* my fine Siſter in Law, (who becauſe her Husband hath a weak head, (though

(though he sat like a Parliament man once in *Richard Cromwels* time for three days, as since I have been informed) must have an assistant to carry on the business. The contents of this Letter were neer to this purpose,

SIR,

I Am unknown to you, but hearing that your Son Mr. John Carleton *hath married a Woman of a pretended great Fortune, and high birth, I thought fit to give you timely notice of what I know, and have heard concerning her, that she is an absolute Cheat, hath Married several men in our County of* Kent, *and then run away from them, with what they had; If it be the same woman*

woman I mean, she speaks several languages fluently, and hath very high Breasts,&c.

I was at the Exchange Tavern, as it was designed, when this Letter was brought, and thereupon their countenances were set to a most melancholly look, and pale hue, which shewed a mixture of fear and anger: presently I was brought before the inquisition of the Family, and examined concerning the said Letter, which I constantly, innocently, and disdainfully denyed, so that they seemed something satisfied to the contrary, and so my Husband and I went home in a Coach, but that very same night, all the gang, with one Mrs. *Clark* a Neighbour to *King*, came

came to my lodging where after moſt vile language, as Cheating Whore, and the like, they pulled me up and down, and kept me ſtript upon a bed, not ſuffering my Husband to come neer me, though I cryed out for him to take my part, and do like a man to ſave me from that violence, who at a diſtance excuſed it, by putting all this barbarity upon his Father; In fine they left me not a rag, rincing every wet cloath out of the water, and carrying them away, The whole, was a moſt unwomanly and rude Action at the beſt of it, if I had been ſuch as they pretended me to be, and not to be parralleld, but by a ſtory I have lately heard of the ſix woman ſhavers in *Drury-Lane*.

See

See the fickleness and vanity of humane things, to day *embellished*, and adorned with all the female Arts of bravery and gallantry, and courted and attended on by the best rank of my sex, who are jealous observers what honour and respect they give among themselves, to a very punctilio; and now disrobed and disfigured in mishapen Garments, and almost left naked, and haled and pulled by Beadles, and such like rude and boysterous fellows, before a Tribunal, like a leud Criminal.

The Justices Name was Mr. *Godfrey*, by whose Mittimus, upon an accusation managed by Old Mr. *Carleton*, that I had married two Husbands, both of them in being, I was committed to the *Gate-house*. Being interrogated

interrogated by the Justice, whither or no I had not two Husbands as was alledged, I Answered, if I had, He was one of them, which I beleive incensed Him something the more against me, but I did not know the Authority and dignity of his place, so much am I a stranger to this Kingdom.

There were other things and crimes of a high nature objected against me besides, That I cheated a Vintner of sixty pounds, and was for that committed to Newgate, but that lye quickly vanished, for it was made appear, That I was never a Prisoner there, nor was my name ever recorded in their books; And that I pickt a Kentish Lords pocket, and cheated a French Merchant of Rings,
Jewels

Jewels and other Commodities, That I made an escape, when sold and shipt for the *Barbadoes*, but these were urged onely as surmises; and old *Carleton* bound over to prosecute onely for Bigamy, for my having two husbands.

Thus the world may see how industrious mischeif is to ruine a poor helpless and destitute Woman, who had neither money, friends nor acquaintance left me; yet I cannot deny that my Husband lovingly came to me at the Gatehouse the same day I was committed, and did very passionately complain of his Fathers usage of me, meerly upon the disappointment, as he said, of their expectations, and that he could be contented to love me as well as ever, to live with

with me and own me as a wife, and used several other expressions of tenderness to me.

Nor have I less affection and kind sentiments for him, whom I own and will own till death dissolve the union, and did acquaint him with so much there, and protested my innocence to him, nor do I doubt could he have prevailed with his Father, but that these things had never happened. If now after my vindication he prove faithless and renege me, his fault will be doubly greater, in that he neither assisted my innocence when endangered, nor cherished it when vindicated by the Law.

In this prison of the Gatehouse I continued six weeks, in a far better condition then I pro-

promised my self, but the greater civilities I ow to the Keeper: as I am infinitely beholding to several persons of quality, who came at first I suppose out of curiosity to see me, and did thereafter nobly compassionate my calamitous, and injurious restraint.

All that troubled me was an abusive pamphlet which went under my Husbands name, wherein, most pitifully he pleaded his frailty and misfortune, and intituled it to no lesser precedent then *Adam*, which I suppose was had out of the new *Ballad*, of *your Humble Servant*, a hint whereof, please the Reader to take in this Abridgement.

Reader,
  I shall not give my self the

the trouble, to recollect and declare the several motives and inducements that deceitful, but wise enough, Woman used to deceive me with, &c. Her Wit did more and more ingage and charm me: Her Qualities deprived me of my own; Her Courteous Behaviour, her Majestick Humility to all persons, her Emphatical speeches, her kind and loving expressions; and amongst other things, her high detestation of all manner of Vice, as Lying, &c. Her great Pretence to zeal in her Religion; her modest Confidence and Grace in all Companies, Fearing the knowledge of none; her demeanour was such, that she left no room for Suspition, not onely in my opinion, but also in others both Grave and Wise. And all this is real and not feigned, and

and more convincingly and apparently true, by this foil of his own setting, As for his undertaking to tell the Story of the management of the businefs betwixt us; he is so far from doing me justice herein, that he wrongeth me and his own soul by lying.

For Confutation of which, I refer the Reader to the ensuing Tryal; Onely there is one passage that I am unwilling to let slip, that is, he saith there, that my Father was in Town upon my Commitment, and did acknowledge me to be his Daughter, and that I had played many such tricks. It's strange this Father of mine could not be produced at the Tryal, if that had been true.

And yet a little before this, upon

upon his visiting me in the *Gate-house*, where I was destitute of money and subsistence, at my first coming in he seemed very tender of me, and charged the Keeper I should want nothing, for as far as 40*lb.* went, he would see him payd, which I beleive he must ere long, and after that sent me a Letter, which is the onely paper I have by me of his, the other amorous and loving scriblings being lost and taken from me, the same time that they plundered me of my Jewels, I do not know what I may do for them, but I hope I shall never cry for those Epistles. This done in these words, so that my Love and my Dear, could be hot and cold almost in an instant.

My

My Dearest Heart,

ALthough the *manner of your Usage may very well call the sincerity of my Affection and Expressions to you in question;* Yet when I consider, That thou art not ignorant of the Compulsion of my Father, and the Animosity of my whole relations, both against You and my Self for Your sake, I am very confident your goodness will pardon and pass by those things which at present I am no way able to help; And be you confident, That notwithstanding my Friends aversion, there shall be nothing within the reach of my power shall be wanting, that may conduce both to your liberty, main-

shall

tenance, and Vindication. I shall very speedily be in a condition to furnish you with Money, to supply you according to your desire. I hope Mr. Bayly will be very civil to you; and let him be assured, he shall in a most exact measure be satisfied, and have a Requital for his Obligation. My dearest, always praying for our happy meeting,

I rest, Your most affectionate Husband.

May the 11th.
1663.

John Carleton.

Other

Other of my Husband's Friends came to Visit me in the *Gate-house*, (of the many hundreds of other I shall say nothing) one of them said, Madam, I am one of your Husbands Friends and Acquaintance, I had a desire to see you, because *I* have heard of your breeding. Alas, said I, *I* have left that in the City amongst my Kindred, because they want it.

Another in his discourse delivered as an Aphorism, *That marriage and hanging went by Destiny*. *I* told him, *I had received from the Destinies Marriage, and he in probability might Hanging.* To waive many others of the like nature.

My innocence furnished me with several of those answers, and

and repartees to the mixt sort of visitants, who either for novelty or designe came to trouble me. I was advised indeed to seclude my self from such company, but because there might be no disadvantage pretended by reason I kept close, and evidence might be puzled, not having seen me in so long a time, as afterwards at my Tryal might have been suggested, I gave all persons the freedom of my Chamber. But for the Nobler sort, I may in some measure thank my stars, that out of this misfortune extracted so much bliss, as the honour of their acquaintance, which otherwise at large I had been in no capacity to attain.

The time of the Sessions of the Peace for *London* and *Middlesex* being arrived, I was conveyed from the Gate-house to Newgate; where by the civility of the Master of the prison I had lodgings assigned me in his own house, which adjoyns to the Sessions-house-yard; and there I was publickly seen by all comers: that my enemies might want no advantage of informing their witnesses of my Person, Age and condition, and so square their Evidence: but my innocence and my good Angels preserved me from the worst of their malice.

From thence, on Wednesday, *June* the third, in the evening, the first day of the Courts sitting in the *Old-Bayly*, I was brought down to the Bar: and there an Indictment upon my Arraignment was read against me, me; to which I pleaded Not guilty: and, as instructed by my friends, and a good conscience, (being altogether ignorant of the Laws and Customs of this Kingdome) put my self for my Triall upon God and the Country, without making any exception, or ever so much as examining what my Jury were.

And because they approved themselves men of honesty, judgment and integrity, and did me so much justice, I can do no less then take occasion here to return them my humble thanks, that they would regard the oppressed condition of a helpless prisoner; and not give credit to the wicked asseverations of a wretch, who onely swore to the purpose against me: and to let the world know my particular gratitude, I will transcribe into this my *Case*, as one of the happiest and fairest

The Case of 75
faireſt remarks therein, the names of thoſe upright Jurors, *viz.*

William Rutland,
Arthur Vigers,
Arthur Capel,
Tho. Smith,
Fran. Chaplin,
Robert Harvey,
Simon Driver,
Robert Kerkham,
Hugh Maſſon,
Tho. Weſtley,
Richard Clutterbuck, and
Randolph Tooke.

The Indictment was *in hæc verba.*

That ſhe the ſaid Mary Moders, late of London Spinſter, otherwiſe Mary Stedman, the wife of Tho. Stedman late of the City of Canterbury in the County of Kent Shoomaker, 12 May, in the Reign of his now Majeſty the ſixth, at the Pariſh of St. Mildreds in the City of Cant.

in

in the County aforesaid, did take to husband the aforesaid Tho. Stedman, and him the said Thomas Stedman then and there had to husband. And that she the said Mary Moders, alias Stedman, 21 April, in the 15 year of his said Majesties Reign, at London, in the Parish of Great S. Bartholomews, in the Ward of Farringdon without, feloniously did take to husband one John Carleton, and to him was married, the said Tho. Stedman her former husband then being alive, and in full life: against the form of the Statute in that case provided, and against the Peace of our said Soveraign Lord the King, his Crown and Dignity, &c.

After which being set to the Bar, in order to my Trial, I prayed time till the morrow, my witnesses not being ready; which was granted: and all persons concerned were ordered to attend at nine of the Clock in the Fore-noon.

Being

Being returned to my lodging, where some Gentlemen gave me a visit to counsell and advise me; my Husband Mr. *Carleton* came thither to take his leave of me, as I understood afterwards by his complement: but my Keeper knowing of him, thought him not fit company for me, who was one of the causers of my injurious usage: but notice at last being given me of it, I gave order for his admittance, and treated him with that respect which became my Relation to him; though he, to add trouble to me, fell into more impertinent discourses concerning the shortness of my dayes, and speedy preparation of Repentance for another world; and that he would pray for me, and the like: to the which I replied, Pray my lord let none of those things trouble you; I thank God I am as well as ever in my life, and do of all things least fear hanging: and as for your prayers, are you righteous or no? if not, they will so little availe me, that they will not profit your self. Hereupon a Gentleman to break off this discourse drank to him in a glass of Canary; which my Lord unhandsomely declining to accept, I could not forbear to tell him, I was sorry to see his Lordship's slender breeding could not suffer him to be civill.

Thus the world may see how these mine Adversaries had already swallowed my life and my credit, and devoted them to the Gibbet without redemption: the onely security of all their past injustices towards me. —— *Per scelera sceleribus est iter*: they must end as they have begun. Thus the Devill and his imps were here frustrated.

For

For, on Thursday *June* the fourth, I proceeded to Trial, according to appointment; but my fathers bandogs being not ready, my husband came into the Court very spruce and trim, in one of his wedding-suits, and prayed the Court, that in respect his father and his witnesses were not yet come together, or rather had not concinnated their lies to be found in one tale, that the Trial might be deferred for halfe an hour. I could not but smile to see my deare husband labour so to make sure of my death, and with so little regard to pass by his dear Princess without so much as vouchsafing a look to her; as if he were angry at his eyes for having beheld so much already. But to abrupt these thoughts, and to continue the discourse: the Court growing impatient of these uncivil

civil delayes, and telling my father-in law that they were not bound to wait on him or his witnesses; they were now produced before them, and sworn; and with old *Carleton* himself were six in number: namely, *James Knot*, one that will almost cleave a hair; *William Clark*, and *George Carleton* her brother-in-law; Mr. *Smith* the Parson, and one *Sarah Williams*; which for fuller information of the world, I will give, with a review of the whole Triall, according to the exactest copy of it, which was taken in short-hand at my desire.

James Knot. My Lord, and Gentlemen of the Jury, I gave this woman in Marriage to one *Thomas Stedman*, which is now alive in *Dover*, and I saw him last week.

Court. Where was she married?

Knot. In *Canterbury.*

Court.

Court. Where there?

Knot. In St. *Mildreds*, by one Parson *Man*, who is now dead.

Court. How long since were they married?

Knot. About nine years ago.

Court. Did they live together afterwards?

Knot. Yes, about four years, and had two children.

Court. You gave her in marriage, but did the Minister give her to her husband then?

Knot. Yes, and they lived together.

Jury. Friend, did you give this very Woman?

Knot. Yes.

Court. What company was there?

Knot. There was the married Couple, her sister, my self, the Parson and the Sexton.

Court. Where is that Sexton?

Knot. I know not, my Lord.

Court. You are sure they were married in the Church, and this is the woman?

Knot. Yes, I am sure of it.

Court. How long ago?

Knot. About nine years ago.

Court. Did you know this woman before the Marriage? and how long?

Knot. Yes, I knew her a long time; I was an Apprentice seven years near her Mothers house in *Canterbury*.

Court. Then she's no forreign Princess? Of what Parentage was she?

Knot. I did not know her own father (and in that he might be believed) but her father-in-law was a Musitian there.

Court. You see her married: what words were used at her marriage, and in what manner?

Knot. They were married according to the order of the Land, a little before the Act came forth touching Marriages by Justices of the Peace.

Court. Was it by the Form of Common-Prayer, any thing read of that Form?

Knot. I did not take notice of that: I was but a young man, and was desired to go along with them.

William Clark being sworn, said, My Lord, I was last week in *Dover*, in company with this *James Knot*, and *Thomas Stedman*, and he the said *Stedman* did own that he did marry one *Mary Moders*, a daughter of one in *Canterbury*, and that *Knot* gave her, and that he had two children by her, and declared his willingness to come up to give evidence against her, but wanted money for his journey: And I have understood that a person here in Court was of a Jury at *Canterbury*, at a Trial.

Triall between *Day* and *Mary Stedman* at the Bar for having two husbands.

Court. Was she cleared?

Clark. I cannot tell.

Young *Carletons* father sworn.

My Lord, I was at *Dover* the last week on Wednesday; I saw the husband of this woman, and the man acknowledged himself to be so; and did say that *James Knot* was the man that gave her in marriage to him.

Court. Where is this man her husband? Hearsays must condemn no man: what do you know of your own knowledge?

Carleton the Elder. I know the man is alive.

Court. Do you know he was married to her?

Carleton. Not I, my Lord.

Sarah Williams. My Lord, This Woman was bound for *Barbadoes*, to go along with my husband,

band, and she desired to lodge at our house for some time, and did so; and when the ship was ready to go, she went into *Kent* to receive her means, and said she would meet the ship in the *Downs*; and missing the ship, took boat and went to the ship. After severall dayes remaining there, there came her husband with an Order and fetched her ashore, and carried her to *Dover*-Castle.

Court. VVhat was his name that had an Order to bring her on shore again?

Sarah Williams. His name was *Thomas Stedman.*

Court. Have you any more to prove the first marriage?

Carlton the Elder. No, none but *Knot*; there was none but three, the Minister dead, the Sexton not to be found, and this *Knot* who hath given Evidence.

Court. What became of the two

two children, *Knot?*

Knot. They both died.

Carlton the Elder. *Stedman* said in my hearing, that he had lived four years with her, had two children by her, and both dead; five years ago last *Easter* since she left him.

Court. Mr. *Carlton*, VVhat have you heard this VVoman say?

Carlton. My Lord, she will confess nothing, that pleases him.

Court. Mr. *Carlton*, did you look in the Church-Register for the first marriage?

Carlton. I did look in the Book, and he that is now Clerk, was then Sexton (just now not to be found;) he told me, that Marriages being then very numerous, preceding the Act beforementioned, the then Clerk had neglected the Registry of this Marriage.

Marriage. If she intended this Trade, she likewise knew how to make the Clerk mistake Registring the Marriage.

Young *Carlton*'s brother sworn, who said,

My Lord and Gentlemen of the Jury, I was present at the Marriage of my Brother with this Gentlewoman, which was on or about 21 *April*, 1663. They were married at Great St. *Bartholomews*, by one Mr. *Smith* a Minister here in Court, by Licence.

Mr. *Smith* the Parson sworn.

My Lord, all that I can say, is this, that Mr. *Carlton* the younger told me of such a business, and desired me to marry them; they came to Church, and I did marry them by the Book of Common Prayer.

Court. Mr. *Smith*, are you sure that is the Woman?

Parson.

Parson. Yes, my Lord, it is; I believe she will not deny it.

Prisoner. Yes, my Lord, I confess I am the Woman.

Court. Have you any more witnesses?

Carlton. We can get no more but *Knot* to prove the first Marriage; the last is clear.

Judge *Howel.* VVhere is *Knot?* Remember your self well what you said before. You say, you know that VVoman at the Bar; that you had known her a great while; that she was born near you in *Canterbury*; that you were present at her marriage; that Parson *Man* married them; that none were present but your self, the married couple, Parson, Sexton, and her sister.

Knot. Some others came into the Church, but none that I knew; I am sure none went with her, but those I named.

Court.

Court. Who gave her in marriage?

Knot. I did.

Court. How came you to do it?

Knot. I was *Stedmans* shopmate, and he desired me to go along with him.

Court. VVere her Parents then living, or no?

Knot. Her Mother was.

Jury. How old are you?

Knot. Two or three and thirty years.

Jury. How long ago was this marriage?

Knot. About nine years since.

Court. Then he was twenty three, and might do it. What is your Trade of life?

Knot. I am a Cordweyner, otherwise, a Shoomaker; *Stedman* was so too: we wrought both together.

Jury. We desire to know whether she had a Father and Mother

ther then living.

Knot. She had a Father-in-law.

Court. Did you know her Mother?

Knot. Yes.

Court. How long before that Marriage did her own Father die?

Knot. I did not know him. He said so before indeed.

Court. What age was she when married?

Knot. I suppose nineteen or twenty.

Prisoner. May it please your Honours, and Gentlemen of the Jury, you have heard the several witnesses, and I think this whole Country cannot but plainly see the malice of my Husbands Father against me; how he causelesly hunts after my life: when his Son, my Husband, came and addressed himself to me, pretending

ding himself a person of honour, and upon first sight pressed me to marriage; I told him, Sir, said I, I am a stranger, have no acquaintance here, and desire you to desist your suit: I could not speak my minde, but he (having borrowed some thred-bare Complements) replied, *Madam*, your seeming virtues, your amiable person, and noble deportment, renders you so excellent, that were I in the least interested in you, I cannot doubt of happiness: and so with many words to the like purpose, courted me. I told him, and indeed could not but much wonder, that at so small a glance he could be so presumptuous with a stranger, to hint this to me; but all I could say, would not beat him off: And presently afterwards he having intercepted my Letter, by which he understood how my affairs stood,

stood, and how considerable my means were, he still urged me to marry him; and immediately by the contrivance of his friends, gaping at my fortune, I was hurried to Church to be married; which the Parson at first did without Licence, to secure me to my Husband, and sometime after had a Licence.

And my Husbands Father afterwards considering **I had a considerable fortune, pressed me, that in respect I had no relations here, and because, sayes he, we are mortall, you would do well to make over your Estate to my Son your Husband**; it will be much for your honour, satisfaction of the world, and for which you will be chronicled for a rare woman: and perceiving he had not baited his hook sufficient (with some fair pretences) to catch me then, he and his Son, who

The Case of

who were both willing to make up some of their former losses in circumventing me of what I had, they robb'd me of my Jewels, and Clothes of great value, and afterwards pretended they were counterfeit Jewells; and declared, that I had formerly been married to one at *Canterbury*, which place I know not; and this grounded on a Letter (of their own framing) sent from *Dover*, with a description of me; that I was a young fat woman, full brested; that I spoke severall languages; and therefore they imagined me the person; and so violently carried me from my lodging before a Justice of Peace, only to affright me, that I might make my Estate over to them. The Justice having heard their severall allegations, could not commit me, unless they would be bound to prosecute me; which

which my husband being unwilling to, the Juſtice demanded of his Father whether he would proſecute me, ſaying, they muſt not make a fool of him; and ſo after ſome whiſperings, the Father and his Son were both bound to proſecute; and thereupon I was committed to priſon: And ſince that, theſe people have been up and down the Country, and finding none there that could juſtifie any thing of this matter, they get here an unknown fellow, unleſs in a priſon, and from thence borrowed, you cannot but all judge, to ſwear againſt me. My Lord, were there any ſuch Marriage as this fellow pretends, methinks there might be a Certificate from the Miniſter, or place; certainly if married, it muſt be regiſtred: but there is no Regiſtry of it, and ſo can be no Certificate, no Miniſter

ster nor Clerk to be found: and if I should own a marriage, then you see that great witness cannot tell you, whether I was lawfully married, or how? but it is enough for him (if such a paultry fellow may be believed) to say, I was married. I was never yet married to any but *John Carlton*, the late pretended Lord: But these persons have sought alwayes to take away my life, bring persons to swear against me, one hired with five pounds, and another old fellow perswaded to own me for his Wife; who came to the prison, and seeing another woman, owned her, and afterwards my self, and indeed any body. If such an old inconsiderable fellow had heretofore wooed me, it must have been for want of discretion, as *Carleton* did for want of money; but I know of no such thing. Several

ral scandals have been laid upon me, but no mortall flesh can truly touch the least hair of my head for any such like offence: they have framed this of themselves. My Lord, I am a stranger, and a forreigner; and being informed there is matter of Law in this Trial for my life, my innocence shall be my Counsellor, and your Lordships my Judges, to whom I wholly refer my Cause. Since I have been in prison, several from *Canterbury* have been to see me; pretending themselves (if I were the person as was related) to be my school-mates; and when they came to me, the Keeper can justifie, they all declared that they did not know me.

Court. Knot, You said she lived near you at *Canterbury*; What woman or man there have you to prove she lived there?

there? have you none in that whole City, neither for love of Justice nor Right, will come to say she lived there?

Knot. I believe I could fetch one.

Court. Well said, are they to fetch still?

Prisoner. My Lord, I desire some Witnesses may be heard in my behalf.

Elizabeth Collier examined. My Lord, my Husband being a Prisoner in the *Gatehouse*, I came there to see my Husband, and did work there a dayes; and there came in an old man, his name was *Billing*, he said he had a wife there; says Mr. *Baley*, Go in and finde her out; and he said I was his wife, turned my hood, and put on his spectacles, looks upon me, and said I was the same woman his wife; and afterwards said I was not, and so to others: I can say no more.

Jane Finch examined.

My Lord, there came a man and woman one night, and knockt at my door; I came down, they asked to speak with one *Jane Finch*. I am the person, said I. We understand, said they, you know Mistriss *Carleton* now in prison. Not I, said I, I onely went to see her there. Said they, Be not scrupulous: if you will go and justifie any thing against her, we will give you 5 *l*.

Court. Who are those two?

Finch. I do not know them, my Lord.

Mr. *Baley* examined.

My Lord, there has been at least 500. people have viewed her; severall from *Canterbury*, fourty at least that said they lived there; and when they went up to her, she hid not her face at all,

all, but not one of them knew her.

Court. What Country-woman are you?

Prisoner. I was born in *Cullen* in *Germany*.

Court. Mr. *Carleton*, How came you to understand she was married formerly?

Carlton the elder. I received a Letter from the Recorder of *Canterbury* to that purpose.

Prisoner. They that can offer five pound to swear against me, can also frame a Letter against me: they say I was nineteen years of age about nine years ago, and I am now but one and twenty.

Court. Mr. *Carlton*, you heard what *Knot* said; he said she lived near him four years a wife: why did not you get some body else from thence to testifie this?

Carleton. Here was one *Davis*

that was at her Fathers houfe, and fpoke with him ⸺

Court. Where is he?

Carlton. I know not; he was here.

Court. You were telling the Court of a former indictment againſt her, what was that for?

Carlton. She was indicted for having two husbands, *Stedman* of *Canterbury* her firſt Husband, and *Day* of *Dover* Chirurgion, her ſecond Husband. The indictment was Traverſed the year before His Majeſty came to *England*, ſhe was found not guilty.

Court. who was at that Trial?

Carlton. One here in Court was of the Jury; but that party ſaid there was ſuch a trial, but knows not that this is the Woman.

Judge *Howel.* Gentlemen of the Jury, you ſee this indictment is againſt *Mary Moders*, otherwiſe wife *Stedman*, and it is for having two husbands, both at one time alive; the first *Stedman*, afterwards married to *Carlton*, her former husband being alive. You have heard the proof of the first marriage, and the proof doth depend upon one witness, that is *Knot*; and he indeed doth say, he was at the marriage, gave her, and he names one *Man*, the Parson that married her, that he is dead; none present there but the married couple that must needs be there, the Parson, this witness, her sister, and the Sexton; that he knows not what is become of the Sexton. All the Evidence given on that side to prove her guilty of this Indictment, depends upon his single testimony. It is true, he says she was married at *Canterbury*, but the particulars, or the manner of the marriage he doth not well remember; whether by the Book of Common Prayer, or otherwayes: but they lived together for four years, had two Children. If she were born there, married there, had two children there, and lived there so long, it were easie to have brought some body to prove this; that is all that is material for the first marriage.

For the second, there is little proof necessary: she confesses her self married to *Carlton*, and owns him; the question is, Whether she was married to *Stedman*, or not?

You have heard what defence she hath made for her self, some Witnesses on her behalf; if you believe that *Knot*, the single witness, speaks the truth so far forth to satisfie your conscience, that that was a marriage, she is guilty. You see what the circumstances

stances are, it is penal; if guilty, she must die; a Woman hath no Clergy, she is to die by the Law, if guilty. You heard she was indicted at *Dover* for having two husbands, *Stedman* the first, and *Day* the second. There it seems by that which they have said, she was acquitted; none can say this was the woman: that there was a Trial, may be believed; but whether this be the woman tried or acquitted, doth not appear. One here that was of that Jury, says, there was a Trial, but knows not that this is the Woman. So that upon the whole, it is left to you to give your Verdict.

 The Jury went forth, and after some short Consultation, returned to their places.

Clerk. *Mary Moders*, alias *Stedman*, hold up thy hand; look upon her Gentlemen, what say you? Is she guilty of the Felony whereof she stands indicted, or not guilty?

Foreman. Not guilty. And thereupon a great number of people being in and about the Court, hissed and clapped their hands.

Clerk. Did she flie for it?

Foreman. Not that we know.

Afterwards I desired, that my Jewells and Cloaths, taken from me, might be restored to me: The Court acquainted me, that they were my husbands, and that if any detained them from me, he might have his remedy at Law. I then charging old Mr. *Carleton* with them, he declared they were already in the custody of his Son her husband. So that if they had been counterfeit, as they all along pretended, I doubt not

not but that they would have had so much confidence and justice for themselves, as to have acquainted the Court with so much, to the bettering the envy and scandal of their gross abuses: but concerning the real worth of those Jewels, I shall have further occasion to speak presently.

Being thus fairly acquitted, *I* was carried back to my former Lodgings; where, among other visits, *I* had one from my Husbands near Friend, who but two hours before had swore and threatned my death: yet to feel my temper in this disappointment of their bloody designe against me, he was sent with an impertinent story into my company, where he began to glaver, and offer me a glass of Wine; (above which their generosity yet never reached:) but my passions fions were fo high at the very fight of him, that *I* bid him get him out of the room, and not trouble me with his company: which he did, by flinking from me, as the Dog in the Proverb that had loft his Tayl.

They thought being thus freed *I* would have ranted and vapoured, and gave them fome further unwary hint of my condition, as being now out of danger: but *I* (that knew my felf not to be in any) was tranfported with no fuch exultation, but kept the fame equanimity and conftant tenour; no lefs affected with the triumphs of Juftice, then thofe of my Honour and Reputation.

Hitherto they have not found any thing unbecoming the perfon I am, or what they made me to be, except in my neceffities, and that frequency of company

to

to which they have subjected me by false imprisonment, and other scandals; which I could not better remove, then by my barefac'd appearance to all comers: so that that which other women hide and mask for modesty, I must shew and set to publick view for my justification.

On the sixth of *June*, being Saturday, I was discharged of my confinement, (having been all along most civilly used by the Masters and Keepers of both the Prisons where I was in durance; but indeed rather in the suburbs of a Prison, then a Prison it self; for which I am their Debtor) and did expect that my husband, by whom I was committed, that is, by his Relations, would have brought me out; and I stayed there to that purpose two days after my acquittal and purgation: but no such matter; they had
got

got my Estate, I might do what I would with my person; the groundless slaunders they had cast upon that, should yet serve turn to infame my bed; and the Counterfeit, though after conviction of the falshood thereof, must be separated and divorced: but the counterfeit Jewels they'll *Hug* and *Embrace*, and *part* withal at no rate.

And therefore in stead of my lawful and true Husband, they endeavoured to put a counterfeit upon me: but too much are they stupified, in stead of being sublimed in this mysterious way of cheat, which as in melancholy people, works still in their fancy that they sent me the most ridiculous Dotard for Husband-Gentleman-Usher, that ever woman laid eye on: a Fellow that could be no younger then brother to Mother *Shipton*, and had his
Pro-

Prophetical Spectacles to fit him for a Legacy.

It was one of my pretended husbands, by whom a Bill was preferred (but not found, as I said before) by *Billing* the Brick-layer. Upon *Whitsun-Monday*, the 8th of *June* instant, the said *Billing* came to *Newgate*, demanded of the Keepers to deliver his Wife to him. The Turn-Key, and other subordinate Officers of the Goal, told him, They had none of his Wife. He insisted upon it, and with-stood all denial, mentioned my name, and the particulars of my Trial. The Keepers remembring there was a former mistake of the same person, given in Evidence on my behalf at the Trial, called one *Grizel Hudson* a Convict, a pretty Woman, and in good habit: the Turn-Key asked *Billing*, Whether this was his Wife?

Wife? *Billing* replied, *Yes*; and askt her, Why she did not come to him upon his first sending for her? She told him, That the Keepers would not permit her to stir out of the Prison, in regard her Fees were not paid. *Billing* said, He would pay the Fees; and whispered her in the Ear, saying, That they had a minde to hang her (meaning the *Carletons*) but he would not prosecute her. True it was, he had put in an Indictment against her, but he could not help that. Well *Moll*, said he to her, *Have ye all your things?* She said, *Yes*. But, said he, *Moll, Why do you stay here amongst such wicked company, Rogues and Whores? I see their Irons about their Legs.* Why, said she, *I have left some Linnen ingaged in the Cellar*. To the Cellar the Keeper carried them both; and there *Billing* left a note under his hand,
to

Madam Mary Carleton.

to pay five shillings to the Tapster: VVhich Note he hath to produce, to satisfie any that shall make further Enquiry in this particular.

He further said, That she had cheated him of fourty pounds, and that he would pawn the Lease of his house, rather then she should want Money, although she was a wicked Rogue, if she would but live with him: she promised she would. He told her he would give her a Sky-colour'd Silk Petticoat and Wastcoat, and a Podesway Gown, new *Holland* for Smocks, and all other things necessary. *Billing* turning himself to the Company there present, said merrily, *That she had cost him much before when he married her, but he never lay with her, but he had kist her, and felt her a hundred times.* *Billing* askt her again, if she would leave these wicked

wicked Rogues, and go along with him. She said, she had another Debt to pay: He askt what it was; She said, twenty pounds to such a one, a stranger then present, unto which person he gave a note to pay 20 *l.* in one moneth after the Date thereof: (it's more then probable he will be made so to do.)

He further said to her, *That now it will trouble me to pay all this Money, and then you to run away from me in a short time.* Withall, said he, *Moll, You need not, for I have a better estate then the young man that tried you for your Life.* So gave the particulars of his Estate, what in Money, Houses, Leases and Land. He added moreover, that he did love her out of measure, notwithstanding she had done him other mischiefs, then what he had before mentioned. She askt him, what they

they were? He said, She had stollen from his Daughter a Knife and a wrought Sheath, a Handkercher, and a Seal'd Ring. With that, the standers by told him, that he was mistaken, that this *Grizell Hudson* was not the person. He swore it was, and that he knew her well enough; that he saw her in the *Gate-house*, and that she knew what passed between us there: *But*, said he, *Moll, Thou art a cunning Rogue; I desire nothing of thee but to be honest, and live with me*; the which she promised, and he parted with great content thereupon.

This affront and indeed disgrace *I* put to the other; but am very sorry the poor old Fellow should be abused so by my Relations; the second part or worse of the cheat of a cunning Gypsie, who having inveagled his affections, and set him on
edge

edge by some lascivious gesture, entangled him in a marriage; and for the better port and celebtation of the Nuptials, procured him twenty pound from a friend of hers, for which he gave Bond, (the Duplicate of this story) and when bed-time came, and the rusty Bridegroom had prepared himself, he ran away in the dark with most of the money, and some odd things, as Linen, and the like, and never after appeared, till those skilful Conjurers of *Grey Fryars* (*in quo peccamus, in eo plectimur*; where my fault was in deserting my first station among the Religious, from the like demolished place am *I* punished) raised up my white name, and made me personate the baseness of that Imposture.

To proceeed: I might now very well be said to be set at libetry, berty, having no where to go, or where to betake my self: for the Verdict did not reach to give me possession of my Husband, whose Wife *I* was declared to be, (the Jury telling my young Lord, upon his asking of them the Verdict, as they were coming through the Garden of their Sessions-House into the Court, *That he must make much of his Princess, and keep her to himself:*) Nor was it easie to avoid the trouble of twenty several Courtiships for Lodgings, which *I* well considered might give further occasion of reproach, and abuse of my Credit.

But Mr. *Carleton* not appearing, which gave me suspition of some further designe, I took Lodgings in *Fullers Rents*, where in privacy I resolved to wait the reduction of him to better and honester thoughts; and that when

when they his friends had all prejudice laid aside, and considered the duty and obligation that lay upon him, they would have restored and returned him to me, But this neither had its designed end, though the danger that I threatned his father with, brought him to me.

This was on Sunday in the Evening, *June* the sixth, when he came to me, accompanied with Mr. *George Hewyt* his Master, a Barrister of *Grays Inne* in *Coney-*Court; where after some discourses, and perseverance of my resolved manner of proceeding against his Father in the same method, and at the same Bar where he had arraigned me; he did most submissively supplicate me, and adjure me by all respects to him, falling upon his knees to move me the sooner, that I would promise him not to prosecute

cute his father for my Jewels, or any other account: adding moreover, That if I did it, he should presently murther himself; with such-like cowardly Bravado's as he had used to the over-ruling of my affections, when he pretended he would do an hundred more mischiefs to himself, if *I* would not consent to marry him.

And now he resumed his first kindnesses, in hope *I* would do what he intreated; kissed me, and offered his embraces: though I could not so easily admit such danger into my bosome, having so lately felt the viperous sting: but this loving humour, like a time-serving passion, soon abated by the interposition of Mr. *Hewyt*.

I do suppose, that if he had been alone, and out of the custody and tuition of that person,

son, he would have stayed with me all night, and perhaps for the future; but that person who hath surfeited may be, and hath had too much of a woman, had now so little respects for our sex, as to curse it in generall: but let him beware, as froward and as great a woman-hater as he is, lest he expiate those Maledictions, by some notable feminine revenge a steeping and preparing for him.

Next day I sent a Letter to my husband, and left it for him at Master *Hewits* Chamber: but through his means, as I can conceive no otherwise, I received no word of any answer; so that I resolved once for all to go and make a demand of my said goods and Jewels of old Mr. *Carlton*; which I did on *Fryday* night, the 19th of *June*, at his house at *Gray-Friars*; and knocking at Door,

Madam Mary Carleton.

Dore, he himself asked who was there: I answered, Your Daughter when a Princess, but now your sons wife: he demanded my business; I told him I came to demand my Jewells, and other things he had taken from me, and also my husbands Person. He replied in short, the old Gentlewoman pulling him back from further discourse, That for the Jewels, my husband had them; and for himself, he was gone.

There being no more to be said or done, I bid them look to their hits, and departed: having on all occasions, after so many injuries sustained, proffered a reconciliation, being willing to cohabit with him, and have left no means unattempted to bring us together, that the world might see I am not such a loose irregular leud woman as I am slandered ed to be, by my carriage and demeanour in that relation of a wife, which title I am more ambitious of then any other yet put upon me: but since it must be otherwise, I doubt not so prudently and innocently to behave my self, as I shall not want a husband, much less the trouble of so impertinent and fickle a person as my husband, whom I would willingly exchange for my Jewels, and give him liberty to look after another Princess where he can finde her.

And now for that *Hocus Pocus*, the delaying of those counterfeit Jewels, as they talked, I shall make it no difficulty to prove that those Gems they had of me were none of their Bristol-stones, or such-like trumpery: for not long after my tryal, they were offered in *Cheap-side* to the view of a Goldsmith, and he demanded

manded what they might be worth; who having steadily and considerately lookt them all over, said, they were worth 1500,*l*. At which the Trustee, or Fiduciary, in whose hands they were, askt the Gold-smith if he was mad, or knew what he said. Yes, that I do, replied he, and will presently lay you down so much money for them, if you have power to sell them: whereupon my Gentleman put up his counterfeit ware with a more counterfeit face, saying, he came only to try his skill, and departed.

And now let all the world judge of the Cheat I have put upon this worshipfull family of the *Carletons*. I have of theirs not a thred, nor piece of any thing, to be a token or remembrance of my beloved Lord, which I might preserve and lay up as a sacred relique of a person

son dear to me (I think indeed the dearest that ever woman had.)

But it may be they intend to furnish my Lord with this portable and honourable furniture to the second part of this *Gusman*-story, against he shall knight-errant it abroad; and having found the way, marry some other great forreign Lady, and in stead of Boys whooping and hallowing at him here, be revered and adored by subjects, as his great spirit alwayes divined and suggested to him he should be some-body, though to little purpose: but I hope to prevent that designe, and to have speedy redress against all this fraud and violence that hath been acted against me.

And now I have concluded the Narrative, and I hope to the satisfaction of the world: and if there be any thing not so elegantly and clearly expressed as my cause requires, let it be known it is my fathers, not my fault, which hath in some places disturbed and muddied my fancy, and in others reserved a hiding place and obscurity for my pursued honour.

I hope the ingenuous will pardon and admit of this defence, considering the nature of it. No man is bound by any law to set forth more then what he is directly interrogated and questioned to; and there I have for my innocence sake exceeded. And for the ignorant and malicious, let them wonder and slander on; and when they shall give me worthy occasion, which is not in the capacity of their shallow brains, or in their dishonest intentions, to a further vindication; that is, when my relations shall have

have returned me what they took from me, and leave me *in statu quo*, by any handsome expedient, I shall not faile of making this discourse most evident demonstration, and descend to such undeniable proofe of every particular here, that shall make their impudence and rash folly one of the leudest stories of the Age.

The world usually and frequently judges as it likes and affects, and is altogether swayed by interest and humour; and even by that, amidst all those industrious calumnies, I dare stand or fall. Let my quality and condition alone, and he is not weighed in the common scales; yet the fair conduct and the harmless example deserves no censure. Let both alone, my sex is to be pittied and respected, and my person not to be hated. But I will not prostitute my
fame

fame to them: to his Highnefs I have appealed, and to him I fhall go. Not doubting but what the ftrictnefs and nicety of the Law doth at prefent withhold him, we fhall by his gracious protection of innocence be freed from fuch incumbrances; and fome eafier folution found for thofe intricacies, then my Lawyers can at prefent expedite.

I am advifed howfoever to profecute my adverfaries in the fame manner, and at the fame Bar where they arraigned me for a fufpition, of a real fuit of Felony, for that riot againft the publick peace committed upon my perfon: which I am refolved to do, in cafe I receive not better fatisfaction from them before the Seffions: nor fhall my husbands dilating intreaties and perfwafions befool me any longer.

Either love me, or leave me,
And do not deceive me.

The fashions and customs here are much different from those of our Country, where the wife shares an equal portion with her husband in all things of weal and woe, and can *liber intentare*, begin and commence, and finish a suit in her own name; they buy and sell, and keep accounts, manage the affairs of houshold, and the Trade, and do all things relating to their severall stations and degrees. I have heard and did believe the Proverb, *That* England *was a Heaven for women*: but I never saw that Heaven described in its proper termes: for as to as much as I see of it, 'tis a very long prospect, and almost disappears to view; It is to be enjoyed but at second hand, and
all

all by the husbands title; quite contrary to the cuſtome of the *Ruſsians*, where it is a piece of their Divinity, that becauſe it's ſaid that the Biſhop muſt be the husband of one wife, they put out of orders, and from all Eccleſiaſtical function ſuch Clergy men, who by the Canon being bound to be married, are by death deprived of their wives; ſo that their tenure to their Livings and Preferments clearly depends upon the welfare and long life of their yoake-fellows, in whoſe choice, as of ſuch moment to their well-being, they are very curious, as they are afterwards in their care and preſervation of them.

 I could inſtance in many other cuſtomes of nearer Nations, in reſpect to female right and propriety in their own Dowers, as well as in their husbands eſtates:
but

but, *cum fueris Romæ, Romano vivite more.* I will not quarrel the English Laws, which I question not are calculated and well accommodated to the genius and temper of the people.

 While I mention these customes, I cannot forbear to complain of a very great rudeness and incivility to which the mass and generality of the English vulgar are most pronely inclined, that is, to hoot and hallow, and pursue strangers with their multitudes through the streets, pressing upon them even to the danger of their lives; and when once a cry, or some scandalous humour is bruited among them, they become Brutes indeed. A Barbarity I thought could not possibly be in this Nation, whom I heard famed for so much civility and urbanity. This I experiment.d the other day in *Fan-church-*

church-ſtreet, as *I* was paſſing through it upon ſome occaſion, which being noiſed and ſcattered among the Prentices, *I* was forced to bethink of ſome ſhift and ſtratagem to avoid them, which was by putting my Maid into a Coach, that by good hap was at hand, and ſtepping into an adjoyning Tavern; which the Herd miſtaking my Maid for me, and following the Coach as ſuppoſing me there for the convenience thereof, gave me the opportunity of eſcaping from them. A Regulation of this kind of uproar by ſome ſevere penalties, would much conduce not onely to the honour of the Government of the City, but the whole Nation in general; having heard the French very much complain of the like injuries and affronts: but thoſe to me *I* may juſtly place to my husbands account

count, who hath expofed me to the undeferved wonder, and to be a May-game to the Town.

And to his debility and meanneſs of ſpirit, I am likewiſe beholding for ſome other ſcandalous Libels and Paſquils divulged upon this occaſion of our marriage; chiefly for the Ribaldry of ſome pitiful Poetry, entituled, *A Weſtminſter-wedding*, which equally reflects as much upon himſelf as me. This tameneſs of his doth hugely incenſe me; and I ſwear, were it not for the modeſty of my ſex, the bonds of which I will not be provoked to tranſgreſs, I would get ſatisfaction my ſelf of thoſe pitiful Fellows, who by this impudent and ſaucie ſcribling, do almoſt every day beſpatter my honour. At leaſt, I wonder my husband doth not vindicate himſelf, and aſſert his own individual Reputation,

tation, having threatned so much in print against a civil person that formerly & first of all endeavoured to clear and justifie mine.

But when I consider how apt his kindred are to return to their vomit of slandering me, and reckoning the nine days wonder of their great cheat discovered is over, are like those that have eat shame and drank after it; I did the less wonder at his stupidity and senslesness of those indignities done him: and commonly those that have no regard to anothers honour, have as little respect for their own; as he is Master of another mans life, that is a Contemner of his own.

I shall therefore omit all the subsequent sneaking Lyes, raised by the same kindred, when they saw their more mighty and potent Accusations helped forward with such prejudices, noise and often-ostentation, were at once disappointed and blown to nothing: such are those Chimæra's of their framing and fancying, that *I* was seen in mans apparel, with a Sword and Feather, in designe to do mischief to some body; and that I have used to do so: and so punctual are they in this Lye, as to name both the time and place: that I resolved to set up a Coffeehouse, and at last to turn Player or Actor: with an huhdred other flams to sully my Name, and of a multitude of the like, to make one or other of those Calumnies and Reproaches to stick upon me.

Whereas on the contrary I do resolve, as soon as my cause is heard, and justice done me by the supreme power, if I cannot otherwise attain it, to retire and return back, though not immediately to my own home, yet to make

make such approaches at necessary distance for the present, that I might be in a readiness and view of all transactions there, as soon as this bluster shall be so laid here, that I shall not fear the tayl of this Hurricane pursuing me: yet shall I always have my heart and my Arms open to Mr. *Carleton*, as a person whom for his Person and Naturals I do and shall ever affect, as his wife and my husband, maugre all those practices (as for my part) of rendring us mutually hateful and suspect to each other.

And while *I* thus open the way to a composure of this unhappy business, and am willing to put up so many private injuries, and publick contumelies and disparagements, in tendencie to, and in consideration of the relative state of marriage, which my conscience commands me to prefer

fer before any advantage, respect or honour of mine own individual particular; and have not refused, but rather by all fair means, and too mean condescentions have courted an Accommodation and Agreement; what Injustice is it upon Injustice, Oppression upon Cruelty, refined Malice like Salt upon Salt, to pierce and exasperate that bosome which is full of so much indulgence to, and dallyance with their worst of injuries, in expectation that time would give them to see their mischievous errour?

But neither Time nor Truth it self will reclaim them, without Angels appear to confirm them in it. And *I* do in some part not blame them for it: for the excess and lofty structure of their hopes hath so dazled their looks downwards, that they can see
no-

nothing aright, nor in any true proportion or colour. Their dejection and fall from the pinacle of their ambition, hath quite ſtunned them, that they will hardly recover the dizzie miſtake that lies between a *Princeſs* and a *Prentice.*

They are angry their golden Mountains have travelled and been in labour with a Mouſe, and that they cannot finger any of my Eſtate; and very importunate they are for me to declare it; and this they ſay is the onely argument to prove me no Cheat, and *I* ſay and believe it is the onely argument to prove me a fool; and with that, of all other their ſlanders and durtineſs, they ſhall never abuſe me.

But may not *I* with a great deal more reaſon enquire for, and demand my Joynture and Dowry?

Dowry? and those Mannors, Leases, Parks, Houses, and the like Rhapsodies and Fictions of an Estate, meer castles in the Air; and as one merrily since told me, he believed they were Birds Nests? It is sure a greater imputation and shame to them to be found such Cheats and Lyars, then it can be the least blur to me, who never avowed any such thing, nor boasted of my Quality and Fortune.

As to the Letters they intercepted of mine from my Steward, I wonder they do not produce them: but they are ashamed of their most ridiculous simplicity therein. I knew very well the uncertainty of my condition here; and therefore the Letters were meerly Cyphers, and under those terms of Moneys, &c. an account was given me of another affair

affair at home : the diftafte whereof made me comply with, and fo foon yeild to thofe importunate and love-fick follicitations of my Lord.

But what will they be the better for a Rent-roll, or particulars of an eftate in *Germany*, the Tenure and Cuftomes of whofe propriety and nature of claime if they did know, yet could they not tell how to make their Title to it ? I could eafily name places, and difcover my own Hereditaments perhaps without danger, and they never the wifer: nor will the impartial Reader be better fatisfied. But if my fifter *King*, or any of my kinsfolk long for fome *Baccharach* grapes, I'll fend to my Steward for them, and he will convey them from mine own vineyard as foon as they are ripe;

ripe; and I can furnish her husband with *Westphalia* Hams, which run in my woods gratis. All those fine things I have store of: and when Mr. *Carlton* pleases to make it a surer match, and be married the third time, all things shall be done in ample manner: I will make a resignation of my whole estate, and have nothing setled in lieu of it, but a necessitous despised condition of life, and be taught to sing *Fortune my foe* to the pleasant new tune, or eccho of a *Cheat*.

But I trust Providence will better govern me, and put me upon no necessity of abandoning good and just resolutions I have made to my self, whether in case of separation or re-union, which I shall not over-fondly press, or urge

urge from them who love not me but mine, and require signes and wonders, and love to be no less then Principalities.

FINIS.

The Arraignment, Tryal and Examination of Mary Moders, Otherwise Stedman, now Carleton (Wing A3764) is reproduced by permission of The Huntington Library. The text block measures 150 × 92 mm.

The following pages are mis-numbered in the original: 9 for 7 *et seq.*

Hard-to-read words in the original:
2.2: Shooe-
2.3: maker, 11 May, in the Reign of his now Majesty the sixth,
2.4: at the Parish of St. Mildreds in the City of Cant, in the

THE ARRAIGNMENT, Tryal and Examination OF Mary Moders,

Otherwise
ST EDMAN, now CARLETON,
(Stiled,
The German Princess)

At the Sessions-house in the *Old Bayly*, being brought Prisoner from the Gatehouse *Westminster*, for having two Husbands; viz.

THO. STEDMAN
of *Canterbury* Shooemaker,
AND
John Carleton of *London*, Gent.

Who upon a full Hearing was acquitted by the Jury on Thursday, *June* 4. 1663.

LONDON:
Printed for *N. Brook*, at the Angel in *Cornhil*, near the Royal Exchange. 1663.

(1)

THE
Arraignment, Tryal & Examination
OF
MARY MODERS, alias STEDMAN,
STILED,
The GERMAN PRINCESS,

At the Sessions in the *Old-Bayly*, Wednesday the third of *June*, 1663.

At Justice-Hall in the Old-Bayly.

THe Court being sate, a Bill of Indictment was drawn up against *Mary Moders*, alias *Stedman*, for having two Husbands now alive, viz. *Tho. Stedman* and *John Carleton*. The Grand Jury found the Bill, and was to the effect following: Viz.

That she the said Mary Moders late of London Spinster, other-

otherwise Mary Stedman, the wife of Tho. Stedman late of the City of Canterbury, in the County of Kent Shoemaker, 11 May, in the Reign of his now Majesty the sixth, at the Parish of St. Mildred, in the City of Cant, in the County aforesaid, did take to husband the aforesaid Thomas Stedman, and him the said Thomas Stedman then and there had to husband. And that she the said Mary Moders, alias Stedman, 21 April, in the 15 year of his said Majesties Reign, at London, in the Parish of Great St. Bartholomews, in the Ward of Farringdon without, feloniously did take to husband one John Carleton, and to him was married, the said Tho. Stedman her former husband then being alive, and in full life: against the form of the Statute in that case provided, and against the Peace of our said Soveraign Lord the King, his Crown and Dignity, &c.

Afterwards the said *Mary Moders*, alias *Stedman*, was called to the Bar; and appearing, was commanded to hold up her hand: which she accordingly did; and her Indictment was read to her as followeth.

Clerk of the Peace. Mary Moders, alias Stedman, Thou standest indicted in London by the name of Mary Moders late of London Spinster, otherwise Mary Stedman, the wife of, &c. And here the Indictment was read as above. How sayst thou, Art thou guilty of the Felony whereof thou standest indicted, or Not guilty?

Mary Moders. Not guilty, my Lord.
Clerk of the Peace. How wilt thou be tryed?
Prisoner. By God and the Country.
Clerk of the Peace. God send thee a good deliverance.

And afterwards she being set to the Bar in order to her Tryal, she prayed time till the morrow for her Tryal: which was granted; and all persons concerned were ordered to attend them at Nine of the Clock in the Fore-noon.

The

The Reader is desired to take notice of the following Passage.

After she was Arraigned, and going back to the Gaol, her Husband the young Lord told her, He must now bid her Adieu for ever. To which she replyed:

Nay, (My Lord) 'tis not amiss
Before we part to have a Kiss.

And so saluted him, and said, What a quarter and noise here's of a Cheat! You cheated me, and I you: You told me you were a Lord, and I told you I was a Princess; and I think I fitted you. And so saluting each other, they parted.

June 4. 63.

Clerk of the Peace. The Court was sate, Proclamation was made: O Yes, all manner of persons that have any thing more to do, &c. Set Mary Moders to the Bar; where she accordingly stood.

Clerk of the Peace. Mary Moders, alias *Stedman,* hold up thy hand: which she did. Those men that you shall hear called, and personally appear, are to pass between our Soveraign Lord the King and you for your life: if you will challenge them, or any of them, you must do it when they come to the Book to be sworn, before they are sworn. And then were called,

William Rutland,	Simon Driver,
Arthur Vigers,	Robert Kerkham,
Arthur Capel,	Hugh Masson,
Tho. Smith,	Tho. Westley,
Fran. Chaplin,	Richard Clutterbuck, and
Robert Harvey,	Randolph Pooke.

And she challenged none, but were severally sworn by the Oath following.

Look.

(4)

Look upon the Prisoner: You shall well and truly try, and true deliverance make between our Soveraign Lord the King and the Prisoner at the Bar, whom you shall have in charge, according to your evidence. So help you God.

Clerk of the Peace. Cryer, make Proclamation: O Yes, If any one can inform my Lords, the Kings Justices, the Kings Serjeant, or the Kings Attorney before this Inquest be taken between our Soveraign Lord the King and the Prisoner at the Bar, let them come forth, and they shall be heard; for now the Prisoner stands at the Bar upon her deliverance: and all others that are bound by Recognizance to give evidence against the Prisoner at the Bar, come forth, and give evidence, or else you'll forfeit your Recognizance.

The Witnesses being called several times, and not appearing, young *Carleton* came into the Court in a rich Garb trimmed with Scarlet Ribbands, and prayed, that in respect his Father and the rest of the Witnesses were not all ready, the Tryal might be deferred for half an hour; and he going back, and passing the Prisoner his Princess, who stood there in a black Velvet Wastcoat, dressed in her hair, trimmed also with Scarlet Ribbands, she (veiling her face with her fan) laughed at him, to the great observation of the Court: and so the young Lord left the Court, (by advice of his friends) and betook himself to an adjoyning house, where he stood the whole Tryal.

After some stay, the Witnesses came into the Court, and the Prisoner set to the Bar, and silence being commanded, the Indictment was again read.

Clerk of the Peace. Upon this Indictment she hath pleaded Not guilty, and for her Tryal hath put her self upon God and the Country; which Country you are. Your charge is to enquire whether she be guilty of the said Felony or not guilty: if you find her guilty, you shall enquire what Goods and Chattels she had at the time of the Felony committed, or at any time sithence: if you find her not guilty, you shall enquire whether she did flee for it: if you find that she fled for

for it; you shall enquire of her Goods, &c. as if she had been guilty: if you find she be not guilty, nor that she did flee for it, say so, and no more, and hear your evidence.

Several Witnesses were sworn by the Oath following:

The evidence that you shall swear between our Soveraign Lord the King and the Prisoner at the Bar, shall be the truth, the whole truth, and nothing but the truth. So help you God.

James Knot. My Lord, and Gentlemen of the Jury, I gave this woman in marriage to one *Thomas Stedman*, which is now alive in *Dover*, and I see him last week.

Court. Where was she married?

Knot. In *Canterbury*.

Court. Where there?

Knot. In St. *Mildreds*, by one Parson *Man*, who is now dead.

Court. How long since were they married?

Knot. About nine years ago.

Court. Did they live together afterwards?

Knot. Yes, about four years, and had two Children.

Court. You gave her in marriage, but did the Minister give her to her husband then?

Knot. Yes, and they lived together.

Jury. Friend, did you give this very Woman?

Knot. Yes.

Court. What company was there?

Knot. There was the married Couple, her sister, my self, the Parson and the Sexton.

Court. Where is that Sexton?

Knot. I know not, my Lord.

Court. You are sure they were married in the Church, and this is the woman?

Knot. Yes, I am sure of it.

Court. How long ago?

Knot. About nine years ago.

Court. Did you know this woman before the Marriage, and how long?

Knot.

Knot. Yes I knew her a long time, I was an Apprentice seven years near her Mothers house in *Canterbury*.

Court. Then she's no Forreign Princess? Of what Parentage was she?

Knot. I did not know her own Father (and in that he might be believed) but her Father-in-law was a Mulitian there.

Court. You see her married: what words were used at her marriage, and in what manner?

Knot. They were married according to the order of the Land, a little before the Act came forth touching marriages by Justices of the Peace.

Court. VVas it by the Form of Common-Prayer, any thing read of that Form?

Knot. I did not take notice of that, I was but a young man, and was desired to go along with them.

William Clark being sworn, said, My Lord, I was last week in *Dover* in company with this *James Knot* and *Thomas Stedman*, and he the said *Stedman* did own that he did marry one *Mary Moders*, a daughter of one in *Canterbury*, and that *Knot* gave her, and that he had two Children by her, and declared his willingness to come up to give evidence against her, but wanted money for his journey: And I have understood that a person here in Court was of a Jury at *Canterbury*, at a Tryal between *Day* and *Mary Stedman* at the Bar for having two Husbands.

Court. Was she cleared?

Clark. I cannot tell.

Young *Carletons* father sworn.

My Lord, I was at *Dover* the last week on Wednesday; I saw the husband of this woman, and the man acknowledged himself to be so; and did say that *James Knot* was the man that gave her in marriage to him.

Court. VVhere is this man her husband? Hear-says must condemn no man: what do you know of your own knowledge?

Carleton the Elder. I know the man is alive.

Court. Do you know he was married to her?

Carleton. No, my Lord.

Sarah

Sarah Williams. My Lord, This Woman was bound for *Barbadoes*, to go along with my Husband, and she desired to lodge at our house for some time, and did so; and when the ship was ready to go, she went into *Kent* to receive her means, and said she would meet the ship in the *Downs*; and missing the ship, took boat and went to the ship. After several days remaining there, there came her Husband with an Order and fetched her ashore, and carried her to *Dover* Castle.

Court. What was his name that had an Order to bring her on shore again?

Sarah Williams. His name was *Thomas Stedman*.

Court. Have you any more to prove the first marriage?

Charlton the Elder. No, none but *Knot*; there was none but three, the Minister dead, the Sexton not to be found, and this *Knot* who hath given Evidence.

Court. What became of the two Children, *Knot*?

Knot. They both died.

Charlton the Elder. *Stedman* said in my hearing, that he had lived four years together, had two Children by her, and both dead; five years ago last *Easter* since she left him.

Court. Mr. *Charlton*, What have you heard this Woman say?

Charlton. My Lord, she will confess nothing that pleases him.

Court. Mr. *Charlton*, Did you look in the Church Register for the first marriage.

Charlton. I did look in the Book, and he that is now Clerk, was then Sexton (just now not to be found,) he told me, that Marriages being then very numerous, preceeding the Act before-mentioned, the then Clerk had neglected the Registry of this Marriage. If she intended this Trade, she likewise knew how to make the Clerk mistake Registring the Marriage.

Young *Charlton's* Brother sworn, who said,

My Lord and Gentlemen of the Jury, I was present at the Marriage of my Brother with this Gentlewoman, which was on or about 21. *April*, 1663. They were married at *Gre-*

St. *Bartholomews*, by one Mr. *Smith* a Minister here in Court by Licence.

Mr. *Smith* the Parson sworn.

My Lord, all that I can say, is this, That Mr. *Charlton* the younger told me of such a business, and desired me to marry them; they came to Church, and I did marry them by the Book of Common Prayer.

Court. Mr. *Smith*, are you sure that is the Woman?

Parson. Yes, my Lord, it is; I believe she will not deny it.

Prisoner. Yes, my Lord, I confess I am the Woman.

Court. Have you any more witnesses.

Charlton. We can get no more but *Knot* to prove the first Marriage, the last is clear.

Judge *Howel.* Where is *Knot?* Remember your self well what you said before. You say, you know that Woman at the Bar; that you had known her a great while; that she was born near you in *Canterbury*; that you were present at her marriage; that Parson *Man* married them; that none were present but your self, the married couple, Parson, Sexton, and her sister.

Knot. Some others came into the Church, but none that I knew; I am sure none went with her, but those I named.

Court. Who gave her in marriage?

Knot. I did.

Court. How came you to do it?

Knot. I was *Stedmans* shopmate, and he desired me to go along with him.

Court. Were her Parents then living, or no?

Knot. Her Mother was.

Jury. How old are you?

Knot. Two or Three and thirty years.

Jury. How long ago was this marriage?

Knot. About 9 years since.

Court. Then he was Twenty three, and might do it: What is your Trade of life?

Knot. I am a Cordweyner, otherwise a Shoomaker, *Stedman* was so too; we wrought both together.

Jury.

Jury. We desire to know whether she had a Father and Mother then living?

Knot. She had a Father-in-law.

Court. Did you know her Mother?

Knot. Yes.

Court. How long before that Marriage did her own Father die?

Knot. I did not know him; He said so before indeed.

Court. What age was she when married?

Knot. I suppose about Nineteen or twenty.

Prisoner. May it please your Honors, and Gentlemen of the Jury, you have heard the several Witnesses, and I think this whole Countrey cannot but plainly see the malice of my Husbands Father against me; how he causlesly hunts after my life, when his Son, my Husband, came and addressed himself to me, pretending himself a person of honor, and upon first sight pressed me to marriage: I told him, Sir said I, I am a stranger, have no acquaintance here, and desire you to desist your suit; I could not speak my minde, but he (having borrowed some thredbare Complements) replied, *Madam*, your seeming vertues, your amiable person, and noble deportment, renders you so excellent, That were I in the least interested in you, I cannot doubt of happiness; and so with many words to the like purpose, courted me, I told him, and indeed could not but much wonder, that at so small a glance he could be so presumptuous with a stranger, to hint this to me; but all I could say, would not beat him off: And presently afterwards he having intercepted my Letter, by which he understood how my affairs stood, and how considerable my means were, he still urged me to marry him; and immediately by the contrivance of his friends, gaping at my fortune, I was hurried to Church to be married, which the Parson at first did without Licence, to secure me to my Husband, and sometime after had a Licence.

And my Husbands Father afterwards considering I had a considerable fortune, pressed me; that in respect I had no relations here, and because, sayes he, we are mortal, you would do well to make over your Estate to my Son your Husband,

Husband; it will be much for your honour, satisfaction of the world, and for which you will be Chronicled for a rare woman: and perceiving he had not baited his hook sufficient (with some fair pretences) to catch me then, he and his Son, who were both willing to make up some of their former losses in circumventing me of what I had, they rob'd me of my Jewels, and Cloths of great value, and afterwards pretended they were counterfeit Jewels, and declared that I had formerly been married to one at *Canterbury*, which place I know not; and this grounded on a Letter (of their own framing) sent from *Dover*, with a description of me; that I was a young fat woman; full breasted; that I spoke several languages; and therefore they imagined me the person; and so violently carried me from my lodging before a Justice of Peace, only to affright me, that I might make my Estate over to them. The Justice having heard their several allegations, could not commit me, unless they would be bound to prosecute me; which my Husband being unwilling to, the Justice demanded of his Father whether he would prosecute me, saying, they must not make a fool of him; and so after some whisperings, the Father and his Son were both bound to prosecute, and thereupon I was committed to prison: And since that, these people have been up and down the Countrey, and finding none there that could justifie any thing of this matter, they get here an unknown fellow, unless in a prison, and from thence borrowed, you cannot but all judge to swear against me. My Lord, were there any such marriage as this fellow pretends, methinks there might be a Certificate from the Minister, or place; certainly if married, it must be registred: but there is no Registry of it, and so can be no Certificate, no Minister nor Clerk to be found: and if I should own a marriage, then you see that great witness cannot tell you whether I was lawfully married, or how: but it is enough for him (if such a paultry fellow may be believed) to say, I was married. I was never yet married to any but *John Charlton*, the late pretended Lord: But these persons have sought alwayes to take away my life, bring persons to swear against me, one

hired

hired with Five pounds, and another old fellow perswaded to own me for his Wife; who came to the prison, and seeing another woman, owned her, and afterwards my self, and indeed any body. If such an old inconsiderable fellow had heretofore woed me, it must have been for want of discretion, as *Charleton* did for want of money; but I know of no such thing: Several scandals have been laid upon me, but no mortal flesh can truly touch the least hair of my head for any such like offence; they have framed this of themselves. My Lord, I am a stranger, and a forreigner; and being informed there is matter of Law in this tryal for my life, my Innocence shall be my Counsellor, and your Lordships my Judges, to whom I wholly refer my Cause: Since I have been in prison, several from *Canterbury* have been to see me, pretending themselves (if I were the person as was related) to be my school mates; and when they came to me, the Keeper can justifie, they all declared they did not know me.

Court. Knot, You said she lived near you at *Canterbury*; What woman or man there have you to prove she lived there? have you none in that whole City, neither for love of Justice nor Right, will come to say she lived there?

Knot. I believe I could fetch one.

Court. Well said, are they to fetch still?

Prisoner. My Lord, I desire some Witnesses may be heard in my behalf.

Elizabeth Collier examined. My Lord, my Husband being a Prisoner in the *Gatehouse*, I came there to see my Husband, and did work there a dayes; and there came in an old man, his name was *Billing*, he said he had a wife there; sayes Mr. *Baley* go in and find her out; and he said I was his Wife, turned my hood, and put on his spectacles, looks upon me, and said I was the same woman his wife; and afterwards said I was not, and so to others: I can say no more.

Jane Finch examined.

My Lord, there came a man and woman one night, and knockt at my door; I came down, they asked to speak with
one

one *Jane Finch*; I am the person, said I; We understand, said they, you know Mrs *Charlton* now in prison; No, I, said I, I only went to see her there; said they, be not scrupulous, if you will go and justifie any thing against her, we will give you 5 *l*.

Court. Who are those two?

Finch. I do not know them, My Lord.

Mr. *Baley* examined.

My Lord, there has been at least 500. people have viewed her; several from *Canterbury*, 40 at least that said they lived there; and when they went up to her, she had not her face at all, but not one of them knew her.

Court. What Countrey woman are you?

Prisoner. I was born in *Cullen* in *Germany*.

Court. Mr. *Charlton*, How came you to understand she was married formerly?

Charlton elder. I received a Letter from the Recorder of *Canterbury* to that purpose.

Prisoner. They that can offer 5 *l*. to swear against me, can also frame a Letter against me: They say I was 19 years of age about 9 years ago, and am now but 21.

Court. Mr. *Charlton*, you heard what *Knot* said; he said she lived near him 4. years a wife, why did not you get some body else from thence to testifie this?

Charlton, Here was one *Davis* that was at her Fathers house, and spoke with him——

Court. Where is he?

Charlton. I know not; he was here.

Court. You were telling the Court of a former Indictment against her, what was that for?

Charlton. She was indicted for having two husbands, *Stedman* of *Canterbury* her first Husband, and *Day* of *Dover* Chirurgion, her second Husband. The Indictment was Traversed the year before His Majesty came to *England*, she was found not guilty.

Court. Who was at that tryal?

Charlton. One here in Court was of the Jury; but that party said there was such a tryal, but knows not that this is the Woman.

Judge

Judge Howel. Gentlemen of the Jury, you see this Indictment is against *Mary Moders*, otherwise *Stedman*, and it is for having two husbands, both at one time alive; the first *Stedman*, afterwards married to *Charlton*, her former husband being alive. You have heard the proof of the first marriage, and the proof doth depend upon one witness, that is *Knot*; and he indeed doth say, he was at the marriage, gave her, and he names one *Man* the Parson that married her, that he is dead; none present there but the married couple that must needs be there, the Parson, this witness, her sister, and the Sexton; that he knows not what is become of the Sexton. All the Evidence given on that side to prove her guilty of this Indictment, depends upon his single testimony. It is true, he says she was married at *Canterbury*, but the particulars or the manner of the marriage he doth not so well remember; whether by the Book of Common Prayer, or otherwise, but they lived together for four years, had two Children. If she were born there, married there, had two Children there, and lived there so long, it were easie to have brought some body to prove this; that is all that is material for the first marriage.

For the second, there is little proof necessary, she confesses her self married to *Charlton*, and owns him; the question is, Whether she was married to *Stedman*, or not?

You have heard what defence she hath made for her self, some Witnesses on her behalf; if you believe that *Knot*, the single witness, speaks the truth so far forth to satisfie your Conscience, That that was a marriage, she is guilty. You see what the Circumstances are, it is penal, if guilty, she must die; a Woman hath no Clergy, she is to die by the Law, if guilty. You heard she was Indicted at *Dover* for having two Husbands, *Stedman* the first, and *Day* the second. There it seems by that which they have said, she was acquitted; none can say this was the Woman, that there was a tryal, may be believed; but whether this be the woman tried or acquitted, doth not appear? One here that was of that Jury, says, there was a tryal, but knows not that this is the
Woman.

(16)

Woman. So that upon the whole, It is left to you to confider of the Evidence you have heard, and fo to give your Evidence.

The Jury went forth, and after some short Consultation, returned to their places.

Their names were called, and all answered.

Clerk of the Peace. Are you all agreed of your Verdict?

Jury. Yes.

Clerk. Who shall say for you?

Jury. The Foreman.

Clerk. Mary Moders alias Stedman hold up thy hand; look upon her Gentlemen, what say you, Is she guilty of the Felony whereof she stands indicted, or not guilty?

Foreman. Not guilty. And thereupon a great number of people being in and about the Court, hissed and clapped their hands.

Clerk. Did she flie for it?

Foreman. Not that we know.

Afterwards she desired, that her Jewels and Cloaths taken from her, might be restored to her: The Court acquainted her, that they were her Husbands, and that if any detained them from her, he might have his remedy at Law: She charging old Mr. *Charlton* with them, he declared they were already in the custody of his Son her Husband.

FINIS.

The Replication, Or Certain Vindicatory Depositions (Wing C585A) is reproduced by permission of the Newberry Library. The text block measures 160 × 103 mm.

THE REPLICATION,

Or Certain Vindicatory Depositions,

Occasioned by way of Answer, to the Various Aspersions, and False Reports of Ignorant and Malicious Tongues, and the Printed Sheets and Pamphlets of Base DETRACTORS,

Concerning the Late Acted

CHEAT

Written by *Iohn Carleton* of the Middle Temple *London*, Gent.

Printed by the Authors Appointment in the Year, 1663.

Judicious Reader,

I Am not Ignorant, (though I have been willingly silent) of the Various Rumours, Reports, Stories, Fancies, dayly encreasing Fables, and Proteus Shapes wherein the Different Humours, and Dispositions of the World bring forth the late acted Project, and Cheat. And though I might be justly angry with some, yet I scorn to take notice of any. For should I begin to un-dress all these prodigious shapes, and set them out singly in the naked truth, into what a Confused Chaos should I bring my self? How endlesse should I make my sufferings? how many years might I lead my life in discontent, before I could hear answer and satisfie the many Niceties, Questions, Curiosities and Objections of the Giddy-headed Vulgar. Qui non adveritatem rei, sed ad opinionem prospiciunt. I am satisfied, that as a little time will make a distinction between the report and the reality, so it will put a conclusion to both, by burying them in Oblivion.

I shall not give my self the trouble to recollect and declare the several motives Acts, Inducements, and protestations so often and so highly expressed, by that (Wise enough indeed, but) deceitful Woman, that provoked and stirred up that faith and credit in me, as to enter the list of sacred Matrimony. Neither shall I go about to vindicate my self much (for that the Law will do) or greatly to vilifie her, that her infamous Actions will best make appear. Nor shall I endeavour to procure a great Credit in any one, especially in such whose narrow soul and single threaded faith, cannot believe the Vindicative Oath of a Christian; Which I dare take to any Assertion that I shall modestly, and I protest without any thing of singularity, or Affectation, hereafter lay down, concerning the reality of my Intentions and Actions; Neither will my troubled thoughts, (Courteous Reader) give me leave to look at the lofty style, nay not time to salute the Garment of that Noble pleading and Worthy Orator Cicero: And indeed it best becomes truth to be naked, and glosses of Eloquence, in some peevish Humours, might invoke jealousies of the intended reality; but as I respect the least approbation of the Wise and Judicious, so I neglect and disdain the greatest censure of the Ignorant and Malicious. I seek for no ones soothing applause, nor I care for no persons rigorous censure; I only beg every Ingenuous Reader (to whose setled and discerning Judgements I submit) to make a Charitable Construction, and to passe by all errors you may without doubt find in this little Book, which my Discomposed judgment will not at this time permit me to see; And I may say of these lines, as discontented Ovid said of his Verses.

Lib. I. Eleg. I. Ovid Trist.   Carmina proveniunt animo deducta sereno,
                               Nubila sunt subitis, tempora nostra malis.

But I hope and wish for a greater serenity, and do expect a calm after this Storm, and then (Worthy Reader) I shall be ready not only to acknowledge and blush at all faults, but to correct and amend them.   Qui non est hodie, cras magis aptus erit.

Yours in all Friend-ship,   JOHN CARLETON.

Cicero was wont to say,

Non Recte amat Uxorem, qui corpus amat potius quam animum.
That is,
He doth not love his second self rightly, that loves the parts of her body, rather then the gifts of her Mind.

MArriage is my Theam, and I cannot but look at Happiness, and I think it is a very great Blessing, when the hand of Providence bestows on Mortals, a suitable conjunction of Vertuous and Good Conditions in VVed-lock, without which parity none can be really happy therein: And they know not what marriage is that onely know how to lust. I shall not stand to Comment, but will come nearer to my present Condition. I was unwilling to write at all, but I will not write much. It was my happy, unhappiness, about the 25th. day of *March* last, accidentally to happen into the House, where that (in some things worthy) unworthy Woman was, she being in the Company of a Person or two of Honour; of whose being there when I was informed, I was willing to return an acknowledgment of my Gratefulness, for then late received Courtesies, It being the first oppertunity that was offered to me, after the receit of them; Among whom also I was willing and did spend some time for a diversion. She, as She hath protested to many persons several times since, at my entring of the room, was suddenly possessed with a strange kind of an affectionate passion, and could not satisfy her self till she had made a strict enquiry who I was; nor did it cease there, for presently after She imployed a Friend of mine to desire the Continuance of my Company, as She hath since declared.

Here I thought good to insert the Original of our acquaintance, that the

the world may the better perceive her cheating designe: though it hath pleased the scurrilous Scribler, that either hath no name, or else is ashamed of it, in a late Pamphlet to demonstrate a very great Friendship to that *Distressed Lady*, as his Pedantick Pen terms her; and though he speaks without Book, as most if not all do besides him; yet he endeavours to make it credible that it was She that carried on a humour and my Relations with my self a Designe, which I deny on both sides, and here attest, that not any of them to whom I owe the Duty of a Son, or the Love of an own Brother, did ever see her until many dayes after Contraction, nay not untill three dayes before Marriage, and then never entertained any discourse to promote, but rather to hinder the Proceedings; For She of her own accord, upon a Visit she gave them, told them of her Affection and Intention, and did Politickly and freely declare to them her Great Birth and Fortune. But to return to our first Acquaintance; I understanding her Fancy, and finding those Excellent parts she was possessed with, cold do no lesse, then poize things in my mind: And considering her Endowments, supposed that she wanted nothing that might cause a likeing, nor had she any Defect, that might procure a loathing. I pressed her to the Reason of her Fancy, She replied *Love gives none*. I minded her of the Inequality between mine, and her then thought High Descended Birth and Fortune: She Answered *Love knows none*. I Objected again, (she telling me, that she ever Related to me the least of both) and put Cases of great Danger, to be called in Question, beyond all Law; She Replyed, *Love knows no Lawes*; *Let her Judgement alone to secure both*. Her Wit did more and more Charm me, Her Qualities deprived me of my own; Her Courteous behaviour, Her Majestick Humility to all Persons, in all her Actions, Her Emphatical Speeches, Kind and Loving Expressions, and amongst other things, her High Detestation and Checks to an untruth, though Jestingly uttered by any; Her great Zeal to her Religion, her Modest Confidence, and Grace in all Companies, fearing the knowledge of none; Her variety of Tongues; Her neat limned, and ready answers to all, and all manner of Objections, that I, or the most Critical Person in the World, (without disparaging any ones Judgement) could in point of Honor, make and put to her, whereby to discover her, she would so Nobly, and Seriously Salve, that she left no room for Suspition; Which did not onely work the belief in me, (that hath wrapped me in this present Misfortune) But also in many Persons of great Wisdome, Gravity, and Quality; All which in a growing Acquaintance and Conversation,

did

did encrease our Credit. She desired nothing of me but my Love, (And that as She told me and others, was alwayes her intention to Marry a Private Gentleman, whom She could Love, that She might oblige him highly to love her by her Nobility and Estate;) An Excellent bait indeed). And I thought She did nobly deserve that. She ever protested a Fervent Love, and I could not promise an unfaithful. And finding in her so Noble a Perfection, who could mistrust a reall Affection and Intention? None but did Esteem her Pearlesse in all qualities of mind. Who could have called her Honour and Honesty into question, when they both, (I must say seemingly) were so great? But the Scene was soon changed, though I could not so soon believe it. And in a strange manner there was a suddain discovery of the truth, which is too long a story to insert here, though in a short time it was made appear that She was such a cheating person, as before a Majestrate She was proved to be. Such a suddain alteration, might (like those that looked on *Medusae*'s Head) have turned me into a Stone; I could hardly put out my former belief; Nay I protest, when I seriously reflect on all the passages of her former Expressions & Actions (not in the least thinking of the last Act) I can believe still; For what person living, that is a Christian, or bears the name only, or knows the meaning of that title (which She in a High manner did own) Nay, what *Turk*, *Jew*, *Infidel* or *Heathen* that sees, wonders at, and Worships the Sun, Moon and Stars, and that never heard the Name of the Great *Jehovah*, could Counterfeit and Religiously glosse over so many haynous and detestable Crimes, without fear of a suddain and mighty Judgement? Sure she thought to Hood-wink Divine Providence: The Devil himself, that old Sophister, might be cheated by her, but that he is so well acquainted with her; Without doubt he would have trembled to have invoked those Direful Judgements which She wisht might befall her, upon clearing some doubts, if such things were not true, which are as false as God is true. And amongst all her Protestations I will name only one, which was the onely thing we desired to know the truth of, that was this, upon the Attestation of one or two strangers to us, who upon the first sight knew her, she having lodged at their Houses; they related of her several Husbands she had living; We pressed her to speak the truth, and in the presence of several persons upon her knees, she wisht for a sudden Judgement to befal her, and that she might Eternally hang in Hell (for so were her words) if ever she was Contracted, Married to, or knew any man besides my self. Oh Miserable Creature! I hear so many things dayly of her of truth enough, that I think

she

she hath the best part of a score, and she hath cheated the best part of a Hundred persons of good Worth, and others; I dare not say, what, least I run into extreams; it is enough, I now find her Honour Dishonour, her Protestations Pretences, her Faithfulness Fickleness; and though her Policy did undermine me, her practises will over-throw her self. Who would have imagined that deceit, the Divels great bait, should have lodged here, or that so Noble a mind (though She hath basely Acted) should descend of such an Ignoble Race, or that so great and Discerning a Capacity should proceed of so base and undeserving Progeny? Base indeed, for her Father in Law (her grand Agent and factor) did in the presence of a person of quality, and another Gentleman and my self, upon our entring into discourse of the News of *London*, when we left it, and of the great Cheat, and so proceeding in the story of it, he fell into such a great rage, and said, *It was no News to him, for he was in Town all along, and was with her in the Prison that day she was Committed*, and declared *her Name*, and that She was his *Daughter in Law, for it will be known* said he; That unworthy low spirited, though hot sottish-headed fellow deserves a further strict Examination. I need not relate where he lives, nor what he is, former Prints speak truth in that. But to return to her, the World still finds in her the same Wit, and they will shortly find lesse honesty then any did Imagine: would She had less Wit, and I better fortune; but though my won affections have stung my self and fortunes, they shall kill neither. Had she been but honest, I should have taken her discourses of Nobility and Wealth, but as a neat Romance to glosse over the want of a happy being, which my Relations and my self did really inform her, she should have, could she vindicate and prove her honesty. Would her High pretended Honour had been but reall intended honesty. I am not alone in the Cheats of Marriage, (for I believe scarce one in twenty proves true, and answers all Expectations) though perhaps not in so high a nature. There are many Presidents higher then this, nay more then I mean to recollect: *Menelaus* after his ten years War won but a strumpet. There is nothing new under the Sun, though new to them that suffer it. I can now shake hands with my Old Grand-sire *Adam*, and say with him, *The Woman beguiled me, and I did, &c.* I could pitty her rather then punish her, and yet the Law must punish her, because she did not pitty her self, knowing how narrowly she hath escaped the Execution of Judgement after her former Tryall. The fairest fly is soonest taken in the spiders Web. Indeed she weaved a fine one to catch me, it is well if she hangs not her self in it. I trust-

ing

ing to her outward talk, was betraid by her inward treachery. But though she won me, she hath not overcome me; and the chiefest Victory will be, that I can overcome my self, and prevent the dangerous consequences and sad effects that unhappy accidents and discontents might cause. My sore, though it be angry I can salve it; And indeed, as it argues much folly in any person to let the Afflictions and Censures of the World come so near ones heart, as to let out or inflame ones blood, so it is a great part of wisdom in my Estimation to suffer admittance so near as to raise ones spirits to understand an affliction by a serious consideration and reflexion. How mixed with mercies, and in the Highest way we Mortals can retaliate, (if I may so speak) to return and expresse a holy gratitude to Divine protection: for we must so bear our afflictions, that as our grief may not utterly deject us, so we must have the sence to feel and apprehend it: All the actions of a mans life, are mixt with bitter ingrediences, like Chequer-work, black and white. There is no armour against our fates, and they are as uncertain as unevitable. I am contented with mine, and I hope now the bitter part of my fortune is past, I may once tast the sweet; if not, I shall be contented, knowing from whose hand it comes; I am satisfied, that as I have done nothing dishonestly, so I care for no reports.

Cic. *Qui injuriam faciunt infaliciores sunt quam qui patiuntur.*

It is better to be Passive then Active in an Injury.

But I have exceeded my Intention, and unless I mean to make a Chronicle of the whole, must stop all further expression. And here I would end, but upon second thoughts, in point of Reputation, I find my self engaged highly, to take greater notice of abuses done to others my Acquaintance then to my self; and now I must be angry, for it concerns me to be so, and it should quickly be seen that the fancy pen of that Audacious and Injurious Libeller should soon be cut by several persons, were it but known where that Corrupted and Diseased soul hath its being, which shall not want for a strict enquiry. I wonder how he durst presume to insert in his Libel termed (*The Ladies Vindication*) the name of that Virtuous and Noble Lady which I will not here denominate, The Salt-water Grave Cox-comb hath published it too much already; Or that his Confidence should permit him to discover any thing of her Actions in *Hide-Park*, which though there may be

some

some little thing of truth, yet it is falsely set out. And indeed I am much troubled that that deceitful woman, to whom I then thought my self Related, knowing her own Condition, should offer to play upon that Worthy Ladyes Civility. And I cannot but take notice that this base Detractor should be so impudent as to throw a dart against that deserving Gentleman my *Friend*, that performed the sacred Office of Matrimony. I am not willing to insert any ones Name, you may understand me by description. Who prompt him to insert the report of a double Marriage? And that Politick lye of so great a gratuity as fifteen pounds; I will not satisfie his weak brain what it was, it is enough to let him know that my friend was satisfied, and I did so much as became a Gentleman.

Lastly, I will clear but one thing more as to her Name, by which she was Contracted and Married to me, which was *Henrietta Maria De Wollway*, though she hath since learned so much Confidence as to deny it, or else some one for her; And here I make a full stop, wishing all the World better fortune.

Si Populus vult dicipi Decipiatur.

FINIS.

A Witty Combat: Or, The Female Victor (Wing P2998) is reproduced by permission of the Folger Shakespeare Library. The text block measures 138 × 92 mm

A
Witty Combat:
OR, THE
FEMALE VICTOR.

A Trage-Comedy.

As it was *Acted* by Persons of Quality in *Whitson*-Week with great applause.

Written by T. P. Gent.

LONDON,

Printed for *Tho. Roberts*, and are to be sold at the *Royal-Exchange*, *Fleet-Street*, and *Westminster-Hall*, 1663.

Actors Names.

Old Mr. *Carleton*.
Mr. G. *Carleton* his Eldest Son.
Mr. J. *Carleton* his youngest Son in love with the Germaine Princess.
Mr. *King*. his Son in Law.
A *Parson*.
Two or three *Gentlemen*.
Two or three *Young Clarkes*.
Two *Watermen*.
Drawers.
A *Cellarman*.
Fidlers.
Mrs. *King*.
Madam *Moders*.
Old Mrs. *Carleton*.
Cook *Maid*.
Constable, and Officers.

A Witty Combat:
Or,
The Female Victor.

Actus primus, Scæna prima.

Enter two Watermen, as in an Alehouse at Billingsgate, and a Boy with a full Pot of Ale.

1 *Waterm.* Thou should'st have brought half a dozen Boy, this will not wet, one Pot of Ale is no more in our Bellies, then a man in Paules. 2 *Waterm.* That's right: I prithee fetch a couple more, for what we do, we must do quickly, and not make a dayes work on't.

Boy. I swear I can hardly spare another Pot, the House swarms with several Companies, that we have scarce Pots enough to serve their turnes; but drink as fast as you will, I'le fill as fast, I'le warrant you.

1 *Waterm.* Away, away, a man may baul his heart out before thou wilt hear him: bring us another Pot, and by that time this will be ready for thee to fill.

Boy. Well I'le try my Skill. *Exit Boy.*

1 *Waterm.* Come, here's half this to thee, fear it not, 'twill warme us within man. 2 *Waterm.* I know it, and will pledge thee and it were a whole one. 1 *Waterm.* Passing good Ale, it goes down merrily.

2 *Waterm.* I believe there's no Bones in't: I have heard of Cock-Ale, Lambeth-Ale, China-Ale, Rosemary-Ale, Mint-Ale, Wormewood-Ale, Orange-Ale, Lemon-Ale. And I know not how many sorts more that are the Gentlemens drink as they call 'em; All is but Ale still, made of Water that runs by Billingsgate. And

B for

for my part, when all is done give me the plain wholsome Ale of *England* without welt or guard as they say, or a deal of mixtures; but of all drinks, I hate that of Coffee, it dries Mens Braines and makes 'em write *Hudibrasses* a plaguy hard Word, and jangles like the breech of a Drum. *Enter Boy.*

Boy. Here Gentlemen I am provided for you.

1 *Waterm.* Gentlemen! you Knave! we may be drunk as Lords if we sit by't, but soft and fair, two words to a bargain, the Fidler play'd no such matter.

2 *Waterm.* No, no, we are for a touch and begone, here fill us this to, and make hast; Presto. *within why*

Boy. With a high pass and a repass I am gone, *Boy.* can I be here and there to, I'me coming. *Exit Boy running.*

1 *Waterm.* Have at thee agen. *drinks.*

2 *Waterm.* Do thy worst Boy, come, to thee agen, the Parish is but short Man. *drinks.*

1 *Waterm.* 'Twill be welcome when it comes, off with it and it were a mile to the bottom. 2 *Waterm.* See, I am a clean Drinker; *Super naculum*: boy, I hate to spill good Liquor, and throw away the bottom, a man may want it before he dies.

1 *Waterm.* I, so the Parson told us this morning in the Boat, we had a jolly Company of Passengers, but what she should be that is gone with the Parson my Noddle cannot imagine.

2 *Waterm.* A notable perrilous witty Wench I warrant her, let her alone for leading her men. 1 *Waterm.* She'l lead the Parson besides his Text I'me afraid; how she handl'd him?

2 *Waterm.* Nay, marry he would have handl'd Her, by your leave friend.

1 *Waterm.* You say very right, but she was too cunning for him, She was Courted by better Men in the Boat, but she was too hard for them all, I wonder the Parson should carry Her away.

2 *Waterm.* Who would think that such a Yea and Nay man should carry so much wickedness in his Hide.

1 *Waterm.* Oh hang 'em, there's no Whore-master, like the slye Whore-master: the zealous old Scot Doctrin'd Whore-master of the Tribe of *Henderson*.

2 *Waterm.* What was he? what was he?

1 *Waterm.*

Or, the Female Victor.

1 *Waterm.* What, what was he? why he was the Pope of Scotland.   2 *Waterm.* Of *Rome* thou mean'ſt Man?

1 *Waterm.* I ſay of *Scotland*, I know what I ſay well enough, and *Marſhall* and *Calamy* were two of his Cardinalls.

2 *waterm.* Lord who would think it,   *Enter Boy with* but thou wilt talke any thing in thy Ale.   *more Ale.*

1 *Waterm.* Under the Roſe I may, Oh art thou there Boy, thou art he that does the Liquor bring, though not the Bottle.

Boy. I promiſe you I made what haſt I could, but our houſe is ſo peſter'd. I'me coming---did you ever   *within* hear the like? but d'ye hear me?   *why Boy.*

2 *Waterm.* Who told you we did not?

Boy. Well, will you hear me then, there is a Gentleman inquires for you without.   1 *Waterm.* What is he for a Man?

Boy. I tell you he ſeemes a Gentleman.

1 *VVaterm.* Though he be not what he ſeemes, 'tis all one to us; if he has any Money he ſhall be welcome, and ſo let him in.

Boy. Well, I ſhall tell him what you ſay.   *within* I come, and I come again Sir.   *Exit.*   *Boy, boy.*

1 *VVater.* Now ſhould I laugh if it were ſome good fellow come to pay our reckoning.   2 *VVaterm.* No, no, They are Fiſh too hard to catch; how e're drink about man.

1 *VVaterm.* That's quickly done, here's towards thee.

2 *VVaterm.* T'other Pot, and away.---

Enter Gentleman and Boy.

Gent. Where are the Watermen.   *Boy.* They are there Sir.

Gent. How now honeſt Lads, cloſe at it, you ſeldome ſleep I think.   1 *VVaterm.* Yes troth Maſter we were juſt thinking upon it, I think and't pleaſe you, you came up with this Tyde in our Boat.   *Gent.* I did ſo.   1 *VVaterm.* We had a Company of merry Paſſengers, not to lye; truely, and worthy Ones, or elſe I am very much miſtaken   *Gent.* You had ſo, but one eſpecially.   2 *VVaterm.* If I do not know where he be now ne're truſt me.   *Gent.* Why I am here.

2 *VVaterm.* I know that too, but I know where you would be.

Gent. That's a hard matter my friend.

2 *VVaterm.* Do you not mean a Gentlewoman.   *Gent.* There were many.   B 2   *2 w,*

2 VVaterm. But I do mean *the* Gentlewoman, she that sat next the Parson.   *Gent.* Now you hit me.

2 VVaterm. And would not you be with her now, with all your heart and a piece of your Liver?   *Gent.* I cannot tell, but I must give thee half a dozen of Beer for thy conceits sake.

1 VVaterm. Ale is the life of a Waterman Sir.

Gent. Why then Ale let it be.

Boy. You shall have it with all celerity Sir.   *Exit.*

2 VVaterm. Will your Worship or Honour, or I don't know what, be pleased to sit down and take part of our Cup.

Gent. I came to that purpose.

2 VVaterm. Blessing on your heart, I do not love a proud Gentleman, methinks a right Gentleman should not be proud by your favour Sir, here's even to you, and to all our Company however dispersed now on Shore.

Gent. I'le pledge you, but my honest friends cannot you tell me what is become of that pretty thing.

1 VVaterm. Pretty thing quoth a, she was worth ten pretty things; she was a thing to thank God for.

Gent. You say well.   *Enter Boy*

Boy. Here's your quickning Ale Gentlemen.   *with Al.*

Gent. Set it down, and begon.

Boy. I come, I come presently.   *Exit Boy.*

Gent. My friends here's to you both.

1 VVaterm. One at once Sir, and we are for you.

Gent. Is there no way to find her out?   *2 VVaterm.* Way quoth a, it is a shame for you all, so many Gentlemen aboard her, and let a dry bon'd Parson carry her away! *Gent.* Pox on't, I lost her in a mist; I know not how she whipt away.

2 VVaterm. You know not whether?   *Gent.* Very true, but I hope thou do'st?   *2 VVaterm.* We know nothing Sir, the Streets are wide and many.   *Gent.* Let this for once corrupt thy knowledge, she cannot be far off?   *Gives him*

2 VVaterm. If I thought so.------   *money.*

Gent. She must be some where?

2 VVaterm. That's certain if she be any where Sir, as doubtless she is, and now I think on't.   *Gent.* I prithee then think on't.

1 VVaterm. *London* is a wide place Brother, have a care what
you

you do.   *Gent.* I prithee hold thy prateing, I'le content thee too.   1 *VVaterm.* I say no more, but Brother have a care.

2 *VVaterm.* And now I think on't.   *Gent.* I, go on.

2 *VVaterm.* London is a wide place indeed, and a Man may as soon find a Needle in a Bottle of Hay, as a woman-stranger in this City, yet I would advise you.   *Gent.* To what?

2 *VVaterm.* To have her Cry'd in every Parish.

Gent. Pish, I see thou art but a baffling fellow; give me my money agen.   2 *VVaterm.* Yes, when can you tell? did you ever know a Waterman guilty of that fault, to part with money when he had got it in his clutches. I am sorry I cannot serve you, and there's all, the time was you might have serv'd your self.

Gent. Thou say'st right, how cursedly was I mistaken! much good may do you with your money.

1 *VVaterm.* 'Twill serve to pay the reckoning, Sir I wish you may find her.   *Gent.* Since you cannot informe me, my hopes, and search is ended, fare you well.   *Exit.*

VVatermen. We'l drink a health to your good fortunes Sir.

VVatermen. So, 'tis an ill wind blowes no body good, Boy take your reckoning, and now we'l   *Enter Boy.* take a good smart Nap, and then to the work agen.

Boy. All's pay'd in the Rose, and you are *Welchmen* Gentlemen.

1 *Waterm.* Thou art a wag Sirrah.   *Exeunt.*

Actus primus, Scæna Secunda.

Enter Parson, and Madam Moders.

Pars. In verity it is a cold bleak morning, a little of the Creature would do well: a Glass of Malligo is very comfortable, yea, even unto the Spirits, with a Toast; it does regenerate, and quicken much, and in a way does elevate, and stir the blood to action; it does assuredly.   *Mod.* I apprehend not that, (Sir) but I fear you give your self too great a trouble, thus to follow me, I cannot reach your meaning.   *Pars.* Verily 'tis sincerity of love I bear to strangers, as we are exhorted even so to do by the most learned Authors; Yea, we are all but strangers here, and therefore assuredly we should love one another, yea, so the Word is,

even

even as one another. And see, Oh see, indeed law, look ye yonder, there is a door open to Comers surely, which we have not till now found in our way; I hope my courtesie, your Gentleness, will not refuse, yea truly I hope not.

Mod. I must house some where: faine I would be rid of this impertinent Coxcomb, yet methinkes I'me chain'd unto him as some fate hung o're me, he may prove fortinate.---

Parf. How say you beauteous Creature?

Mod. In truth I say Sir you do so abound in Courtesie, I shall fall short in my endeavours to requite it. *Parf.* 'Tis an easie, yea, even a very easie matter surely will do't if you so please,--- where is the Man o'th house here? *Enter Mr. King.*

King. What is your will? *Parf.* Nay, is it your will, that we may have a special Glass of Malligo.

Mr. King. The best in all the Town I warrant you. Where are you there? *Enter Drawer.*

Parf. We are but newly come off the Water in verity: and something that's warme is not a miss truly; how say you Sir? with this fair Creatures good leave, I think it is not assuredly.

Mr. King, Shew a Roome presently d'ye hear, and draw a Pint of the best Malligo, that's next----d'ye hear, do you see, do you understand me. *Exit Mr. King.*

Draw: I shall Sir---will you please to walk into a Roome.

Parf. Yea verily, how say you forsooth? *Mod.* I am at your disposal Sir.

Parf. In verity I wish you were else, for ah-- *He rubs* ah- -pray give me leave to take you by the *his Elbow.* hand forsooth ah--ah--'tis as soft as Velvet. *Exeunt.*

And enter again at the other end of the Stage, where there is a Table and Stooles set forth.

Parf. A very pretty close convenient Roome this is assuredly; how say you beauteous Creature. *Mod.* Why truly Sir the closeness of it does not at all concern me; if it were ten times wider I should like it a great deal better. *Enter Drawer*

Parf. Assuredly I think not so; yea, I can *with VVine.* give you many reasons for it, Divine, and Morrall, Hyperbolicall, or Tropologicall,---but here's the creature come, that's the wine,

now

now this should have a fellow, that is a Toast, where is the other Creature?

Draw. Even at the fire Sir, To receive its Tryal.

Mod. The fellow jeers him.

Parf. You answer'd well young man, yea verily; but let it not be burnt.

Draw. It shall not be a Martyre; he will turne first assuredly   *Exit.*

Mod. Why this is excellent.

Parf. A good ingenious young man verily, I warrant him well notion'd, that's to say in truth one that has somthing in him, yea certainly, but as I was about to say; to draw my reasons to a head, that is to tell you what they are, assuredly and first.---   *Enter Drawer.*

Mod. The Toast is ready Sir.   *with the Toast.*

Parf. You assure me right.

Draw. Yea, and it has got a new Coat by turning.   *Exit.*

Mod. Ha, ha, ha,

Parf. Assuredly your mirth is comfort to me, what might occasion it, I pray if that---

Mod. A Toy came in my head.

Parf. Your Sex have many: but in so sweet a thing as you, they do appear (methinks) commendable, yea verily.

Mod. In that opinion you deceive your self, me you cannot Sir.

Parf. Not for Worlds on worlds! and yet the Weather may allow us to come neerer one another, verily, without offence, or misconstruction; for it is raw and cold, yea very cold.   *offers to*

Mod. The Roome is warm, good Sir, keep your seat.   *remove.*

Parf. Strangers I love, and strangers should love me, in verity they should Ia; else we do deny the sense, bids us love one another; yea, verily we do, I'le try how warme you are, and truly by a sweet conjunction we may warme one another, yea assuredly.   *drawes his Chair neer Her.*

Mod. Sir I understand you not.

Parf. I hope you will, an understanding Woman is a Jewel, yea, yea, a precious Jewel in the Eares, and hearts of Princes and wise men assuredly, in sundry places we do find it so, yea verily; ah, ah, ah, ah, this hand yea this same hand of yours.

Mod. And what of it Sir?

Parf. It melts like Butter 'gainst the Sun believe me, I would come neerer verily, that is unto your Lip,   *Enter Drawer.*

in

A Witty Combat:

in verity it would affourd me sweetness in abundance, truly assuredly it would, I pray, I pray.--- *Mod.* I am a strainger to your sense and Person: keep farther off Sir, or indeed I shall,---
Pars. Yea, yea, *Draw.* Nay, nay, are you so rampant; 'Parson, I thought I knew your meaning *Aside.* by your Gaping; are you so hot? I'le send a cooler to you. *Exit.*
Pars. Ha--ha--ha--ha--ha.-- *Mod.* What's your meaning Sir?
Pars. The Spirit boyles within me, ye *Enter Mr.* assuredly, and if it be not look'd to, certainly *King.* the Liquor will run over, yea in truth, la.
Mod. You are th'uncivill'st man that e're I met with, and undeserving of the Coat and Title you do assume; hands off.---
Mr. King. A civil Gentlewoman I warrant her.
Mod. You rude fellow you. *Pars.* Yea, as the Wise man said, a Womans Tongue is Wormwood, yea verily Gaul and bitterness. *Mr. King.* A man of your Coat d'ye see to do these things d'ye see, it is a shame d'ye see, d'ye marke me, that.
Pars. Assuredly I will pay for the Malligo and the Toast, yea I will. *Mod.* I scorn your courtesie Sir. *Pars.* In verity I will. *Mr. King.* Let him Mistress d'ye see, he has sworn d'ye fee. *Pars.* Assuredly I will, what is it pray?
Mr. King. But Twelve-pence do you see.
Pars. Twelve-pence is just a Shilling verily, and there it is assuredly; fair one, I greet you well; but will conclude with the wise Man, he that takes a Woman for his friend takes a wrong Sow by the Ear; yea verily. *Exit Parson.*
Mr. King. I do perceive d'ye see you are a stranger.
Mod. A very stranger to this Town indeed Sir.
Mr. King. And 'tis very likely d'ye see you have a charge about ye. *Mod.* I have so Sir. *Mr. King.* If you please d'ye see to make use of part of my House, d'ye see you need go no farther, here you may be safe d'ye see, I see you are a civil Gentlewoman, and 'tis pity d'ye see you should happen into a place that would abuse you, there are some such in Town; d'ye see that will prey upon strangers d'ye see, but you shall find no such thing here believe me. *Mod.* I do Sir, and kindly do imbrace your proffer
Mr. King. You shall want nothing in my house d'ye see, if you
pleas

please to see your Chamber? much for this civility. *Mod.* Sir you oblige me *Exeunt.*

Actus Secundus, Scæna Prima.

Enter Mr. King and his Wife.

Mr. *King.* SWeet Heart, I have a secret to impart to thee, and a very precious one, d'ye see, it may be worth us pounds wench, nay, if I said hundreds I should not lye, d'ye hear me? provided we order our matters well, and carry 'em in the right way, d'ye see. And therefore I must conjure thee by all loves and nuptial kindnesses that has or may pass between us at Bed or at Board, d'ye see.--- *Wife,* What is all this for?

Mr. *King,* For it is no petty ordinary common thing d'ye see, but a thing of profit d'ye see, and credit d'ye see, and honour may come on't d'ye see. *Wife,* What is it? what is it?

Mr. *King,* If a man cannot reveale a thing to his own Flesh and blood, d'ye see, who shall he do it to then d'ye see?

Wife, I pray Sweet-heart let me know your meaning?

Mr. *King,* Womens hearts are like Cullenders, d'ye see, or Loop-holes, d'ye see, but if a man cannot trust his own wife, his second self! d'ye see, I know not what to say d'ye see.

Wife, Good Sweet-heart let me understand you, do you doubt me Sweet-heart? Mr. *King,* I doubt no body d'ye see, but a secret is a secret, d'ye see, and ought to be kept safe, tender as the Apple of ones eye, d'ye see, or the heart in ones bosome, d'ye see. *Wife,* Lord, lord, how I long to know it.

Mr. *King,* Yes you may long d'ye see, and shorten agen, d'ye see, but who payes for't d'ye see. *Wife,* Nay, I prithee Sweet-heart.

Mr. *King,* This it is d'ye see, to have a carefull Husband d'ye see, that riseth early and sits up late, d'ye see, while you she things, you lazy drones, you heavy ey'd wives d'ye see, run to your roost e're it chymes tenn, d'ye see me, there snug and snore till ten next morning, d'ye see; out upon such huswifes I cry.

Wife, I, but Sweet-heart, what needes all this? good, now let me know this secret, this secret you talk of. Mr. *King,* He that

goes

A Witty Combat:

goes to bed with a Cap of cares on his head is an early riser, d'ye see, he takes time by the fore lock, d'ye see, and must thrive d'ye see, as it is seen in Cynder women, and Small-cole men d'ye see, who have a penny in Purss to spend when the sluggish man does want it d'ye see. *Wife,* You weary me, good Sweet-heart to the purpose. Mr. *King,* It is a secret d'ye see, that you must keep as close d'ye see, as you do your sins, d'ye see, and reveale it to no body d'ye see, without my privity d'ye see.

wife, You have charm'd me chuck, pray let me know it.

Mr. *King,* Why then, d'ye see?--- *wife,* You know I do, dear heart you know I do, if you love me do not trifle thus,

Mr. *King,* Why then I must tell you and exhort you, d'ye see, not to lye so long a bed, you may get Fleas d'ye see, but no wealth there; a stirring Wife is the only woman d'ye see, when all is done, d'ye think my Brother *Bloodworth* would ever have come to be an Alderman or a Knight if his wife d'ye see had not had a care of the Kitchin, and been stirring? *wife,* Well, well, I'le begone Sweet-heart, I see you have a mind to mock me; prepare me for a secret to no purpose. Mr. *King,* Yes, it shall be to a purpose d'ye see, and a good purpose too d'ye see, this very morning e're the Crow had pist d'ye see, I got into my Barr d'ye hear, and as good fortune would have it d'ye see, in comes a Parson and as sweet a thing d'ye see, as modest and as comely as ever strod o're Threshold d'ye see, with him d'ye see, they drank a pint of Wine, and I found the Parson was ill inclin'd d'ye see; and his Coat lin'd with letchery d'ye see. *wife,* I pray Chuck by the way, where does that Parson preach? Mr. *King,* That's not to my matter d'ye see, I found her to be a vertuous Gentlewoman d'ye see, a stranger, and a Person that had a charge about her d'ye see, yea Jewells and Treasure d'ye see. *wife,* And what then Chuck?

Mr. *King,* Why, then I discharg'd the Parson d'ye see, after he had discharg'd the Reckoning d'ye see, as it was fit, but not before d'ye see. *wife,* So then, and what became of the Gentlewoman? Mr. *King,* Why she had a charge about her d'ye see, and you may think I would take care of her d'ye see, she is forth comeing. *wife,* Where, good Husband where?

Mr. *King,* In no worser place then our own house d'ye see.

wife,

Or, the Female Victor.

wife, Now blessing on thee Chuck I shall have a Companion.

Mr. *King,* Hold there child, d'ye see, we must go wisely to work d'ye see, and find out what she is d'ye see, for certainly she is a Gentlewoman of some quality, and therefore you must use her with all respect becoming her Person d'ye see; and when we find how matters stand let us alone to make our Markets d'ye see, if we don't hang me d'ye see. *wife,* Sweet-heart, believe me if there be any confidence to be put in Woman, your secret is lockt here in this Cabinet of which none keeps a key but your self; and if you think I retain any thing of a mothers wit in me let me alone to sift her out; were she as subtle as the great Grandmother of us all.

Mr. *King,* Be wise d'ye see, keep things close d'ye see, and then I warrant ye d'ye see. *Exeunt.*

Actus Secundus, Scæna Secunda.

Enter Madam Moders, and the Maid of the House.

Maid, My Mistress will waite upon you immediately forsooth, and I am sent in the meane time to know what you want.

Mod. I returne my equal thankes to your Master and Mistress, and tell them if they can spare me a Glass bigger then this I travail with, to dress me by, they will do me a kindness, and d'ye hear sweart a little Paper too, prithee, and I will pay for it. *Maid,* And Pen, and Inke forsooth? *Mod.* No, I never am without one 'tis so necessary. *She opens a little Cabinet & spread some Jewels and money upon the Table.*

Maid, Do you want nothing else, forsooth.

Mod. Not at present, *Maid,* I'le returne withall speed forsooth. *Mod.* Do so. *Exit Maid.*

Madam Moders alone.

Mod. These People are highly officious, I have not met the like civility in any place, what e're the reason is; if it continue thus, it will be wonderfull: I am a Stranger, and I must be so in my Deportment, as the sight of these drawes on respect, so a becoming distance in me is necessary; to be too familiar renders a woman light, though she be honest, and to be *pointing to her Jewels.* sowre

sowre and surley is as bad, and argues want of breeding, to avoid the censure of either, I'le walk between both, and as I find my Company, appear neither too Jocand, nor yet too severe.

Enter Maid.

Maid, I have brought the Glass, and the Paper forsooth.

Mod. You have done very well, set 'em down, I thank you.

Maid, My Mistress is just upon coming; forsooth.

Mod. She gives her self too great a trouble then, but she shall be most welcome.   *Maid,* I'le tell her so forsooth, God bless you forsooth.   *Mod.* I thank thee Wench, *gives her* thy prayer deserves something, and thou shalt have it.--- *money.*

Madam, Oh lack-a-day forsooth, no, no forsooth, but if it must be so forsooth I humbly thank you.

Mod. Farewell, this must be done; A grain *Exit Wench.* or two cast on a fruitful Soyle may multiply. The Wench looks not like one would be ungratefull, and I have gain'd experience by my Travail, that 'tis a thrift thus to be prodigal.   *Enter* Mrs. This should be the Gentlewoman of the house,   *King.* I should meet her now---but stay a little. --

Mrs. *King,* I fear I entrude forsooth; you are busie.

Mod. I cry you mercy Mistress, some Letters I am fitting for the Post, but no great business; to let my friends know where I do reside, that I may hear from them, that's all.

Mistress, And that's enough for me.   *a side*

Mod. Will you please to seat your self?   Mrs. *King,* I came indeed to invite you down to Dinner, goodness how these hangings look for want of brushing, what an idle Wench is this, the Curtaines and Vallance too, and the Chaires and Stooles too, what Windowes are here, I dare say they have not been well rub'd this week; the very Flore forsooth if you will believe me have shin'd so, you might have seen your face in't, goodness my Husband is such a man to put a Gentlewoman into a Roome,---Oh fie upon't, I fear forsooth you are but ill pleas'd as you are ill fitted, but indeed I promise it shall be amended.   *Mod.* It needes not Mistress, methinks 'tis very well, and so long as I am contented, you need not trouble your self.   Mrs. *King,* That is your goodness forsooth, but will you be pleased to walk down to Dinner, or will you have

Or, the Female Victor.

a Dish of Meat brought up? *Mod.* No, Mistress I dare not take that State upon me as to dine by my self, if I dine at all 'twill be with you, but truly I do not know how--- Mrs. *King,* If your Letters be all the hinderance, you have time enough to dispatch them forsooth. *Mod.* But I am all unready.
Mrs. *King,* You need not fear Strangers, my Husband and my self are all. *Mod.* Say you so Landlady, then I dare venture.
Mrs. *King,* Will you please to lead the way forsooth.
Mod. No, I hope you will leave me in Possession of my Chamber.
Mrs. *King.* Oh because of shutting of the door, 'tis very right, Lord how forgetfull I am, pray pardon me forsooth. *Exeunt.*

Actus Secundus, Scæna Tertia.

Enter Young Carleton and the Celler-man.

Y. Carlet. Where's my Sister? *Cellerm.* Who do you mean, my Mistress. *Yo. Carlet.* Prithee fool whom else?
Cellerm. Why then my Mistress your Sister is. ----
Yo. Carlet. What art thou drunk, where is she?
Cellerm. Drunk, what is that word drunk? did you ever know me drunk? let Coblers and Tinkers be drunk, did you ever know a Cellerman drunk? *Yo. Carlet.* Leave this fooling, where's my Sister? *Cellerm.* drunk! drunk! how can he tell any thing that is drunk? yes I know where your Sister is.
Yo. Carlet. Come where is she. *Cellerm.* You may go look, drunk! if I did know I would not tell you; drunk! *Yo. Carlet.* Go you are a Sot.--- *Cellerm.* A Sot! you Scriveners Boy, you Pen and Ink-horn, a Sot you Shittafritter. *Yo. Carlet.* Sirrah I shall box ye if you be thus sawcy. *Cellerm.* Box me, you cocaloach, you Tinder-box of a Clark, you Rump of a Lawyer, you box me, come, boy come, come an thou darst *Enter Drawer.* here I stand. *Yo. Carlet.* Very hardly, art not thou a base Rascall to abuse me thus I could kick thee about like a Foot-ball thou dirty fellow thou. *Cellerm.* Who *he offers to kick* me, kick me! Boy, boy, I'le kick thee boy, *and falls down.* thou spindle thou. *Draw.* Why how now, what's the matter?

ter? what down man? up again and take another. *helps him up.*

Cellerm. Drunk, and sot, and a Foot-ball to be kickt very fare, come kick for kick, I'le so tofs thee.   *Yo. Carlet.* welfare a good friend, you had given your self the other tofs else.

Draw. Come prithee get thee in.   *Cellerm.* He sayes I am drunk.   *Draw.* Why so thou art insufferably, cursedly drunk.

Cel'er. Thou liest in sober sadnefs, cursedly, to say so, though thou wert my brother ten times over.   *Draw.* No more of this; go, go thy wayes to sleep.   *Cellerm.* Sleep, Pox of sleep, I care not for sleep, I did not sleep ten wincks all last night, I never sleep, am up early and late for my Masters profit, yes *Carleton,* I am *Carleton,* what say you to that now *Carleton,* hah!

Draw. Prithee go thy wayes up Stares, or into some by Roome I prithee brother do.   *Cellerm.* Yes, I shall but d'ye hear *Carleton*, if ever I meet you *Carleton.*---   *Draw.* Thou'lt give him a Glafs of Wine.   *Cellerm.* What then? it may be so I will, and the best Wine in the Celler too; *Carleton* without being drunk *Carleton,* what say you to that *Carleton,* or a Sot, *Carleton,* or a Foot-ball *Carleton,* how think you of that *Carleton*?

D. Very well, prithee begone.   *Celler.* I will not tell I've ta'ne him by the hand.   *Draw.* Why that's well done.   *Cellerm.* Why you must think I cannot but love the man for the Womans fake, I do so Mr. *Carleton,* fhe is my Miftrefs Mr. *Carleton,*   *weepes.* and you are her Brother Mr. *Carleton,* Flefh and Blood Mr. *Carleton,* is very neer Mr. *Carleton.*   *Draw.* Now his kindnefs over-flowes: wilt thou go in?   *Cellerm.* I will have a pint of Canary first to drink to Mr. *Carleton,* I pray fetch it Brother I'le pay for it, honest Mr. *Carleton,* my Miftreffes Brother, but I am not drunk Mr. *Carleton,* nor a Sot Mr. *Carleton,* nor a Foot-ball Mr. *Carleton,* I may be a fool Mr. *Carleton,* but I love you Mr. *Carleton.*

Yo. Carlet. Thou art an honest fellow.   *Cellerm.* Yes, and ever was Mr. *Carleton;* yet I will creepe on all four to do you good Mr. *Carleton,* and yet I am not drunk Mr. *Carleton.*

Draw. Thou art not, thou art not.   *Cellerm.* It may be I am so, so, as they say in a fair way, but drunk I hate to be drunk.

Draw. Wilt thou go into a Roome.   *Cellerm.* I will not ftirr a foot, nor a leg, nor a finger, nor a thumb, unlefs Mr. *Carleton* commands

Or, the Female Victor.

commands me, and sayes honest Rogue I love thee.
Yo. Carlet. Why honest Rogue I love thee. *Cellerm.* Why so now; is not this better then to say you are drunk, a sot, and I'le kick you like a Foot-ball:——why now you are a Gentleman; and if you will go down into the Cellar I will not wast your Brothers Goods but what you drink there I'le pay for, a man can say no more. *Draw.* Another time Brother, another time.
Cellerm. Why what's that to thee, thou wilt be medling with other mens matters. *Draw.* No more quarrelling good brother: prithee go in. *Cellerm.* Do you say I shall go in Mr. Carleton, if you say the Word I am gone. *Yo. Carlet.* I, honest Rogue prithee begone. *Cellerm.* Why then I fly. *Stumbles.*
Draw. Hold there man. *Cellerm.* A pox of these Tobacco Pipes, they lie in a mans way basely: d'ye hear brother, if company come in you know where to find me: *Exit Cellerman.*
Draw. Fast asleep in the Cellar. *Yo. Carlet.* 'Tis a very honest fellow, did not this drink abuse him. *Draw.* 'Tis wonder'd where he gets it; in Company he shuns it, unless the sent of the Celler makes him drunk, no man can guess it, or drinks with his own shaddow. *Yo. Carlet.* Alas poor fellow; but where is my Sister? *Draw.* At dinner Sir, or neer upon't, with a most dainty Creature, a sweet modest thing. *Draw.* What is she? *Draw.* A meere stranger happen'd in here by chance; she is worth your seeing Sir. *Yo. Carlet.* Say'st thou so; I confess I'me something bashfull, but I'le venture.
Draw. I would I durst. *Exeunt.*

Actus Tertius. Scæna Prima.

Enter Young Carleton and Mistress King.

Mrs. *King.* Good lack *John* that you should be so simple to come so late, you know we dine betimes, especially when we have little Company; but if thou'lt take a snip such as it is, thou knowest thou art welcome *John.* *Yo. Carlet.* Pough, I care not for a dinner; I am vext I mist the sight o'th Lady.
Mrs. *King.* What Lady? *John?* *Yo. Carlet.* You think that

A witty Combat:

I know nothing; what Lady was it that came in this morning early, very early.   Mrs. *King.* Why *John* as I am a Woman.---
  Yo. Carlet. You know there was a Gentlewoman or Lady, stranger, came hither this morning as I said before; fie Sister why do you make it so strange to me your natural brother.---
  Mrs. *King.* Lord, how dost thou know this.
  Yo. Carlet. What do I not know ?   Mrs. *King.* Well now it is out; I ever took thee for a *Conjurer* by the scrawles thou us'd to make at home; nay in my conscience I think verily if thou would'st confess *John,* thou mak'st Almanacks *John,* and fortune Bookes *John;* Oh thou wer't alwaies a wag *John.*
  Yo. Carlet. Away fool; But may not I see this stranger ?
  Mrs. *King.* Well thou art a very Witch *John,* if I was not sworn to secrecy, yea by my own Husband let me be hang'd now, and thou by thy craft, thy wicked craft,(for so it is) hast found out all; but *John* thou canst not see her now for all thy cunning.
  Yo. Carlet. Why so, Sister ?   Mrs. *King.* In troth she's despatching Letters to be sent by the Post *John,*but to morrow *John.*
  Yo. Carlet. What then Sister ?   Mrs. *King.* We shall feast our friends *John,* and cannot in civility do less then invite her *John,* being a sojourner in our house *John,* and then thou shalt have thy belly full of seeing of her *Iohn,*but no words *Iohn;*if thou lov'st me; she is a wellbred Woman, I perceive that *John,*already *John;* but no words as you love me.   *Yo. Carlet.* Not a word I.
  Mrs. *King.* Be sure you come betimes, and be very neat *John,* 'twill be for your credit,and you may find the benefit of it in time *John.*   *Yo. Carlet.* Well, well, you know Sister I can be as spruce and finicall as another when I please.   Mrs.*King.* I know it *John.*   *Yo. Carlet.* And so adue Sister.   Mrs. *King.* fare you well brother *John.*   *Exeunt severally.*

Actus Tertius, Scæna Secunda

Enter madam Moders and the Maid of the House.

  Mod. Sweet heart shall I trouble thee.   *Maid.* No trouble forsooth to serve you.   *Mod.* Only to get a trusty messenger

Or, the Female Victor.

to deliver these Letters for me at the Post office, they are of concernment, and their miscarriage will much prejudice me; and therefore good sweet heart get one you know, and are assured of.

Maid. I'le carry them my self forsooth with my Mistresses leave.

Mod. That would do well indeed, but I fear thy mistress cannot spare thee. *Maid.* Yes I warrant you forsooth.

Mod. shall I not be too troublesome.

Maid. Oh no forsooth. *Mod.* I would not give her occasion of distaste. *Maid.* You need not fear it forsooth, she is of a better disposition then so. *Mod.* Well sweet heart I'le trust to your care then, there's money for 'em. *Maid.* They shall be safe delivered forsooth. *Exit.*

Mod. I find these people's over kindness mixt;
With greyness of subtlety; their plausibility
Gives only Credit to their busie purpose:
My Landlady like to one Grandam Eve,
Covets to know more then she ever shall;
Yet I'le afford her to tast of the Apple,
And since she'l needes trouble her self 'bout matters
That unconcernes her, I have fitted her,
My Letters which I know she'l intercept,
And pry into, to satisfie her longing,
(Though it be most inhospitable and base,)
I've fram'd accordingly there let her nibble,
Upon the bates I've laid and please her self,
With thinking she knowes all, when she knowes nothing:
Whil'st I've seem still a stranger to her meaning,
The more respects she shews me, I will be
The more reserv'd which will draw greater on,
With some continuance, poor shallow thing
To hope to sift me out in my affaires,
My Education has not been so slender,
Nor my Wit left naked of Rudiments,
To be a Price for thee and thy designes;
All bold inquisitors ought thus to be
Deluded with some shew of certainty.

D   *Enter*

A witty Combat:

Enter Maid of the House.

Maid. The Letters are delivered forsooth. *Mod.* Art sure on't? *Maid.* Sure on't forsooth, I deliver'd 'em with my own hands I'me sure. *Mod.* Say'st thou so, thou hast made hast then I'le promise thee. *Maid.* Have you any more service to command me forsooth? *Mod.* Not to night wench. *Maid.* Shall I not help to undress you forsooth?

Mod. I was not drest to day, and having nothing on but what I can cast off without thy help wench, I acquit thy diligence.

Maid. Good rest to your Ladiship. *Exit.*

Mod. Ladiship! so, now it begins to work,
Will it rest there! no, their conceits fly higher;
A forraign Princess, that for love of some
Brave *Englishman*, has left her Native Soyle,
And privately is here Arriv'd, or so;
But that's too lame, I'd rather have it thus.;
A Noble Person that to view the World
With an experienc'd eye, throwes off her State,
And like to the late active *Sweedish* Queen,
Retires into a Hut without her Retinue.
This meetes my fancy and comes neerest to
Their Wit (if they have any) here's a Field
For us to play in; as I see 'em move,
I'le poyse their admiration, and their love. *Exit.*

Actus Tertius, Scæna Tertia.

Enter Mr. King and his Wife.

Mr. King. Good sweet heart d'ye see, I would not have you so busie d'ye see, sweet heart a body does not know what may come on't d'ye see sweet heart. *Wife.* Prithee chuck hold thy tongue she's a brave Woman, nay, she must be a gallant Woman, I know what I intend well enough, take you no care, the businefs is mine chuck. *Mr. King.* Nay, d'ye see, I will not cross you sweet heart d'ye see, I wish all may go well, but you know she is but a stranger d'ye see, and a body may be deceiv'd d'ye see, of

what

Or, the Female Victor.

what you hope for d'ye see.   *Wife.* Let the fault lie on me then chuck, look here's my brother *John*.   *Enter Yo. Carleton.*

Mr. King. Brother you are very heartily welcome d'ye see, indeed you are d'ye see, I cann't dissemble d'ye see, in truth I cannot.

Yo. Carlet. I know it, what needes all this brother?

Wife. You are very early *John*, and very smug *John*.

Yo. Carlet. I came just from the Barbers, but where's the Lady?

Mr. King. What Lady? I know no Lady I protest d'ye see, but my own Wife your Sister d'ye see, who is the only Lady and Mistress of the house d'ye see.   *Wife.* Oh fie chuck, fie, you know, you know.   *Mr. King.* True, there is a strange Gentlewoman sojournes here d'ye see for some time, but I know no more on't d'ye see.   *Yo. Carlet.* Why then a Gentlewoman let her be, so I can but see her.   *Mrs. King.* I think thou long'st for't *John*, hearken and thou may'st hear her *John*, 'tis her   *sings above.* voice I promise thee.   *Yo. Carlet.* 'Tis a sweet one,---hold good Sister hold, I love a good voice as I love my life.

SONG.

    Away, away, flatter no more
    My easie faith, for now I see
      What thou in me seem'd to adore
      Thou mak'st thy pleasures property;
      No more, no more will I believe
      The man that can so soon deceive;

Yo. Carlet. Excellent, excellent,---Oh good   *She goes on.* Sister listen a little.   SONG.

    Nor was it flattery that did,
    Betray my heart, but that I lov'd,
      For which my Reason hath been chid,
      And I the said effects have prov'd;
      Then go, and I no more will see
      The man that has abused me.

Yo. Carlet. Incomparable! the Voice of Nightengales are hoarse to hers: shall I see her Sister?   *Wife.* Yes brother *John* you shall see her, but I must prepare her first, you will not know her else, she'l not be seen till Dinner time.   *Yo. Carlet.* Would it were ready, I shall be starv'd till then.

A witty Combat:

  Mr. *King*. Rather then so d'ye see, we have a bye Bit for ye.
  Yo. Carlet. You do not understand me brother.
  Wife. No, no, *John*, heaken to me, she that I shall call Couzen when we are at Dinner is the Party; and by that word *John* you may know her, but let none else take notice of it.
  Yo. Carlet. If her person be answerable to her voice, she will be taken notice of, whether I will or no.   Mr. *King*. He sayes right Wife d'ye see, the truth is I would not have my brother d'ye see, take any notice of her more then as a stranger.
  Wife. That is my meaning chuck.   Mr. *King*. for she may be a person of Quality d'ye see, and she may not d'ye see, all is not Gold that glisters.   *Yo. Carlet*. Good brother do not forstall the Market, when I know not how to carry my self you shall instruct me.   Mr. *King*. Nay, brother I do not speak for your carriage d'ye see, but for your good d'ye see, I would not have you ensnar'd d'ye see.   *Wife*. Ensnar'd Love! dost thou think that I, who am his natural born Sister, flesh, blood, and bone, would bring him into a snare love!   Mr. *King*. No chuck, but thou may'st be mistaken in the thing it self d'ye see chuck.
  Yo. Carlet. I perceive my Brother is not minded I should see the Gentlewoman, fare you well Sister, I'le not be troublesome.
  Mr. *King*. Good lord d'ye see, my own heart is not welcomer to my Bosome then you are to it d'ye see, but I speak by way of caution d'ye see, because I love you,   *Yo. Carlet*. Certainly I'me neither fool nor mad-man, I have my Wits about me.
  Wife. I *John* that thou hast *John* to my knowledge, more wit then twenty of 'em, and I am no fool neither *John*, thou knowest it, and I know more *John* then I will speak; be rul'd by me *John*, let me alone I'le order the business if thou hast a mind to her.
  Yo. Carlet. When I have seen her I will tell you more.
  Wife. And that thou shalt *John* for all his pettishness.
  Mr. *King*. Nay, I have done d'ye see, I'le medle no more in't.
      Enter two Gentlemen, with a Drawer.   *Exeunt.*
  1 *Gent.* Are the Guess all come.   *Draw.* Now you are come Gentlemen.   2 *Gent.* Are we the last Couple in Hell then.
  1 *Gent.* I believe not; is *Jack Carleton* come?   *Draw.* Yes Sir.   1 *Gent.* Nay then I fear we are tardy in point of time, for he us'd to be alwaies the last man born.   *Draw.*

Or, the Female Victor.

Draw. To day he came sooner then was exspected indeed, but you are not too late, in very good time Gentlemen; will you please to walk up. *2 Gent.* What else. *Exeunt.*

The Scæne of a Celler is discovered, wherein sits the Cellerman, by him a little Table, with a lighted Candle on it, and several sorts of Pots about it.

Cellerm. Here am I plac'd to attend the noice above Staires; I fill and fill, all manner of Vessels from the Gallon to the Gill Pot, and they bawle and call, and take 'em away as fast, but the divel of drop they give me; none has the heart to say honest *Wat* here's to thee, and God-a mercy 'tis good Wine, hang their money, I respect their love, but thou art not belov'd *Wat*, therefore love thy self *Wat*, the Poets say thou art Prince of the Spiggot and art in thy Kingdome when thou art in the Celler, if so the 1 all these are my Subjects, the *French*, the *Dutch* and the *Spanish*, nay I dare say if need be I can command the *Welsh*, the *Irish*, the *Scotish*, and the *English*; then *Wat* do like a Prince make use of thy Subjects as they make use of thee, for they would be musty else.--- *within Wat,* dost thou hear *Wat* thou art call'd upon, thou *Wat, make* must make hast they say him,---so be it, by, and by, *hast.* this must be fill'd with Sherry, this with Canary brisk, this with old Malligo, but d'ye hear me Sherry, Canary *points to* brisk, and old Malligo, there's none of you shall *the Pots.* go 'till I have ta'ne excise---here *Wat*, since no body else will, I'le drink to thee my self, 'tis a cup of pure Sherry, *Wat*, why gramercy---this is something now, here is good fellowship, and no body sees! they say thou hast a good Pallat *Wat*, *fills his Ves-* I'le try it in faith, here's to thee in a Cup *sel and cup.* of brisk Canary, off with it man, and so I will *VVat*, and now what say'st thou to a Cup of old Malligo *VVat*? it cannot but be good, the best in Town *VVat* I approve it, off with it man; doubtest thou me *VVat*? now are we Company for Poets *VVat*, but hold--- wilt thou let thy *French* and *Dutch* Subjects go free *VVat*? No thou wilt be an unjust Prince then, as for the *English*, *VVelch*, *Irish*, and *Scotish*, they are poor, acquit 'em, acquit 'em, then here's to thee in a Cup of Rhenish 'tis cleansing drink *VVat*; off with it, art thou now for a Cup of spruce Claret, or White *VVat*? both; thou shalt

shalt have 'em intire boy, intire boy; rich Wine *VVat*, huge rich Wine *VVat*, damnable searching *VVat*; yea *falls into his* it is so, it is so, it is so. *Chair & sleeps*

Enter two Drawers.

1 *Draw.* Here he is with all his Artillery about him, dormant as a Mouse. 2 *Draw.* Does he not sleep Dogs sleep.

1 *Draw.* No you may hear him to *Hogesden.*

2 *Draw.* I'le waken him. 1 *Draw.* By no means, he sat up late last night, come help up *They carry the Pots off and so* with these Pots. *The Scæne is drawn.*

Enter Mrs. *King, and Young Carleton.*

Mrs. *King.* Now Dinner's done, while they are merry *John* let you and I consider of the matter; how do you like the Person, *John?* *Yo. Carlet.* Exceeding well; good at discourse, and of a modest countenance. Mrs. *King.* Why law ye now, did not I tell you this *John?* and you would not believe me, my Husband like a fool was of the same faith too. *Yo. Carlet.* Pough I did believe you Sister, but has she that estate you talke of too?

Mrs. *King.* What do you doubt me there too *Iohn?* yes she has an Estate and a glorious Estate *Iohn*, but what it is I do not know *Iohn*, yet I can shrewdly guess *Iohn* and if need be.

Yo. Carlet. Is it in her own hands. Mrs. *King.* Why now I see thou art not so wise as I thought thee to be *Iohn*, in whose hands should it be else *Iohn*. *Yo. Carlet.* Where lies it.

Mrs. *King.* Between Heaven and Earth *Iohn*, does not all peoples Estates lie there you fool. *Yo. Carlet.* I would not be made one of good Sister. Mrs. *King.* Nay, if you be there abouts *Iohn* I have done. *Yo. Carlet.* I must confess I never saw a person I ever fancy'd better; Pray Heaven my flames consume me not, they take so soon, and are so fierce. Mrs. *King.* Fear not *Iohn*, I am her bosome *Iohn*, and if she were not for your turne, you should not have her *Iohn*, but you must be rul'd *Iohn*.

Yo. Carlet. In any thing dear Sister thou wilt have me.

Mrs. *King.* Then put your self *Iohn* into an Equipage beyond your self *Iohn*, appear as I would have you like a Lord *Iohn*, with your Coach and Foot-boyes, the sooner *Iohn* the better; were't to morrow, and treat her nobly *Iohn*, were I a man, *Iohn* I could

do

Or, the Female Victor.

do it to the life *Iohn*, I know you want not friends to furnish you, let it be so *Iohn*, for she is a Lady, & none but him is recommended for a Lord will carry her *Iohn*.   *Yo. Carlet.* It shall be done dear Sister; I know where to be provided both with money and Cloaths.   *Mrs. King.* And then let me alone to manage things for thy advancement *Iohn*.   *Yo. Carlet.* I, dear Sister prithee use thy Interest.   *Mrs. King.* If we should not do well for one another *Iohn*, how would the World look on us *Iohn*? I love thee heartily *Iohn*.   *Yo. Carlet.* I know thou dost, and there is no love lost on either side.   *Mrs. King.* I'le lordifie thee *Iohn*, I'le be thy HERAULD: thou shalt no more be plain *Iohn*, nor poor *Iohn*, nor honest *Iack*, as thy friends call thee; but my Lord *Iohn*, I will have it in my thought, and will dream upon't, for man, I must not call you brother, nor you me Sister, observe that *Iohn*, yet I would not have you to forget *Iohn*, that I am your Sister.

Yo. Carlet. Dost think I will? but come, our friends do stay.

Mrs. King. Then my Lord *Iohn* I pray lead on the way. *Exeunt.*

Actus Quartus, Scæna prima.

Enter Cellerman, Drawer, and Cook-maid.

Cellerm. Yesterday was a hot day, a wicked hot day.

Draw. No, 'twas a very cool day; how canst thou call it a hot day when thou wert in the Celler all the while?

Cellerm. Why goodman puppy the Celler is the hotest place in the house.   *Draw.* To thee sometimes it may be so.

Cookm. I know not what it was to him or you, but to me I'me sure it was a very sultry hot day.   *Draw.* I, thou art a Wench that deales in fire, but he is for the other Element.

Cellerm. You, ly you Logerhead I hate Water.

Draw. But thou art quarrelsome in thy Ale.

Cellerm. I hate that too.   *Draw.* Small Beer can never stir thee.   *Cellerm.* I do not much affect that neither, it rots my Guts.   *Draw.* Some secret Liquor, some *Nepenthe* as the Poets call it, inspires thee now and then abominably: but I am taught to tell you Brother mine, and Sister *Eke*, that if you chance to see

this

A witty Combat:

this day a Lord in shape as like Mr. *Iohn Carleton* as Puss to Cat, you must not think it him.   *Cellerm.* What him, what him?
   Draw. Even him, I spoke off Mr. *Iohn Carlet*, yea though you know the Nose upon his face you must not think it him, but.—
   Cellerm. But what?   *Draw.* A Lord.   *Cookm.* A Lord, ha, ha, ha.   *Cellerm.* I shall laugh too, prithee what Lord.
   Draw. The Lord knowes what, but hear me it is no laughing matter mums the word.   *Maid.* May not one winck and laugh?
   Draw. yea winck you may but laugh ye may not.
   Cellerm. Where didst thou get this Tone thou wicked elder.
   Draw. Even of a Parson truly, yea verily it was, that brought the Lady to this place assuredly.   *Maid.* Hold there is a Coach at door, no feasting I hope this day.   *Enter Yo. Carleton*
   Cellerm. 'Tis he.   *Draw.* 'Tis not he.   *with two Foot-boyes.*
   Maid. But I say 'tis he.   *Cellerm.* And I am sure 'tis he.
   Yo. Carlet. What he?   *Omnes.* My Lord.   *Yo. Carlet.* You do well there,—   *Gives them money.*
   Maid. Ne're go now if he ben't   *Exits.*
a hansome Gentleman.   *Draw.* And generous.
   Cellerm. 'Tis pitty he is not a Lord indeed, now my trouble comes on.   *Maid.* Or mine rather.   *Draw.* No I dare assure you the day will not be so hot to either of you as yesterday was.   *Cellerm.* Then I shall be plagu'd with night work.
   Draw. Why all times and seasons are alike to thee so thou dost drink and sleep.   *Cellerm.* Hang ye Raskal I never was a drinker, a thorough drinker in my life.   *Draw.* Not to speak of.
   Maid. Nay truly, VVat is as sober a man when he is not drunk, as any of us all.   *Draw.* Ha, ha, ha, come, come, let's about our business.   *Exeunt.*

Enter Young Carleton, Mrs. King, Madam Moders, and two Foot-boyes.

   Yo. Carlet. Boyes.   *Boyes.* My Lord?   *Yo. Carlet.* Get you down Staires, take a Roome there.   *Boyes.* Yes my Lord.
   Yo. Carlet. And when I call be ready.   *Boyes.* We shall my Lord.   *Mrs. King.* And one of you bid one of my men bring up some Wine, shall it be so my Lord?   *yo. Carlet.* I come not to be idle, 'twas well thought on.   *Mrs. King.* These boyes
are

Or, the Female Victor.

are as bad as young Coach-horses, they   *Exeunt Boyes.*
take up so much time in teaching it wearies one.

  Mrs. *King.* You may remedy it as they say my Lord, and have those that are prepared to your hand my Lord.

  Yo. Carlet. I may so indeed, but many of them have practic'd sawcyness and become surley.   *Enter Drawer*
Oh art thou come; where are my Foot-boyes?   *with Wine.*

  Draw. Below, my Lord.   *Mod.* Do I dream? a Lord *aside.*
since yesterday!   *Yo. Carlet.* Fellow fill some Wine.

  Draw. Yes my Lord.   *Mod.* Can this be real?   *aside.*

  Yo. Carlet. Madam my hearty service to you.

  Mod. You do too much eclips you title in't Sir.

  Yo. Carlet. Not a whit Madam, Honour's bound to serve a person of your vertue and your Presence: will you be pleas'd to take the aire to day, my Coach is *ready*.   *Mod.* Were I dispos'd, I could cammand one Sir.   *Yo. Carlet.* So you may mine Madam.

  Mod. Not I Sir.   Mrs. *King.* Why will not your Ladiship accept his proffer?   *Mod.* You put strange Titles upon people Mistress. *The Lord and Lady went over the Green.*

  Yo. Carlet. A smart wit; would you would honour me so much Madam.   *Mod.* As how Sir?   *Yo. Carlet.* As to walk with me over the green.   *Mod.* No my Lord, I should be wet shod then, *April*'s dew is deep.   *Yo. Carlet.* And therefore sweet.

  Mod. Your Lordship makes that up a vulgar Error.

  Yo. Carlet Well Sister.---   Mrs. *King.* Art mad or *aside.*
foolish.   *Yo. Carlet.* Both; I am not right.   *Mod.* I do believe so.   Mrs. *King.* His Lordship is not well.   *Mod.* A-lack good Gentleman.   *Yo. Carlet.* I beg your pardon; I am forc'd to leave you.   *Mod.* No force Sir, in good time.

  Yo. Carlet. She would be rid of me.   Mrs. *King.* How do you my Lord.   *Mod.* His Lordship would to Coach.

  Yo. Carlet. Again.   Mrs. *King.* Will your Lordship have any Comfortable thing?   *Yo. Carlet.* No I'le to Coach, the Lady has directed me.   *Mod.* In the right way I hope Sir.

  Yo. Carlet. Again! I will not stay, call my Boyes fellow.

  Draw. Why Children,---I forgot my self,---Boyes,---I'le send 'em up an't please your Lordship.   *Yo. Carlet.* No, tell 'em I'me

a going, and 'tis enough.   *Draw.* I shall my Lord.   *Exit.*
  Yo. Carlet. Madam give me leave to kiss your hand,---your servant, your servant Mistress.   *Exit.*
  Mod. His Lordship will be hard put to't, to serve us both.
  Mrs. *King.* Me he cannot, you he may Madam.   *Mod.* Good Couzen, or Landlady, the last is the truest, be not so prodigal of your favours in confering Titles of Honour at this rate.
  Mrs. *King.* Why d'ye think I do not know you to be a Lady Madam.   *Mod.* I should be so were I a Madam really; but you are free in the bestowing it as I suppose upon any person, because the word is common, and therefore Landlady I do abhor it.
  Mrs. *King.* Indeed you mist my meaning Madam, I ne're apply Titles to any person but such as I know deserves 'em, as on your self, my Lord, or so.   *Mod.* But is he, that was here, a Lord really descended.   Mrs. *King.* A very Lord I do assure you Madam.   *Mod.* Since yesterday translated! for then he din'd with us or my memory deceives me.   Mrs. *King.* He did so, but then he was disguis'd.   *Mod.* Not with drink I'me sure.
  Mrs. *King.* No, but in his freikes as they call 'em, and he has many, some times he will go in the Street as he went for a wager, with his Collor all unbutton'd, swetting like a Bull, his Cloak hanging behind him, in one hand his Gloves, the other full of Papers, that one would take him for all the World to be some young Clerk, or one that had Relation to the Law. At another time when he has a mind to be privately merry he throwes his Cloak over his Nose, and in he steales, and is as good Company!----
  Mod. For a mad Lord.   Mrs. *King.* Nay he is not mad, in truth he has some whymseys but they are huge becoming I'le assure you Madam, if you were acquainted with 'em; then he has been bravely bred Madam.   *Mod.* So a Lord should be.
  Mrs. *King.* He's a good *Latinest* they say, and writes a very good Hand.   *Mod.* Those are very good commendations for a Clerk indeed.   Mrs. *King.* Or for a Lord or a Gentleman or any body else believe me Madam; and then he's as sober, as vertuous, and as hansome a young Lord though I say't as any is within a hundred miles of his head, and of as sweet a disposition.
  Mod. Methinkes you dwell too long upon his prayses.

Mrs.

Or, the Female Victor.

Mrs. *King.* If you were but well acquainted with him Madam.---
Mod. I must to my Chamber. Mrs. *King.* And I'le wait on you Madam. *Exeunt.*

Enter Drawer, and a Foot-boy with a Box of sweet Meates.

Draw. How now, did these come from your Lord.
Boy. Yes to the Lady. *Draw.* Where did thy Lord pick thee up? *Boy.* What's that to you Jack-a-napes. I'le tell your Mistress Sirrah. *Draw.* Why how now little impudence will you be lug'd by the Eares Sirrah, does your Lord teach you no better manners you Arss-worme? *Boy.* I cannot tell---I must speak with your Mistress. *Enter Mrs. King.*
Mrs. *King.* Who's there? *Boy.* My Lord presents his love to you forsooth, and desires you would present his service with this Box of sweet Meates to the Lady. Mrs. *King.* Thou shalt see it deliver'd thy self, Boy come in with me. *Boy.* Your man is so unlucky he will not let me alone. Mrs. *King.* fie, fie, meddle with a Child. *Exeunt.*
Draw. There's a young Pimp now, he'l be a stew'd Rogue in time if his Lords Trade continues. *Exit.*

Enter Madam Moders, Mrs. King, and the Foot-boy.

Boy. He bid me tell your Ladiship he'l wait upon you in the afternoon, and have you abroad. *Mod.* Will he, but 'tis a question whether I shall give my self that leisure or not.
Mrs. *King.* By all meanes good madam. *Mod.* How ever boy prithee present my service and thankes to him, *gives him* there's something for thy paines. *money.*
Boy. Your humble servant madam. *Exit.*
Mod. D'you observe Landlady, the word madam is so out of fashion 'tis a Foot-boyes Complement. Mrs. *King.* What shall I call you then? Princess. *Mod.* Away, away, I abandone flattery and do Titles that are misapply'd. Mrs. *King.* Why directly your Presence and excellent parts cannot speak you less,---but saving my tale forsooth, odds so I cry your Ladiships mercy.
Mod. Nay let it go on so. Mrs. *King.* Why then an't please you how d'ye like my Lord? is he not as I told you a sweet condition'd Gentleman? *Mod.* He begines well. Mrs. *King.* And so he'l continue to the end I warrant ye. *Mod.* That's more then
E 2 you

A Witty Combat:

you know Landlady.   Mrs. *King.* My life on't.   M*od.* 'Tis a hard venture in my opinion Landlady.   *Exeunt.*

Enter Young Carleton and Footboyes.

Yo. Carlet. Let the Coach wait, and stay you there.
Boyes. We shall my Lord.   *Exit Young Carleton.*
1 *Boy. Jack* let thee and I crack a Pint together.   2 *Boy.* I have no money.   1 *Boy.* Hang't, I have, the Lady was generous to me this morning.   2 *Boy.* Would she had been so to me.
1 *Boy.* 'Tis all one between thee and I, let's call the Coachman in and see if he will joyne.   2 *Boy.* The more the merrier.

Exeunt.

Enter young Carleton, Madam Moders, and Mistriss King.

Young Carleton. Deare Madam.   *Moders.* Good my Lord do not deceive your self.   *Mistriss King.* My Lord an't please your honour, the word Madam grates her eares she sayes, because it is so common.   *Young Carleton.* Why then my Princess, for so you are asserted in my thoughts, I will assure you most accomplisht Lady.   *Mistriss King.* I, this sounds well, how can you find in your heart to deny his Lordship? most accomplisht Lady.   *Moders.* My Lord, though young, I do perceive has been train'd up in Complements, they are indeed the Courtiers prayers.   *Young Carleton.* Then they should prevaile.

Moders. With Fooles, but not with such have understanding.
Mistriss King. Most accomplisht Lady, even for my sake.
Moders. How will my Credit stand that am a stranger, to be Coach'd out by one, and so soon too, upon so slender an account.

Young Carleton. My heart shall stand betwixt you and all calumny, it shall return the filth into their face that spits at yours.

Moders. You speak Nobly, my Lord.   *Young Carleton.* My Actions shall second my words most singular Lady.

Mistriss King. Most accomplisht, most singular   *aside* Lady----- well *John* thou deserv'st her.

Moders. You do so powerfully importune me, my Lord, I have no fence left for my self, especially your honour being oblig'd to all Civilities.   *Young Carleton.* Count me a Tartar, most horrid Villain if I infringe, or trespass in the least upon your

virtue

Miſtriſs King. Is it granted? moſt accompliſht, moſt ſingular Lady.   *Moders.* For your ſake Landlady, you ſee I can deny nothing that's virtuous and civil, as you ſay my Lord is.

Miſtriſs King. As the innocent Babe, moſt accompliſht, and moſt ſingular Lady.   *Young Carleton.* Will you vouchſafe your hand moſt gracious Lady.

Miſtriſs King. Moſt gracious Lady, that's another.   *Young Carleton.* To me this honour is receiv'd above rules of compariſon unexpreſſible.   *Yo. Carleton takes Moders by the hand.*

Exeunt.

Enter Old Mr. *Carleton, and his Wife, and* Mr. *George Carleton their Eldeſt Son.*

Old Mr. *Carlet.* George you are privy to your brothers ſecrets, how does he find the Ladies pulſe to beat? has he hopes of her.

Mr. George Carlet. Doubtleſs Sir he has.   *Old Mr. Carlet.* He buſſels ſtrangely do'ſt think her worth his charge and toyle?

Mr. George Carlet. If he were not aſſur'd of that (as I believe he is) he would not certainly purſue with ſo much eagerneſs his ſuit, that's my beliefe Sir.   *Mrs. Carlet.* So it is mine, George thy brother is no fool.   *Mr. George Carlet.* That the Town knowes, and if he ſhould miſcarry 'twould be ſtrange, I know not what the power of love may do.   *Old Mr. Carlet.* Doſt think ſhe is the perſon that he ſpeakes her?   *Mr. George Carlet.* Seriouſly Sir her breeding and her habit does denote her a perſon of no ſmall repute and quality, they ſay ſhe ſpeakes the Languages.

Old Mr. *Carlet.* Believe me that's rare in a Woman.

Mr. George Carlet. I'me in a manner a ſtranger to her perſon, (for ſhe is very ſhy, and takes ſtate on her) but ſo I've heard Sir.

Old Mr. *Carlet.* Perhaps by ſome that do not underſtand her.

Mr. George Carlet. I know not that Sir.   *Old* Mr. *Carlet.* Gibberiſh you know ſtartles the ignorant   *Old* Mrs *Carlet.* Let her be what ſhe will I'le ſee her.   *Old Mr. Carlet.* I prithee do, and what then?   *Old* mrs. *Carlet.* Marry I'le know what ſhe is and from whence ſhe came.   *Old* mr. *Carlet.* Do ſo, 'twill appear well in thee, I'le not be ſeen in't.   *Old* mrs. *Carlet.* And know what ſhe has too I'le warrant you before my Son ſhall Bed her.

mr. *George.* My Siſter *King* and my Brother (as I am inform'd) can

can satisfie you in that point forsooth. *Old* mrs. *Carlet.* And so they shall, I'le thither presently. *Exeunt.*

Enter Madam Moders, mr. King and mrs. King.

Mod. Good now, be not so importunate, I'le not see 'em.

Mr. King. Why how comes this d'ye see, I thought that all had been right and sure d'ye see. mrs. *King.* What has he done that has displeas'd you most accomplisht, most singular and most gracious Lady? *Mod.* I'le not be blown upon by every person he brings with him, become the Town talk, have my Credit stale, and buz'd i'th eares of every idle fellow. mrs. *King.* Indeed la if you will believe me, most accomplisht, most singular and most gracious Lady as his Lordship calls you; there is no body with him but his Lady mother and a Banquet of Sweet-meates.

Mod. My Lord (though in himself a nobler person) had never been admitted to my present but for your mighty importunities; I love to be retir'd, not to be shewn like to a piece of *Dutch*-work, newly brought over to all sorts of people; pray let my Lord know where his error lies. mr. *King.* And reason good d'ye see.

mrs. *King.* If we durst be so bold chuck, but his Lady mother waites most accomplisht, most singular and most gracious Lady.

Mod. I cry you mercy and excuse me to her.

mr. King and his Wife go off and bring Young Carleton and his mother in, the sence of his gross error did transport me.

Yo. Carlet. This is my mother and your servant Lady.

Mod. Your Lordship has oblig'd my service to her, your faithfull servant Lady. *Salute.*

Yo. Carlet. Will you vouchsafe to grace this *A Banquet* homely present with your acceptance Lady? *is set out.*

Mod. My Lord you know I am no Chaplaine, nor needes there a preludium to a Banquet. *Yo. Carlet.* My meaning is most precious Lady you'd add a sweetness to the meates by tasting them.

Mod. Coming from you my Lord compos'd of sweetness they need no more addition. mrs. *Carlet.* Words are but wind, you seem to be a Gentlewoman, pray what are you?

Mod. More then I seem. Mrs. *Carlet.* Where were you born?

Mod. At *Billinsgate.* *Yo. Carlet.* Oh, dear Lady.

mod.

Or, the Female Victor.

Mod. Why, should I tell her I was born at *Rome* what's she the neerer. mrs. *Carlet.* Have you an estate, *Mod.* I hope I have. mrs. *Carlet.* Where lies it pray. *Mod.* Where you shall never find it Lady,---why thus inquisitive. Mrs. *Carlet.* Have you the *Languages*, as they say you have? *Mod.* Let your Son try me. *Yo. Carlet.* Oh most precious Lady I am a stranger to the most of them. *Mod.* So am I to your Mothers scrutiny, I could giv't a worse Title, but hereafter if you intend to stock up precious time, pray spare your Visits, for they will be fruitless.

Yo. Carlet. Oh mother your too indulgence has undone *Exit.* me, I'me lost for ever, all my hopes are shipwrackt.

Mrs. *Carlet.* Why so Child? *Yo. Carlet.* She has prohibited me the sight of her, which is as precious to me as my Being.

Mrs. *Carleton.* 'Tis very strange, let her be ne're so high in Birth and breeding, methinks she should not blame the Parents care, for that will be, and must be. *Yo. Carlet.* That's the point I must insist upon; and that no more obstruction may happen to my happiness, my Sister will informe my Father & your self the state of her affaires, which may be mine. Mrs. *Carlet.* Do so and you shall find me Instrumental for thy advancement.

Yo. Carlet. And dear Sister prithee use all thy wit and interest with her. Mrs. *King.* Do ye doubt it brother *John*, no Lord but when she's present. *Exeunt.*

Enter two Drawers, and Cellerman to take away the Voyders.

1 *Drawer.* They have not carry'd away all I see.

Cellerman. No, they have left the Voyders, and something more.

2 *Drawer.* What do you do here, get you to your Garrison the Celler. *Cellerman.* Prithee prate not, this is my Garrison or any other place where I am safe, *They scramble for——* nay if you fall to scrambling I am for you.

2 *Drawer.* These will spoile thy drinking. *Cellerman.* My drinking Jack Sprat, I could box thee sirrah. 1 *Drawer.* No, I dare say you wrong him, he's no drinker. *Cellerm.* Who I? never in my life thou know'st it. 1 *Drawer.* The very stem oth' Celler now and then besots thee, Brother does it not?

Cellerm. That may be, for the Wine fumes and flyes into a mans head most plaguely—— but now stand off—— let me speak the
sense

sense of the Poet to the Auditory.
      I'm not the Person that I seem'd to be,
      Although a Cellerman, I am not he.   *Exeunt.*

Actus Quintus, Scæna Prima.

Enter Madam Moders alone.

Moders. GLory depends on Conquest, I have brought
    (After so many Tryals of my Wit,)
My amorous Lord, and his averse Allyes
Upon their knees to supplicate my love;
This very minute I expect his Lordship
To hurry me into the Armes of Hymen:
For that's their drift I know, let their pretence
Be what it will; and i'le imbrace it.   *Enter young Carleton.*
  Young Carleton. My dearest Lady are you ready.
  Moders. You see I am, but for what end my Lord.
  Young Carleton. To heare the Musick.   *Moders.* I have reason to love it my Lord.   *Young Carleton.* You are the Empresse of it.   *Exeunt.*

Enter Mr. King and his Wife.

  Mr. King. Well they are gone d' yee see, and blessings follow both of 'em d' yee see.   *Mrs. King.* I, now you say so Chuck, but the time has been.   *Mr. King.* What has the time been honey? you know d' yee see, 'twas my care at first d' yee see to preserve her here d' yee see.   *Mrs. King.* I but you never meant her for my Brother *John*, and that my Father takes unkindly Chuck.   *Mr. King.* Who not I sweet heart? I never meant any man else d'yee see, as I am here d' yee see, why you know I love my Brother *John* d'yee see, with all my heart d'yee see, I only did expresse my care of him, being but a young man d'yee see, and I knew not how things stood d'yee see, which it seemes you knew better d'yee see.   *Mrs. King.* Well chuck, what an honour will it be to my Father in his age to have a Prince, or Princesse to his Grandchild.   *Mr. King.* How's that sweet heart?
  Mrs. King. Nay, I say no more. Windows have eares.   *Exeunt.*

Enter

Or, the Female Victor.

Enter Young Carleton, his Brother George, Madam Moders, and several others attended upon by Drawers.

1 *Gent.* A Wedding and no Musick. *Draw.* They are i'th house Sir. *Yo. Carlet.* Prithee let's have 'em; and now most gracious Lady as you have given spirit to my Clay, and made my soul to raper in its Cottage by this blest Conjunction; know I'me still your servant. *Mod.* My Lord I think all Complements ridiculous after this Ceremony. *Enter Musick.*

George Carlet. Come here's a good divertion, what Songs have you? *Fidler.* A hundred and fifty, two hundred if need be, I furnish all the Faires and markets with 'em; I keep a Poet in pay on purpose Gentlemen, which is no small charge to me you must think, 'tis true the Poet is a prety wit, but what's wit or good lines, nothing, unless well Humour'd and well Sung, I sing 'em all my self, though the lines be never so bad I make 'em twang, which sets off a Poet mainly you know. *George Carleton.* Pox take you for a puppy, leave praising your self and let us hear a Song.

Fidler. What Song will you have Gentlemen?
Omnes. Any, any. *Fidler.* What say you to that of the love between a Kitchin Wench and a Chimney Swifter.
Yo. Carlet. Sirrah d'ye know where you are.
Fidler. I cry you mercy Sir, I'le fit you with a rare one. *Sings.*
2 *Gent.* Hold your howling and behang'd, what a mouth he makes, how he grates the words and teard the sense?
1 *Gent.* He's good for nothing, canst thou tumble?
Fidler. Tumble? I don't understand ye Sir.
Yo. Carlet. Come, come, a Dance or two, and so good Night Mr. Fidler. *George Carlet.* 'Tis pitty to keep thee too long from thy happiness. *They play, the company dance.*
Yo. Carlet. There are you pleas'd. *Fidler.* Very nobly we thank your Honour. *Exeunt Musick.*
Yo. Carlet. Now Gentlemen I must crave your pardon, Lady, your hand. *Exeunt.*
Omnes. A good Night to you Both. *Exeunt.*

F *Enter*

A Witty Combat:

Enter two or three Clerks.

1 Clerk. Newes, newes, newes, Boyes. *2 Clerk.* What Newes, what newes? *1 Clerk.* Wonderfull, strange and true newes, newly Printed and newly come forth. *3 Clerk.* Of the downfall of *Grantham* Steeple; the miraculous discovery of old Braziel by a Ship-Carpenter at *Namptwich*, or the horrid murder of *Tom Thumb*, some such paltry stuffe. *1 Clerk.* You are wide of the matter: Mr. *John Carleton* is married.

2 Clerk. Prithee to whom? *1 Clerk.* To no less then a Princess, a *German* Princess believe me. *3 Clerk.* Why then it must be no more Mr. *John Carleton*, but my Lord *John Carleton*.

2 Clerk. Pough, I don't believe it. *1 Clerk.* Thou art an incredulous Coxcomb, I tell thee they keep their Court and State at *Durham* House 'ith *Strand*, there you may see his Lordship if you have a mind to't. *2 Clerk.* If I thought he would not take too much State upon him, I'd put my Holy-day Habit on, and take a day to visit him. *3 Clerk.* Set thy time and we'l go with thee.

2 Clerk. Two dayes hence.

1 Clerk. Agree'd, agree'd. *Exeunt.*

Enter Mr. King, and his Wife.

Wife. What happy Instruments have we been Chuck in this businesss, they talk of giving hundreds of pounds to others, and I'me sure we deserve thousands. *Mr. King.* That's very rightly said d'ye see, but for my part d'ye see, I look not for a penny d'ye see. *Wife.* In troth Chuck if thou dost not, I do, there's the short and the long on't, my Father's gone to see if she will settle her Estate upon my Brother *John*. *mr. King.* And a great deal of reason there is in't, d'ye see Sweet-heart, for he has been at a vast charge d'ye see. *Wife.* Her Estate will make amends for all, and though he is a false Lord now, her Estate will make him currant; money will buy Honour at any time Chuck.

mr. King. I if, it hit right, but there are so many cheates abroad d'ye see. *Wife.* Why I hope thou wavering faith'd man thou dost not think the Princess my Sister one? *mr. King.* If she be such a person, and have such an Estate d'ye see, my Brother may bless the time he ever see us d'ye see, but if she be not the person and has no Estate, why then 'tis a meer cheat d'ye see, and we shall
suffer

Or, the Female Victor.

suffer in our credit cruelly d'ye see.   *Wife.* Lord help thy simple head; I warrant thee man.   *Exeunt.*

Enter Old Carleton, and mr. *John Carleton.*

Old Carlet. Unfortunate boy, thou art undone for ever.

Yo. Carlet. Bless me, Sir, you do amaze me wonderfully.

Old Carlet. After thy loss of time, thy vast expences in riotous Banquettings, perpetual Visits, what hast thou purchas'd?

Yo. Carlet. A reward above my merit Sir; a virtuous Princess of high Endowments, and of ample fortunes, rich in her self, her parts speak her a Dowre, sufficient for a person of my quality had she no other Riches to adorne her.   *Old Carlet.* A very Pusscat, a subtle Carrion, and a cursed cheat.   *Yo. Carlet.* With pardon Sir, I partly do imagine the cause of this your sudden discomposure, you prest her in my absence (like a Father) to settle her Estate on me, which she unwilling to consent to, hath rais'd this storme within your quiet Bosome. *Old Carlet.* An Estate, where lies it? at the Brick-hills, foolish boy; she is not worth a groat, but what thou hast out of thy prodigal affection given her, her Jewels are but counterfeit, and she a base imposture.   *Yo. Carlet.* Good Father let not your passion so deceive your reason, she cannot be so Sir.   *Old Carlet.* Boy, she's a Strumpet, a vagrant, a Wandring Baggage that has two Husbands beside thy self; a paltry Shoomaker is one of them, this I'le make out.   *Yo. Carlet.* You have thrown Daggers to my heart Sir.   *Old Carlet.* Be not troubl'd Boy, I'le hamper her, I warrant thee, come along with me. *Exeunt.*

Enter madam Moders alone.

Mod. I do expect a storme, and suddenly, by my bad dreames; which tell me I must wade through mud and Water; signifying troubles dangerous ones: yet I shall pass them all, cleer as a sheet that has been whiten'd by the whitsters hand.

Enter Old Carleton, Young Carleton, Constable and others.

Old Carlet. That's the Strumpet.   *Mod.* Who do you handle, you unreveren'd Raskalls? why Father, Husband, what do you mean?   *Old Carlet.* To hang you Whore for having of two Husbands   *Mod.* Is that all? Ha, ha, ha.   *Yo. Carlet.* Sure she is innocent, her courage speaks her so.   *Old Carlet.* Away with her Mr. Constable.   *Exeunt.*

Enter Mr. *King and his Wife.*

Mrs. *King.* Oh Chuck, Chuck thou hast defil'd our Nest, and

A Witty Combate.

thrown a speck upon our Family? the Princess is a Whore, a double Whore, she has two Husbands: has your early rising come to this?

Mr. *King.* Why honey 'tis true, I took her for a civil Gentlewoman, and so I entertain'd her d'ye see; now you took her for a Princess d'ye see, and there is the mistake d'ye see: alas I would not have done such a thing d'ye see for a thousand pound d'ye see; nay and more too as poor a man as I am d'ye see.

mrs. *King.* I wish it from my heart thou had'st been sick a Bed chuck when thou'd dst what thou did st; but 'tis no matter, I hope to see her hang'd.

mr. *King* Why that will make amends for all d'ye see. *Exeunt.*

Enter two Gentlemen as from the Sessions-house.

1 *Gent.* I wish I had had your place Sir, you sat neer the Bench.

2 *Gent.* Introth I was weary ou't, I did not like the *Scene.*

1 *Gent.* How does the Princess carry her self I pray Sir?

2 *Gent.* I understand you not Sir, unless you mean a Princess that derives her Title from the powdering Tub. 1 *Gent.* Your pardon Sir, I meane the person now is at her Tryal. 2 *Gent.* You may assure your self she wantes not Confidence, I might say impudence 1 *Gent.* They say her Husband is a hopefall Gentleman. 2 *Gent.* A sweet lad, my heart earnes for him; a man well bred of a good Family, and in a hansome way: thus to be catcht, argues a weaknels, some where a gross oversight, a pittious shallow conception.

1 *Gent.* How do you think 'twill go with him Sir. 2 *Gent.* Not with him Sir, 'twill rather go against him, the Evidence is *A noise within.* defective,—hark,—I dare say she's quit. 1 *Gent.* A hard fate has follow'd the friend *Carleton,* I pitty the Gentleman though a Stranger to me: This business was not manag'd well I fear, but there's away to bring't about again if she be the same person. 2 *Gent.* I believe *Enter madam* so Sir,—bless my eye sight, here's the beast will none *Moders & sev-* spit at her, how she stares & glotes like old *Grimalkin, al others after her.* or mother *Guttons* Cat 'ith Colehole. 1 *Gent.* Is that she Sir?

2 *Gent.* Yes 'tis she Sir, for want of a better. 1 *Gent.* Your servant Sir, 2 *Gent.* I'me yours Sir. *Exeunt severally.*

Enter Moders alone, applying her self to the Auditory.

Mod. I've past one Tryal; but it is my fear
I shall receive a rigid sentence here;
You think me a bold Cheat, put case 'twere so
Which of you are not? now you'd swear I know,
But do not hast that you deserve to be
Censur'd worse then you yet can censure me.
The Worlds a Cheat, and we that move in it
In our degrees do exercise our Wit:
And better 'tis to get a glorious Name
However got then live by common Fame.

FINIS.

Vercingetorixa: Or, The Germane Princess Reduc'd to An English Habit (Wing B65) is reproduced by permission of The Huntington Library. The text block measures 145 × 80 mm.

Hard-to-read words in the original:
A4v.1:   *Lamenting much his sad mishap,*
2.23:   But as on Dunghil Cock doth strut,
2.24:   And proudly throws with Heels up Dirt,
2.25:   So doth he walk with *Yeomans* grace,
2.26:   Or Poultry-Sergeant carrying Mace,
6.17:   Have you beheld the graver Fry
6.18:   When to a Dinner they do hie?
6.19:   How formally they walk at leasure,
6.20:   And very tenderly keep measure?
6.21:   When but for shame with Zealous Tears
7.1:   But by the rowl of 's greedy Eye,
7.20:   Shall of your Grace be seiz'd in Fee,
7.21:   The words this Wight had scarcely sed,
7.22:   When She in's Bosome threw her Head;
7.23:   And bid the weeping Lover rise,
7.24:   And with her Gloue to wipe his Eyes.
7.25:   Then up he stood as tall as *Bevis,*
7.26:   Or little Dwarf drest up for *Mevis*;
18:       [marginalia 1] *The best wits may borrow.*
          [marginalia 2] *A Simile fit enough for the subject.*
          [marginalia 3] *As it too truly fell out.*
          [marginalia 4] *Would he had taken the counsel.*
20:       [marginalia 1] *He was always too modest.*
          [marginalia 2] *It has always been the custome of Knight-Errants to go in quest after their Doxeys.*
26:       [marginalia] *Good advice in a fierce Assault.*
33.1   Where being lodg'd, on the next day
37.17:   Sometimes the Horse was down, and he
37.18:   Was brought upon his little Knee;
37.19:   Then up agen he'd get to Crupper,
37.20:   And with his Jaws begin to mutter;
37.21:   Thence to the head and so to side,
37.22:   And could not at one place abide:
37.23:   At length being tir'd as well as able,
37.24:   Crept to his *Noose,* and shut the Saddle.
37.25:   So gude *Mrs John* 'twixt hope and fear,
37.26:   Was entertain'd with the like Chear;
42:       [Errata] Pag.2. lin.8. read *Check*. l.14.r. *properer*. p.3.l.17.r. *Trance*. l.22.r. *Trance*. p.4.l.2.r. *aw'd*. p.11.l.10.r. *shipt*. p.23.l.9.r. *dust*.

Vercingetorixa:

OR,

The GERMANE
PRINCESS
Reduc'd to
An English Habit.

By *F. B.* Gent.

Why Vercingetorix *we give*
Unto this Book for Name,
Know, German Princess *doth derive*
As By-blow *from the same.*

LONDON:
Printed in the Year MDCLXIII.

To his good Friend
Mr. *F. B.*
Upon his *Germane Princess.*

IN *Stories new, and Stories old,*
   Many Romances have been told:
One sings the Fame of **Cleopatra***,*
Caſſandra*, or of* **Biles atra**
Writes Satyrs, while in humour jolly
Another chants the praiſe of Folly.
Well ſure they did, in mine opinion,
Each to his Muſe to chuſe a Minion:
But thou haſt ſuch a Subject got,
As time fore-going ſhew could not:
A Princeſs in a ſtrange Diſguiſe,
That leads the world with ſuch ſurprize,
That Story of her with deſire
Has been expected Horſe to hire.
And ſince 'tis done, no more we'll ſay,
Our Thanks ſhall all thy Labour pay;
Acknowledging all former Tricks-a
Surpaſs't by **Vercingetorixa***.*

                       T. M.

                       J. C.

J. C. to the Author.

NOw that an Exile I am made,
    And am eclips'd as Moon in shade,
Whilst Pamphleters my Case do cry,
Pray, Sir, will you the Princess buy?
With her kind Husband, Man of Might,
Who's neither now a Lord nor Knight,
But is the same as heretofore,
When bound to Post of Scriveners Door;
And so in Ryme the Wits do cry me,
Whilst I do weep sans Princess by me;
And now as wandring Knight am bound
To ambulate the vast Globe round;
Whilst you 'mongst all have done the right
To me J. C. no Lord nor night.
And now to you I send my thanks,
All that is left of Dowre in Banks,
For making Verse to speak true Story
Of me when in my hopes and glory.
                              J. C.

Dean Dunstable in laudem Authoris.

PRaise thee I would, as Worth requires,
    And offer Wood to make great Fires,
                                        For

For joy that Dame is out of Newgate,
And is in Codpiece put by New-mate:
In Rime I never could do good,
Unless of that like Robbin Hood,
Or Hopkins and his Neighbor Sternhold,
Chaunted by me in getting Tayl-hold.
With Hat in hand I render thanks
For bringing in my May-pole Shanks:
For I in Pye had reading Finger,
But lost conjunction by their Linger;
And closing Mouth lay snug in House,
Watching for Jobb as Cat for Mouse.
But I have done, thy Wit shall fly,
In and beyond my Deanery;
Never forgetting how Tale-Priest
Did humbly bow, and Garment kist.

     W. S. Dean Dunstable,
      à Deska Capellanus.

Skydder a Brawle, to the Author.

AS Phœnix pearcht in spicie Nest,
 Perfuming thee to be burnt Brest;
Expecting when bright Sol will burn
The Bird, and her to Ashes turn:

So I expected have thy Rimes,
To satisfie the longing Times
And my Desires : thy Book shall lie
Pil'd up with my Welch Poetry ;
And fame of Princess, Harp shall sing,
Plaid by Ap-Rise on Cats-Gut string,
To British Bards, my self being one
That shall the fate of Princess moan :
And now I thank thy painful Pen
For bringing Princess into Ken.
But when at large, my Rimes shall run
As swift as Horses of the Sun,
Or Goat on Mountain grazing hie,
Well coucht in Skydders Poetry.

The Martial Doctor to the Author.

YOu that have done the Lady right
   In Story true of City-Knight,
VVho now is vanisht as the dust
Of Coffee made of burnt-bread-crust,
VVho like Gonzales with his Ganders,
Or Thomas Coreat now he wanders
VVith thred-bare Cloak on the Ryalta,
Like to the Gadding Jew of Malta ;
Or like St. Hugh with's Bones at's back,
And Tinker with his Trull and Pack,
                    Lamenting

Lamenting much his sad mishap,
And Lady-Princess unkind Clap:
Or whether he with anger blushing
Be gone to meet his Wealth at Flushing,
We'll not dispute, but let it pass,
Whether he be transform'd to Ass;
And onely speak of thy rare worth,
Which taketh pains for to set forth
(Since scribling Pens have kept a pother,
By telling Lyes all Truth to smother)
The Story whole, and dost indite
With Fancie nimbler then Joe Wright,
Your Wit being just of the same stander
With his that droll'd at young Leander;
And much I fear will spoile our Physick,
Since thou alone canst cure the Tissick,
With Rimes that cause in us such laughter,
'Twill break Impostures fine plaster;
And with the mirth of thy sweet Quill,
Dost quite undoe both Purge and Pill.
Then courage, Friend, and do not sneak,
And fear what men of thee do speak:
But let those Scoffers who do spite
Thy jolly Muse, themselves go write;
Which being compar'd, the world must then
Allow thine for the brisker Pen.

To

To my worthy Friend the Author upon his GERMANE PRINCESS.

ONce a great Work-man by his cunning Art
   Did shape an Image like t' a broke his heart,
Had not Dame Juno gratifi'd his skill
In making it a woman to his will.
Another painted Grapes so to the life,
That it put all the Birds into a strife
VVho first should taste of them. But to speak all,
Thy Pen has given their Pencil a fair fall;
And meerly with two colours, white and black,
Hast laid their Pallas flat upon her back.
All which I apprehend now from thy Muse,
Is that she should through all the world infuse
Such a belief, that thou art the Contriver
Of all this Plot. I durst lay a whole Stiver
It will be said, The Princess did but Act,
And that thou wert the Author of the Fact;
Since thou hast limn'd so to the life this Dame,
Whoere doth see this draught must needs proclaim
Of all men none could come so near the matter
As thou hast done. You know I cannot flatter,
And thus conclude, There's nothing wanting there
But her false Dialect, Yaw, yaw, min here.

                                        P. B.

VERCINGETORIXA:
OR,
The Germane Princess reduced to an English Habit.

Now every one hath verdict spent
  On Princess in the *Gate-house* pent,
And Scriveners Boy (pretending *Templar*)
A *Book* hath writ very exemplar,
Which he doth stile *Vindicative*,
And strives his Folly to retrive;
Rails against Wives, Cheats, Wits and Arts,
Bawds, Pimps, Trepans, & Whores in Carts,
When in good sooth by *Venus* Glass,
Before espous'd one clapt her——
And that he knew; (*but Love is blind*)
And Princess would not out of mind.
But hold (*Sir Prologue*) now let's enter,
And speak of Story true th' Adventure.

             B   When

Vercingetorixa.

When time was come that scribling Cit
Must walk abroad to try his Wit
Amongst *Peripateticke Ladies*,
And kiss his hand to *Cheapside* Babies,
His Cloaths were brusht, Cloak laid in print,
And off was cleanly rubb'd the Lint:
His Joynts were Oyl'd as if for Match,
And on his Cheeks was sable Patch;
A Mark to know his Lordship by:
His Shooes were of the *Gresham* Dye.
So goes to Friend, and in a word,

Who made a good Bargain, had he received the benefit.

Doth quickly borrow *Silver Sword*;
And when put on, pray tell who can
Where he or it was proper man.

B'ing thus Accoutred, out he goes
In places clean, keeps durt from Toes;
And over Shoulders looks to see
Who eyes his City-Gravity:
At last unto the Exchange-Tavern,
Where Sack is kept in a dark Cavern,
The Youth comes in, and calls the Skinker
To shew a Room to good Sack-drinker.

But as on Dunghil Cock doth strut,
And proudly throws with Heels up Dirt;
So doth he walk with *Yeomans* grace,
Or *Poultry*-Sergeant carrying Mace,

Till

Vercingetorixa.

Till out of Window he was fpide
By *One*, that after was his *Bride*.
   It was a Princefs in difguife,
With am'rous Looks and piercing Eyes,
That lay there fecret and moſt fullen,
And lately had efcap'd from *Cullen*:
As rich as *Crœſus*, and as fair
As any well-dreſt *Flanders* Mare,
And was to *England* come to wed
A City-Chick of the *firſt Head*,
Becauſe ſhe would no longer tarry,
And *Germane* Lord confent to marry:
But as bright *Cynthia* with *Endymion*
In Love did burn and weep with Onyon;
Or *Cupid* with his Golden Dart
Venus wounded to the heart,
The Princefs down in *France* did fall,
And in *Teutonick* 'gan to yall.
Th' Alarm given, the Servants ſtraight
Upon the Princefs 'gan to wait;
And Lady Vintner did advance
To bring the Princefs out of *France*.
   But opening of her Eyes, ſhe cride
For Youth ſhe out of Window ſpide;
And ſaid, That now her Fate was done,
And ſtraight into ſtrange Paſſions run.

Vercingetorixa.

The Chamber then was clear'd of all,
And Mistress ow'd as General :
In private then they did converse,
And Mistress pray'd *Her* to rehearse
The occasion of her sudden change,
And noise which reach'd to the Exchange.
With doleful Looks and weeping Eyes,
Half utter'd Words, and quaking Thighs,
  She told her that in *Germany*
A man well read in things o' th' Sky,
(As *British Merlin*, Doctor *Faustus*,
Or *Lilly*, *Trigge* or *John Acostus*)
Her Fate had told, that she should Wed
With English Youth, and with him Bed;
And in a Glass shew'd her by face
Him that her Highness Love should grace.
The same she out of Window saw
Before she fell. At this the Maw
Of Vintners Wife began to rise,
Bidding her Highness wipe her Eyes,
And be content; for she would bring
The Gallant up her Offering.
With that she went unto the Lad,
Who sate alone in Room most sad,
Thinking and chewing the Adventer,
At last *Barre-Lady* she did enter.

Sir

Vercingetorixa.

Sir Knight, quoth she, pray cheer thy looks,
And mope no more like Don on Books;
But be as high as *Lord* or *Yeomen*,
And now begin to study Women:
For lovely Looks and gentle Grace,
Hath deeply wounded Princess face:
(I mean a Lady bred full high,
That hath escap'd from *Germany*)
And hither's come to lie in private,
And is resolved you to drive at:
For she was told by wise Magician,
(Well read in Arts, and great Physitian)
That little man with chitty face
Her Highness should in Wedlock grace;
And *You* are He, as she doth say,
That to the Church must lead the way.
Jewels she hath, as Sanguine Ruby,
Onyx and Saphire with a blew dye;
Diamond and Topaz, with the Opal,
Emerald and Agate, Turquez; take all:
What shall I say? Sh'ath Gems in plenty:
Pray enter on her; Room is empty.

 As Peacock in a Summer-day
Doth swell and brustle in his Gay
And painted Dress, and picks his Plumes,
But looking on his Feet he fumes;

So

Vercingetorixa.

So Gentle Sir arose from's Stool,
And look'd as wise as *Tom* the Fool;
And having set his Wig in print,
Careen'd his Cloak, and given hint
To Damsel for some Water clear
For Face and Hands, and hinde his Ear:
On Shooes Cole-black he cast his Eye;
But when the Dirt he did espy,
And saw the gloss of's shoon bedirted, (ted,
Good God! how's Worship fum'd & snor-
And rav'd 'gainst Mayors, Cities Shreeve,
The Scavenger and under-Reeve,
For keeping Streets in such a pickle,
Enough to hinder Conventicle.
But Maid with Dish-clout thither came,
And wip'd his Shooes; so ended blame.
 Have you beheld the graver Fry
When to a Dinner they do hie?
How formally they walk at leasure,
And very tenderly keep measure?
When but for shame with Zealous Tears
They'd fly about the Custards Ears,
And out of order put the Feast,
Like Knavish Boy on Skittish Beast:
So walk'd our Spark in steps upright,
While Lady-Mistress usher'd Light:
         But

Vercingetorixa.

But by the rowl of's greedy Eye,
He long'd for Principality;
   When Feet into the Room he put,
A Leg he made to Princess Scut;
And kneeling on his bended Knee,
The Tears did fall like drops from Tree,
And said, What's, Lady, your Behest
To Servant newly come from Desk?
Say, gentle Dame, for by St. *Gervase*
My Pen and Ink shall do you service,
For I can write in Prose and Verse,
And can your Greatness well rehearse;
And have *sans* help of VVrit or Pattin,
Acquir'd some ends of broken Latin,
And this by study very hardy;
And now believe I am not tardy.
Your Highness I desire to tell me,
Whether good fortune hath befel me;
And whether *Dulk-man here on Knee [*Observe he was well acquainted with Igno-ramus.]
Shall of your Grace be seiz'd in Fee.
The words this Wight had scarcely said,
When She in's Bosome threw her Head,
And bid the weeping Lover rise,
And with her Clout to wipe his Eyes.
Then up he stood as tall as *Bevis*,
Or little Dwarf drest up for *Mivis*;

And

Vercingetorixa.

And did await Reply of Princess
While Heart in Belly kicks and winces;
Quoth She------

(odds,
Sweet *Ganymede,* for 'twixt you there's no
Thou'rt fit to carry Trenchers to the Gods,
And fit in *Juno*'s Lap like Child in Cradle,
Or be a Groom to *Phœbus* horse in Stable:
From forreign soyle I come, crept out of Cloyster,
And thee have found like Orient Pearl in Oyster.
Do but consent, this Gem I mean to put
Into my Heart, like Pudding made in Gut:
For Lands or Livings, or Bags full of Mony,
Or Warrens stor'd with Cole-black Coney;
Or Coach that rattles in the street,
With set of Horses very meet,
I ask thee not, or test by Letter
Of Pounds laid into City-Checquer;
Or where thy moping doting Grandame
Will leave thee Bags to spend at randame;
Or whether father purging Amber
Hath Bags pil'd up in Money-chamber:
Of these no wants I have, my DEAR,
For I have thousands by the year,

Which

Which thou shalt spend, by old King *Harry*,
If Princess thou'lt consent to marry.
Just like the City-Excrementer,
(The Office-Emptier to the Venter)
When long Pole in the house he puts,
And fathoms not; Oh how he struts,
Reck'ning the Quantity and Gain
To be convey'd in Carts, not Wain:
So greedy Knight when Tale had heard,
He lick'd his Lips, and wip'd * his Beard;   * *Or place*
And having blest his happy Fate   *where he*
That brought him such a vast Estate,   *would have*
Beyond the reach of City-wit,   *had one.*
Or learned Body Politick,
Like Statue made in Ginger-bread,
He neither mov'd his Corpse or Head;
But stood like Bull bedight in Fair,
Or Monkey set up in a Chair:
And after pause, and pause was fit,
He fumbl'd out his School-Boy wit;
And in a stile most humble wise,
(Having like Pole-cat star'd in Eyes)
He said, Most lovely witty German,
Fairer then Negro, strong as Carman,
I do consent, and from this Toe
To Ivory Belly I will go;

C   And

And enter will thy Arched Cloyster,
That gapes for Liquor like an Oyster;
Where I will labour like a Brewer,
Or he that cleanseth common Sewer.

   The answer of the worthy Squire,
Set Lady-Princess all on fire :
To Knight without delay she run,
And hugg'd him as the Childe doth Bun ;
But whether Livery or Seizin
Was taken then, (as was good reason)
I cannot tell, but sure I am
London agreed with *Amsterdam.*

   But I had almost quite forgot
Her Pedigree as broad as *Scot,*
Long as *Cadwallader* the fierce,
(That eats more Cheese then Baily Mess)
Or Low-Dutch *Hogan,* call'd *Van Rutter,*
With Breech of Bacon, Face of Butter :
Then she in private told young Lord
Of great descent in one bare word,
That she was pigged very high,
As from the Toe to top of Thigh,
Call'd *Vulva,* from *de Vulva* born,
As * from the Oak drops the Acorn ;
And could compute from *Eve* the Spinster,
When *Adam* first advanc'd against her :

                                                           But

* *As 'tis elegantly express'd by the Author of* Hero and Leander.

Vercingetorixa.

But being in haste, pursu'd by foe
That trac'd her on the Petitoe,
Her Pedegree drawn out in Vellam
By Germane Herauld, yclep'd Skellum,
'Mongst other things of worth unknown,
VVas into friends kinde Clutches thrown,
Till News was given of her arrival,
And that she wedded Knight Corrival;
Her Goods and Plate full rich emboss,
Should all be stript for English Coast.

   Silence, my Princess, quoth this Knight;
For by the Sable Shades of Night
I'm satisfi'd as well as He
That stuffs his Guts on Apple-tree;
And hasten will our Matrimonials
By *Office Faculty's* Testimonials.
B'ing over full with joy he farted;
And having kist her Lips, he parted.

   Then came grave *Justice* sage and wise,
That us'd at *Sessions* to advise,
Sprung from the Race of *Cambrian* King,
VVho sweeter far then *Bard* could sing
Skyddur----A Brawle surnam'd the *Great*
Andrake, renown'd for Martial feat.

   Madam, quoth he, welcome on Shore
Of *Albions* Isle: I'll praise thee more

                           Then

Vercingetorixa.

Then blitheft *Bard* that ere was drunk
With any * *Heliconian* Punk:
> * A Simile much ufed by him.

I'll make thy Name live when expir'd,
As *Phœnix* born from Neft b'ing fir'd.
Then lowting low on bended Knee,
As if adoring Deity,
With holy *Zeal* and *Sack* infpir'd,
Her Health he drank; and being fir'd
In lofty Tones and Verfe Prophetick,
With Ditty fweet, and not Pathetick,
Her praife he chants, and did fore-bode
Great Race fhould come from *Sable Pode*.
With that he rofe, and gave the Liquor
To Princefs Göll, who gan to fmicker,
Taking caroufe: it fhall go hard,
She faid, but that I will, Dear *Bard*,
Thee much advance for thy fweet Rimes,
Maugre the Poets of the times:
Thou fhalt have Riches, and wears Bayes,
And Laureat be to fing my praife.

Like Butchers Dog in Garden *Paris*,
That mows down Bears as Sythes do Harveft,
And having fore contented Eyes,
Carry'd away the worthy Prize,
In ftreets he walks clofe to the Wall,
And fnarls at's Fellows great and fmall:

So

Vercingetorixa. 13

So pufft-up Youth by Princess graced,
Look't big as Bull with Bull-Dogs traced;
And puffing swelling Sir, appear'd
As big as *Morgans* mighty Beard:
For ev'ry one he met on's way,
Although his Friends, yet would not stay;
But like a Begger born in Cot,
When Wealth and Riches he hath got,
Where ere he comes makes a great pother,
And will not know Father or Mother:
So Blade doth strut upon his high Pins
Like Artist great well skill'd in Nine-pins;
Telling them now they must forbear
With foolish Tales to trouble Ear,
For he was many Stories higher
Since last with them, and now a Squire;
The best in all the English Court
Beneath him was for to consort:
Emp'rors, Kings, Princes, Lords and Earls,
Should his Companions be, not Karles.
At length he came to Daddies House,
And set him down as still as Mouse;
And Cocking Bever, look'd on Sword
That did return him ne'er a word:
Quoth he, *Bright Blade made of good steel,
If thou may pangs of Love didst feel.

* Note, that Knights errant of Yore used to make such like Speeches to their Swords or Horses: as you may see several in the Reverend Legends of Don Quixot.

Thou'dst

Thou'dst out of Scabberd draw thy Mettle,
And make more noise then Drum call'd Kettle:
But now I think on't, keep thy edge,
Princess to guard through Ditch & Hedge;
And when ocasion doth require,
Be thou her Guardian and her Squire.

  VVhen Mother heard her Infant tattle,
And to discourse * like Childe with Rattle,
To him She came, charging the Youth
To tell her all in sober sooth;
For that She fear'd he was * ore-lookt
By evil Eyes, or by some rookt
Into belief of strange adventure,
Which had occasion'd this distemper.

  To satisfie his Mams desire,
And expectation of his Sire,
He did begin, and by-past Story
Repeated o'er like learn'd *Jack Dory*:
And pray'd his Parents by their leave
To keep't as close as Knife in * Sheath.

  * As he that by strange fury led
With strange Chymæra's in his head,
Suppos'd himself to be a Member
In Commons house in times most tender,
Crept into seat, and took his place,
And boldly look'd on *Lenthals* Mace;

margin notes:
* Love is always childish.
* Take heed of Fascination.
* whereby you may note, he intended to be a Courtier.
* Observe that Phrensie runs in a blood.

At

Vercingetorixa.

At length discover'd for a Stray
That had leapt into Brethrens way,
And was ycleped Vintner Master,
That took the House for Common Pasture;
Voted he was for his offence
Unto the Pound, so carry'd thence:
So Parents hearing Sons Relation,
Were both surpriz'd in the like fashion;
Their thoughts being nought but Lord & Madam,
Ne'er thinking on poor delving *Adam*:
But time may make them chew the Cud,
And value Yokes in house of Mud.
Quoth Mother to her aged Husband,
Rejoyce with me, and put on clean Band;
For *John* our Son by Salmons Jowles,
Will rear up House as high as *Powles*;
And make us all by his Adventers
Get more them *Urlyn by Debenters.   *One that traded very much in that Commodity, in Purchasing of the Kings Lands.
Quoth aged Sire, My Dear, enough;
Pray send for Martial Friend in Buff,
And bid him bring with him his Cutter,
And Pocket Pistol: do not mutter,
But hasten to him; for by my Whiskers
More he shall get by this then *Glisters,   *Note, that his Friend profest Physick.
Or riding up and down the street,
Striking of fire with Horses feet.

Bid

Id est, Coffee.

Bid him from me leave Turkish * Julep,
And drink Canary sweet as Tulip.
For such a Man of mighty Spirit,
Undaunted Courage beyond merit,
Our Son must have if 's heart should fail,
To undermine Princesses Tail.
At length the Gallant being come,
And Strangers all put out of room,
The old Man he assum'd the Chair,
By him his Lady, (foul, not fair)
Of one side young Lord sits with Hat on,
On t'other Friend with Iron Cap on.

* *A fit Allusion.*

* Have you beheld the close Committee
When *Oliver* trepann'd the City,
How Gravely they in Council sat,
Like Puss when set to catch a Rat?
So after silence and great leasure,
The Daddy did unfold the treasure
Of Fortune, Beauty, and Descent
Of Lady-Princess to be shent,
And snatcht away by Ink and Pen,
Like Chick by Kite from wary Hen.
When Friend had heard the full Relation
Of Princess come from forreign Nation,
And judging it a thing full desp'rate
That Lady should be made his Copes-mate;

And

And in respect of high-born Linage,
And fortunes fair besides within age,
Adjure he did the Youth with fear
To forbear handling Ladies Gear:
But being resolv'd in Pate so addle
To win the Horse, or loose the Saddle,
He answer fram'd in terms most haughty,
To gentle friend that was not loughty.
  Sir, If my Lady-Princess love me
As I do her, who can reprove me?
I am a man, 'tis true, o' th' Quill,
And use Blank Bonds to fit and fill;
*But what of that? *Crispine* the Cobler   * *Of late*
Was lov'd of Princess, and did down-jobble *there hath*
And many more I can relate   (her: *been many*
That have crept into the same state;   *such examples.*
*Been Generals, made Governors of Islands, * *As these*
Lords of great Castles steep as High-lands: *late times*
And who can tell but I may be   *can testifie.*
Vicegerent in *High Germany*,
And have my Squadrons drest in Buff,
With Pistol, Sword, and Sable Muff?
  When Friend saw Youth as fully bent
As *Cutting Dick* when's money's spent,
That stands at corner of *Hide-Park*,
Robbing both Poor and Rich i' th' dark,

Vercingetorixa.

He did forbear to reason further,
As much as Rabby 'gainst self-murther;
And said, My Lord, pray no more words,
Unless of Cheescakes, Cream and Curds,
To be devour'd on Wedding-day,

* Th: best wits may borrow. When you are fine as *Green* * *Poppay.*
But by the way, to clear all doubts,
* A Simile fit enough for the subject. * As Maiden washes Infants Clouts,
And prevent stain on antient house,
Worser then Beast on Cloak call'd Lowse,
* As it too truly fell out. * Left Lady of the ancient Mannor,
Call'd *Bloomsberry*, where lives no Tanner
Should dress her self in Princely shape,
And you deceive like *Jack*-an-Ape:
Therefore-----
* Would he had taken the counsel. * Take my advice, and be not slow,
But straight unto the Tower go;
See beast there Couchant called Lyon,
That fawns on Princes when cast eye on;
Whereby you'll know if Princely born,
Or else his stern he'll whisk in scorn.
Quoth he,------
No more of that, fair friend of Steel
Such Tryal, Dear, must never feel:
For I do know she's Princess stalk,
As sure as Dames know *Grays*-Inne walk;
And

Vercingetorixa.

And further to confirm the truth
Of my believe, conceive me, Youth,
She'll not confent, or me admit
With her to play at Game * Treytrip,   *The fame
Till her great Riches do come over,   that Peter's
And Land within the Port of *Dover*.   the Betcher's
Befides, in penance once fhe went,   wife.
And met fierce Beaft that was unpent;
Who humbly kneel'd as Friend, not Foe
And all ore-lickt her fweaty Toe.
So ended Gallants high Difcourfe,
Being refolv'd to run his courfe;
As is the Dog when fet at Bear,
Or Groom attempting Ladies Ware.
Quoth he to's Friend, Sir, I cann't tarry,
For Princefs I muft forthwith marry:
Be clofe as night, firm as the ground,
* (For Gag receive two hundred pound)   *The more's
But not till money comes to *London*,   the pity he
Then I am made, or elfe I'm undone.   made not
But till I come to her Eftate,   fure on't.
Be our Companion, and our Mate:
For I refolve when we take Court,
And great Men to us do refort,
Thy little Legs fhall ftrut in Hall,
And thou be call'd our General.

D 2   Be

Be Captain of our Guard of Horse,
Of Troopers tall, fiercer then *Moss*:
Shalt use our Court, Goods, Plate & Money,
And Princess too, excepting Coney.

  When friend had heard this proffer great,
And how the Knight did him intreat,
And offer'd all ev'n to his Jerkin,
Excepting lovely Princess Merkin,
He was full glad that by the end
He had taken such a real Friend:
And thanks to him he then did utter

He was always too modest. *In manner smooth like new-made Butter:
Like Presbyterian, Independent,
When both resolv'd to have *an end on't*,
They in their Canting Hymns did sing,
And hand in hand did murther King:
So Daddy, Mammy, Friend and Knight,
In Judgement one did all unite;
And did agree without long tarry,
That Knight should Lady-Princess marry.
But as the Council was adjourning,
The Lady-sister enter'd mourning;

It has always been the custome of Knight-Errants to go in quest after their Doxeys. Acquainting them that forreign Knight,
*With cole-black hair, & eyes like spright,
Had at the house enquiry made
For Germane Princess, and like Blade,

                         Of

Vercingetorixa.

*Or *Gallant a la mode* did swear,
That heart from body he would tear
Of him that durst crack Princess *Nut*,
Or dare with her to go to Rut:
And wheresoe'er he found the Man
Should dare to usher *Princess* hand,
His Arms he'd cut off to the bones,
And whisk out *Laboring*-Dog-Prick-*Stones*:
Withal he'd give two hundred pound
Princess to see on English ground,
That he might carry her to *Cullen*
With greater Joy then *Anne* from *Bullen*.

Like some of our Modern Hectors.

 Have you beheld a *Millers* Coat,
The white Beard of a *Rammish* Goat?
A New *Thin* Cheese, or *Harry Groat*,
Or *New-turn'd Milk*, (that's very naught?)
So pale and thin lookt Princess servant
When he had heard the fierce Knights er-
Believing that his *Hangers* by   (rant;
For bold attempt should surely die.
The House was all in Chitty Chatty,
And Heart of Knight went Pitty Patty:
At length arose the little Captain
To *Corps de Guard*, before mad Chieftain.

 Courage, Sir Knight, quoth he, be bold,
And quit not Princess strong tayl-hold:

For

For by my flaming Sword of Steel,
This Brave shall Doughty Mettle feel:
Bid Lackey-Boy go call a Coach,
While I the *Knave* on Spit do broach.
The Coach being come, & Boot put down
And Lackey tayling Princess Gown,
Knight put her in as well as able,
And drove to house of *Dean Dunstable*,
As tall as *Meg Westminster* Lass,
And of the make of *Caiaphas*;
Where he agreed to take a Room
For her, and him the good Bridegroom.
But had you seen the Mimick Gesture
Of Reading Priest in his long Vesture,
How humbly he did scrape and bow,
And lickt his Lips, (like Calf by Cow)
With Hat held under arm like Bag-pipe,
Stood he upright like man in Moon-light;
Acquainting in his Gesture featly,
That he could marry them most neatly;
And Churches more could have then Hearers
For to assist such Love-Pickeerers:
And having ask'd advice of Priest
(First charging him for to be hiss't)
Whether 'twas lawful, fit or just
That Scrivener should at Princess thrust;
Pray

Pray think what said the Priest hereat;
Indeed he spoke the words of *Pilate*,
Saying, I find no fault therein;
For Copulation is no sin:
For by such Jobs as these I'm richer
Then twelve Apostles, or St. *Peter*.
At last the Gallants took their farewel
Of Priest in Coat Canonical:
Having 'forehand paid durt for Lodging,
For he and she to play hodge-dodge in,
If not prevented by Tongue-blabber,
Or Information of *Dutch* Swabber.
But being return'd again to *London*,
Enquiring out what Spyes had then done,
They found there fresh pursuits by Letters
To look out Princess though in fetters,
With promise fresh to give more Money
To him should tell where lay Dear Honey.
At this the Knight was sore affrighted,
And star'd like Beast anew bedighted,
Knowing not whither he should go
To shun pursuit of cruel Fo.
The Council being call'd agen,
And sate as close as sheep in Pen,
It was resolv'd at pale Knights instance
For to prevent a further mischance,
That

That marry'd they should be in Church,
And lie no more like *Dogs at Lurch.*
As Loyal-suff'ring Cavaleers
Were lugg'd about like Pigs by th' ears,
By people then, and yet call'd *Saints*,
Upon pretence of great Complaints,
And brought to *Haberdashers Hall*,
Where with Contracts they did 'um mall;
And *Moyer* with his Ferret-Eyes
As red as *Low-Dutch* Ladies Thighs,
Would with one blow of Wooden Hammer
Conclude, sequester, and not stammer:
So aged Sire with Fist fast clutched,
Gave Table blow, and wise Son mutched,
And bid him get him to the Church,
While he went home on Wooden Crutch.

In *Smithfield* liveth a Divine
That loves a Cup of brisk old Wine;
And, though Canonical, can tope
As well as he that plucks the Rope;
And loveth flesh better then fish,
And eats of many a good mans dish;
Pretending a Prerogative
In this to be Dispensative:
To him, the Knight, the Princess friend,
And elder Brother at the end,

Was

Was come along to fee the Wedding,
And be eye-witnefs to their Bedding;
And joyful news to Dad to carry,
And words to hear, *I John take Mary.*
   When Prieft had fet his face in fafhion,
He finifht words of Copulation:
Which being done, they fell a grinning
As loud as Wench let loofe from fpinning;
And Parfon too began to fneat
When eye he caft towards Princefs Gear.
But Licenfe man in black had not ;
Hafte and the fear had it forgot :
But they muft do as *Dick* with *Beffe,*
Go to't and work *de bene effe,*
Till Licenfe was got feal'd before 'um,
They might go to't, though of the *Quorum*
Juftice were by, they had fatisfaction,
And being refolv'd for am'rous action,
They drove away to place call'd *Barnet,*
And with them took their Parfon *Garnet.*
Where being come, they fell a eating,
And hungry Prieft threw Wine & meat in,
Like Mifer at a City-feaft,
That eats ten Meals in one at leaft.
At length their Guts being ftufft with food,
And all being fet on merry mood,
          E   The

The Parson he took off his Girdle,
That binds his Coat as Wyth does Hurdle,
And did begin to dance and caper
Like *Poppet* made up with brown Paper:
Princeſs began a *Germane* Dance,
And friend in Buff like *Mars* did prance:
The Lord did dance in order meet,
And Elder Brother on's bare feet;
An ancient Cuſtome where young Cit
Before his Elder ———— doth hit.
At length the Couple went to Bed,
And Cap was put on young Lords head;
The Poſſet too of Sack was eaten,
And Stockin thrown too, (all beſweaten)
Which Ceremonies being ended,
And that days work by all commended,
The Parſon, Brother, and his Friend,

Good ad- Bid him, Ride ſoftto's Journeys end;
vice in a And Germane Shins forbear to rub,
fierce Aſ- Left ſwallow'd in her Butter-tub:
ſault.
Wiſhing them ſport at very heart,
They left the Lord at Princeſs Mart.
The famous Couple thus at reſt,
And cloſely linkt as Birds in Neſt,
Friends did return, and fell to Toping,
While Lord his Princeſs was a Groping:
And

And elder Brother of the Lord
Being with Liquor over-goar'd,
Went and lay down upon his Bed
To reſt his drowſie drunken head,
While Captain and the worthy Parſon
So ply'd their Cups, they could ſee ſcarce
The Man of *Mars* told *John* of *Leyden* (one.
That he muſt down to fair young Maiden,
And Conjure down the evil Spirit
That Coney hunts as doth the Ferrit.
So down he went, and in a Bed
Cloſe on the ſides and over head,
He found the Kitchin-Damſel ſleeping,
But having wak'd her, he did peep in.
As ſubtle Fox, that crafty Beaſt,
When head gets in, brings on the reſt;
So he his body did get in,
And play'd with * two Bowls & Nine-pin: * *A very ancient Game, and much in uſe.*
And when the Game was fairly done,
Straight to the Parſon he did come,
And gave to him account of all
That in his Journey did befal;
Deſiring him in favour much
Not to acquaint the holy Church:
But Parſon blam'd unkind Companion
That he ſhould mount his Demi-Cannon
'Gainſt

'Gainst Maiden-fort, and let him not
At hairy Sconce to have one shot.
When morning-light began t' appear,
And day was nois'd by Chaunticlear,
The friends and Parson went to Room
Where lay the Bride and the Bridegroom;
And as they enter'd Princess smil'd,
But Knight did look as *Owl* parboyl'd,
And like to Bulrush hang'd his head,
Being more fit for Grave then Bed.
The friends did pity Knight so little
* When they saw him in sweating pickle;
Then Martial Doctor stept to Knight,
And praid him shortly to recite
His last nights labour with the Dame,
And where the Mare held up her Mane.
At this young Lord began to weep,
And Doctor praid counsel to keep,
For that his Princess with hot force
Had spoiled quite his Water-course.
No more, quoth Doctor Steel-Cap then,
There's Cure for you as other men:
In four days time I'll cure your Tool,
And make it sound as Oaken Stool;
Therefore arise, shew signes of mirth,
And pay respect to Royal Birth.

Belike he came out of the Princess Stove much like to Cornelius his Tub.

An unkinde Bed-fellow

Having

Vercingetorixa

Having receiv'd this good advice,
He put on Garments in a trice;
Yet * walk'd like one late all befir'd,
Or like a Horse that's newly tyr'd:
At length being full of Country-air,
Back to the Town they did repair;
Where being come to Fathers Court,
Their friends in Clusters did resort,
To kiss the Hand of Princely Dame,
Meerly for love of Royal Name,
Whilst Lord was clearing of the way,
And access to his Princess gay;
Telling them Proverb very old,
By others to him long-since told,
That after high attempts and pother,
* He had got the Steerage of her Ruther;
And now that maugre all her friends,
Of Princely Dame he had his ends.

   A Banquet then was well drest out
To entertain the City-Rout;
Wine too was given to them in Glasses,
And *drink* they did, and *bray* like Asses,
While Lady-Princess lookt as mute
As doth the Privy Lovers Lute.
The Banquet ended, friends departed
You may conceive not heavy-hearted,

*Blame him not, for he came from hot service.

* He might safelyer have cunnde a Ship then her.

And

And mounted were in Streets I ween,
As *Bergerack* was in *Moon-machine*.

   When house was clear'd of all but friends,
On Princess there was further ends
Intended to be done in instance,
Marri'd to be again with License,
For to prevent the Lawyers bawl
In Court Ecclesiastical:
The which was done, and then old Sur
With Instrument well drawn *sans* blur,
Reciting Princess *Earth* in hand,
And Personal Goods about to land,
Desir'd the same might be made over
To *Lord his Son*, and her great Lover.
To this he hop'd she'd not be shy,
Being to prevent Mortality:
Sir, quoth the Princess, I'll consult
My Pillow, and give you result:
But till I die I think not fit
To part with *State* or *Wealth* one bit:
Besides, your Son's to me but light wood,
And ha'n't receiv'd *Honour* of Knighthood;
Though in regard of my high Birth
He's called Lord, with Caps to th' Earth:
And judge, pray Sir, when friends arrive,
And see their Princess *Scriveners* Wife,

                    Will't

Vercingetorixe.

Will't not disparage high descent,
As Garters in Rump-Parliament?
Like Childe rebuk'd crying for Knife,
Stood Father without Soul or Life;
Or without Fodder Cow in pound,
Or Ape in chain with whip scourg'd round.
At length he spake to Princess face
With home-spun Language, Coblers grace:
May't please your *Highness*; Daughter, I
No harm did think most verily.
Quoth she, Pray, Sir, no more of this,
We do forgive what is amiss;   *A Princely*
And for to satisfie your Will,   *Pardon.*
Time and his Love shall it fulfil.
At this, *Old Eighty Eight* was glad,
And straight acquainted Lord-like Lad,
And of Discourse for future Good,
And how his Lady was all Wood:
But said, they ended in pure Love,
As time to him would shortly prove.
Being thus satisfide at large,
As City-Dames in husbands Barge,
With *Tammy, Willy, James* and *Jack,*
While good men cry, Pray, what d'you lack?
The Father with content fetcht down
In Bags full stuff'd many a Crown:

Bid

Vercingetorixa.

Bid him to treat her like her self,
And let her not to want for Pelf,
Or Garments new the best in fashion,
Or *Hide-Park*-air for recreation;
And to attire his Lordships Body
With Silks and Sattins very hoddy,
And Lodgings new in *Strand* to take,
And Preparations great to make,
To entertain his Royal Kindred,
VVhich now his little *Palace* hindred.

The Lord with Money in his hand
Did trip it neatly to the *Strand*,
And house by house enquiry made
Of Lodging void for Princely Blade:
At length he took up Princess Stall
In *Durham-yard* at Golden Ball;
And thither she in trice was brought
As safe as Cheese in Apple-Loft:
And in good sooth she did appear
Like *Sol* in his bright Hemisphear,
With Gold and Silver all bedight,
And in a Case of Gold, the Knight
VVell shap'd by Painter of Signe-post,
Like Antick in gilt VVood embost,
Hung by her side when enter'd Lodging,
To shew she'd caught a City-Gudgeon:

VVhere

Where being lodg'd on the next day
The Tradesmen set in good array,
Did humbly crave his Lordship straight
For License on his Corps to wait:
One to serve Shooes, another Linnen;
Stockins a third by Loom or Spinning:
A fourth to fit his Pate with Bevers;
A fifth with Swords as sharp as Clevers:
A sixth to make his Periwigs;
A seventh to teach the newest Jigs:
An eighth his Garments for to make;
A ninth to cure the pain Tooth-ake:
A tenth Sweet-powder for to bring,
For Hair and Beard, and Ladies Thing:
A 'leventh and twelfth to furnish Mear,
As Flesh or Fish, old Ling or Neat.
Gentlemen, quoth this worthy Knight,
To me this is a pleasant sight,
And sweeter far then *Hampshire-Honey*,
In places sold for store of Money:
For I rejoyce to see my Servants
For to attend and run on Errants;
And as Dame Fortune gave to me,
So I to you, as you shall see.
Your places take, which is no hard thing
* To be admitted without *Farthing*.

F   Next

*He scorn'd to sell places; a custome now very à la mode.

Next day the Knight did want a Gown
To dress him in, not Russet brown,
Or scribling Coat more rude then Freezes
*The Flee- That's homely made of *Villain Fleeces,
ces of Wool
taken off But Indian-Dress of Pink and Green,
from Scab-
bed Sheep, Fellow to that on *Great Back* seen;
31 Edw. 3.
Cap 5. Which being on, he lookt as stout
As Gem well fasten'd in Hogs Snout;
And did contemn his truest friends
That did assist him in his ends,
And slight he did the Art of 's Pen,
And all converse with vulgar men;
And Captain True-Friend was laid by,
And slighted with a scornful eye:
The Owner of the Silver Sword,
Of Weapon could hear ne'er a word:
These the Lord hated by pure Argent,
As much as broken *Cit a Sergeant*;
And at Bo-peep with them did play,
* As great * At home to morrow, not this day:
men use to
do by their Sometime employ'd in great Concerns,
Duns.
When he was cutting Princess Kerns:
At other times dispatching Orders
To's Stewards on the German Borders,
Requiring an account of Wealth,
And of his Cousin-Princes health.

But

Vercingetorixa.

But while in *Puff-Paste* Lord doth strut,
And studies onely Back and Gut,
Dame Fortune wheel'd her tayl about,
And turn'd his *Lordship* to a *Lowt*:
For Shooemaker by a Petition
In Court did humbly pray admission
To serve them with both Boots and Shoon,
As well to ride as for to run :
But Princess seeing the Address
Of bold Sir *Hugh*, she 'gan to guess
His Errand thither, telling Lord
He Calve-skins cut upon her word;
And that she could not fancie him
'Mongst all the Race of Cobling Men.
The answer of the Princely Spouse,
Hugh and his Bones did forthwith rouse;
For he did kindle like a Taper,
And lookt as pale as any Paper;
And having vindication made
Of Paring-Knife and Awle, (sharp Blade)
Goodness of Leather, Wax and Thred,
And able Work-man called *Ned*,
He packt up Tools, and went his way
With stiffned Whiskers, Beard of Whay,
Contriving in his Horny Pate
Malice against the Lords Bed-mate.

Vercingetorixa.

The next day Lord went to *Hide-Park*,
With him his Princess, (light not dark)
For she did shine as bright as Sun,
But Lord did look as sad as *Dun*,   *The com-
When but one *Hector* doth appear   mon Hang-
To help expence of following year;   man.
Though they were treated in the Park
By Ladies great, and many a Spark ;
Giving right-hand to Royal Madam,
And great respect which much did glad 'um.
But coming home unto their Court,
Sir *Hugh* to Lord did straight resort ;
Told him he could relate sad Story
Would make him weep in all his Glory,
And curse the time that ever he
His *Hawke* at *Hobby* did let flee :
Enough to put him into Lax,
Not to be stard by *Coblers Wax*.

   The Knight did wonder what he meant,
And praid him to declare intent
Of his address : for he did make
His Teeth to chatter, Knees to shake,

   Why then, quoth he, your Lady gay
Is *Kentish* breed, and *Crowders* Spray ;
And marri'd is to a Shooe-maker
That is no Cobler or Translator :

                       And

Vercingetorixa

And hath to boot (take't not in Dudgeon)
Another Husband call'd a Surgeon;
And you in order make the third,
For Princess is not worth a ----

    This made the Lord to fume and fret,
And water drop like Sable Jet:
For he did whine and howl like Dog
When at his Tayl is Wooden Clog;
And sad mishap did oft recount
Of this to-be-imagin'd Count.

    Have you beheld the *Jack-an-Apes*
With Bears and Dogs, his constant Mates,
When Horse was set upon by Dogs,
Being resolv'd to pluck off Lugs
Of little Gentleman in Coat,
How gallantly with them he fought?
Sometimes the Horse was down, and he
Was brought upon his little Knees,
Then up agen he'd get to Grupper,
And with his Jaws begin to mutter;
Thence to the head, and so to side,
And could not at one place abide;
At length being tir'd as well as able,
Crept to his *Noose*, and shut the Saddle:
So gude *Mrs. John's* 'twixt hope and fear,
Was entertain'd with the like Chear.

And

And I dare say by his fierce screeches,
He * *Atkiniz'd* his Wedding-Breeches.
The Lackey-Boy was sent away
To Father and to Mother; Nay,
His Sister too, the good Match-maker,
Of Story true must be Partaker:
Who being come, the Lord did tell
His sad mischance, which made 'em yell,
And to exclaim 'gainst Germane Lady
That had abus'd poor little Baby.
At last they went into Bed-chamber,
Where Princess lay like Dog in Manger,
Till aged Sire did her importune
The truth to tell, if such a fortune,
Or where she was a Germane Princess,
Or who had taken her by th' Inches
'Fore Son did enter Lower Quarters,
Or who wore *Senior Coblers* Garters
When he did marry her in Church,
And who she lam'd and brought to Crutch;
And who it was besides did scrub her,
And what the Surgeon was did *probe* her.
This fierce assault did make the Lady
To stand as mute at Joynted Baby,
And was surpriz'd to hear the Gabble
Of this connext and joyned Rabble,

By

* *A Story so well known, it need not be told again.*

Vercingetorixa.

By which the women thought her guilty,
With hand and knee they hilty-tilty
Most shamefully did her assault,
Which made her Royal Back to hale,
VVhilst antedated Lord stood by,
And like Boy whipt did snob and cry:
At last Old Man as fierce as *Hector*,
Having more of Henbane then of Nectar,
Lay'd hands upon the Ladies Garments,
Jewels and Rings, and her Attirements,
And Gouty Shank was held aloff,
And new Silk-Stockins plucked off:
In fine, they stript her to her Smock,
So fine, you might have seen her Nock.
Then much despis'd by bawling Litter,
Which made before their Chops to twitter.
   When all Indignities were over,
In *German Vest* they did her cover,
With *Justacore* and a *Night-Rayle*,
And Pettycoat all black to th' rayle,
The same reserved by Ships master,
VVhen she escap'd from forraign Cloyster,
Thence brought 'fore *Godfrey* not of *Bullion*,
For this did use her like a Scullion;
And so by Beadle fell and Hostile,
He sent her to the Gate-house *Bastille*:
                    VVhere

Where being come, the Gates flew open,
For to receive *Datch Fro Van Slopen*,
As great Companion come to dwell
In Prison close much like to Hell.

The noise of Princess close restraint,
Sent persons great to hear her Plaint:
But when they heard her to discourse,
They netled were like Pamper'd Horse;
And did applaud her high-bred Parts,
Not to be equaliz'd at Marts,
Or Ladies some with face like Maple,
That spend their time in tittle-tattle,
With great respect they did her treat,
And sent in Money, Wine and Meat,
And Bribes to Keeper to be civil,
As he that Candle holds to Devil:
Where I will leave her to her Fate,
Still great, though in confin'd estate:
And for her high-conceited Lord,
When Reputation he had scor'd
On *Tick* and borrow, then he went
To Chamber where he Body pent,
Believing German Knight would call
His Lordship to account for all
His base abusing Princely Dame,
And using her with so much shame:

And

Vercingetorixa.

And Parents full with shame and ire,
Did mope and dote like Cats by fire.
  But stay, my Muse, now hand is in,
Ore Boots and Shooes; thou'lt never lin,
Though thou be grown as dull and weary
As *Sculler* at the Laboring Ferry:
So cease at present, and let end,
For this time working feet befriend,
Till second part in *Canto* quaint,
Shall write of Princess close restraint;
How long in prison she did stay,
And who for Liberty made way;
How she was brought 'fore Learned Bench,
And treated like her self, (not Wench)
And how she in most learned guise
Defence did make, (to those are wise)
Pleading her Cause like fluent *Cato*,
Or Advocate with a bald Pate-o;
And was with great applause acquitted,
And Father, Son, and all out-witted.
This shall be sung in the next Part,
As second course to cheer your heart.

              G   The

The Princess to her Lord: a Farewel.

There was a time when Skinker Perkin
   Leapt into Prince from a Freeze Jerkin:
Time also was, as't has been sed,
VVhen Fryar Bacon's brazen Head
Spoke monstrous things; but We do tell
Of stranger things that have befel,
How pretty Monkey in disguise
Held * Pescod in her Mouth as prize.
Oh fatal time! how couldst thou be
So cruel in thy Managery?
More fierce then erst thou wast to Fellow,
Who though in rage with Drink more mellow,
Did all his forepast Fancies deem
Of Drunken brain the passing steem.
Oh my sweet Pescod, prethee think
Like him, that all thy hopes was drink.

* A Name she much used to call her Lord by.

FINIS.

ERRATA.

Pag. 1. lin. 8. read check. l. 14. r. properer. p. 2. l. 17. r. Trance. l. 22. r. Trance. p. 4. l. 2. r. aw'd. p. 11. l. 10. r. ships. p. 23. l. 9. r. dust.

The Memoires of Mary Carleton (Wing G35B) is reproduced by permission of The Huntington Library. The text block measures 115 × 67 mm.

THE MEMOIRES
OF
MARY CARLETON,
Commonly stiled, the
German Princess.
BEING
A NARRATIVE
OF HER
Life and Death
Interwoven with many strange and pleasant Passages, from the time of her Birth to her Execution at *Tyburn*, being the 22th. of *January* 167$\frac{2}{3}$.
WITH
Her Behaviour in Prison,
Her last
Speech, Burial & Epitaph.

Juvenal.
Aude aliquid brevibus Gyaris & Carcere dignum,
Si vis esse aliquis. Probitas laudatur & alget.

London, Printed for *Nath. Brooke*, at the *Angel* in *Cornhill* near the *Royal Exchange*; and *Dorman Newman*, at the *Kings-Arms* in the *Poultry*, 1673.

THE
Stationer to the Reader.

Reader,

I Do here present you with the Memoires, or Narrative of the Life and Death, of the German Princess, lately promis'd to be published; and withal do assure you, that the Author had all the help and assistance imaginable to accomplish the Work, and that by order too. Nor has he been negligent herein; but improv'd his time to the greatest advantage, to the end that he might gratifie the World, with the expected true Relation of the Adventures and Atchievements

chievements of this infamous Woman. 'Tis true that the former part of her Life is somewhat obscure, and taken up upon credit, tho' from persons of known integrity. The latter more notorious and certain, being related by those who were eye and ear witnesses of her several particularis'd Actions and Discourses that are mention'd in this Treatise: And if the Contents thereof do but satisfie your expectations, 'tis all the reward that he expects for the care and indefatigable pains that he has been at to perfect this Relation; who subscribes himself

J. G.

TH

THE
Life and Death
OF THE
German Princess.

I Do not design to Pamphlet you into a belief of the Grandeur and Noble Extract of this suppofititious Princefs (as fome have formerly done) for that were to abufe your Faith with a *Canterbury*-Tale; and perfwade you that this Fidler's Daughter of *Kent* was a *German* Princefs of *Colen*: But this

Narrative aspires at nothing more than the satisfaction and diversion of the Reader as to the true Original of the Person, and the Menage of all her Affairs to her last sad Catastrophe.

Impositions of this nature have the kindest entertainment with an Engilshman above all *Europeans*; because he is of an ingenuous temper, and withall so debonair and affable to Forrainers (especially Females) that he is soon caressed to believe any rumour that is maskt with seeming verity, and countenanced by a counterfeit gravity. But to undeceive this facile Nation, the credulous *Britain* ought not to be abused with a fallacy; for that is too ingrateful a return for his courteous disposition; but be gratified with the true History of her Life, as far as Information can direct, or Knowledge certainly inform.

Antiquity is a known mark of Gentility; but the Family of this Mock-Princess is so antient that it is unknown;

known; and her Maiden name (if ever she had any) like the original of the *Egyptian Nile* is inscrutinable and past finding out.

Mary Carleton (for that name she owns) was the aery Issue of an Itinerant Fidler of *Canterbury*, born in the year 1634. A noble off-spring of a more noble parent, that did *Annos ludendo haurire*, sport away his life and time on a Country Crowd.

This Place of her Nativity was once the Regal City of the Kings of *Kent*, and the Ecclesiastical Chair originally fixed there, and by King *Ethelbert*, upon his Conversion, bestowed on *Austin* the Archbishop and on his Successours for ever. And upon my word in the opinion of the Eagle-ey'd Indagators of this Age, this once Regal and now Metropolitical City receives no small additional honour by the Birth of this Modern Princess.

As to her Estate (let the fond populace affirm what they pleafe) it muft needs be very flender, though fhe had a fcraping Father; becaufe his whole livelihood was only a fingle dependance on the two-penny Benevolence, or at moft a four-penny, or fix-penny Largefs of the Clouted-fhooe.

Her Education could not much exceed her Birth and Eftate, if we may be permitted to give our fence and opinion; but that, and that only hitherto tends much to her commendation, and does infinitely aggrandize her natural parts, and fo pronounce her a perfon of very quick Apprehenfion, fhe being Miftris of as many Languages as there are Liberal Arts; but to do Juftice on all fides (give the Divel his due)as to Legerdemain, or any other ingenious contrivance of that nature, nothing ever went beyond her.

Nor is this fo prodigious a thing if all be duely confidered, as fome fay: for fhe infinuated into the favour of a Gentlewoman, who defigned a Voyage into the Low Contreys (obliged thereunto by fome indifpenfable neceffity) and fo waited upon her thither (a poor and beggarly condefcention in a Perfon of her Quality to turn Maid of Honour to one that only writ Gentlewoman) and in procefs of time converfing with the over-obefe and heavy Inhabitants of that Bogg of Chriftendom, there learnt that Tongue of *Myn-Here*, and was fo naturaliz'd, that fhe brought along with her the pilfring (I will not fay debauch'd) and faithlefs humour of the Treacherous Hoghens.

As for the Symmetry and Proportion of her Body, the Apartment of fo Noble a Soul, it was *Dutch*-built, not fo curioufly fabrick'd as that every Lineament would dull the very edge of Rhetorick in its Commendation; nor yet fo defpicable as to create Contempt, or expofe her to the fcoffs of the rabble. A ftout Fregat fhe was, or else she could never have endured so many Batteries and Assaults. A Woman of unexampled Modesty, if she may be her own Herald; but if Fame (which desires not always that abusive attribute of Liar) she was as common as a Barber's Chair, no sooner one was out, but another was in. Cunning, crafty, subtle, and hot in the pursuit of her intended Designs, and as much addicted to dissimulation as any of that Sex.

Being thus qualified both as to gifts of Body and Mind; she trips from *Holland* (or if you please from *Canterbury*) to *Gravesend*, intending for *London* in the Tilt-boat, the next opportunity of the Tide (the first and possibly the last time that lowsie Vessel ever wafted a Princess to the *British* shore:) the waves soon profered their service and grew immediately proud to bear this High-born burthen of Original and Actual sin; and so in a small time she with her Company

arrived

arrived at *Billingsgate*, the fittest place for her Reception; and had she been confined there to the Employ of one of those bawling Wastcoteers; she had treated the Hangman as she did all people that she treated, *viz.* cheated him.

And here by the way observe, that this Voyage was performed in the Night, which contributed much by its darkness to her counterfeit Lustre; for she appear'd like the Firmament, all bespangled with Stars; but when the day approach'd, she was like the Sun, oriental, glistering with pretious Stones; and very richly accoutred, as became one of her Quality, that expected her great retinue in a small time; who were, and for ought I can hear, are still to follow after her.

At length she arrived at *London*, that little World of People, the *Emporium* and *Metropolis* of *England*, and the scene that she made choice of, wherein to act all her future Cheats and

and Impoſtures. Therefore I cannot paſs by this Digreſſion. Let the Proud *Don* boaſt no more of his *Guzman*, *Quixot*, or *Lazarillo*, nor the aery *Monſieur* of his *Francion*, or *Du Vall*, ſince here is a poor *Kentiſh* Girl (I dare not ſay Maid of *Kent*, as formerly) a friſking, fidling *Canterbury* Laſs that hath out-done them all, and would have undone them too had ſhe dealt with them; for like impartial Death ſhe ſpared none of either Sex, or Condition, that ſhe could hook within her Clutches.

Thus ſhe appear'd as a real Princeſs of *Germany*, and ſtiled her ſelf ſo accordingly: where note by the bie, that I make this Obſervation. Had ſhe had as great a ſtock of handſomeneſs as ſhe had of confidence, ſhe would have been the greateſt Beauty either of *Canterbury* or *Colen*. We read in Hiſtory that a Septenary of Cities did contend which ſhould have the honour of being the Birth-place of the

the blind Greek Poet; and here we find that two famous Cities in two more famous Monarchies are ambitious to be the place of the Nativity of this English-German Lady. O brave Kentish *Moll*! 'Tis nobly done to thwart the old Proverb, *Fortune favours fools*: For since the fickle Baggage hath been so propitious to thee; by my consent that saying shall be eras'd out of all Parœmiographers.

But now to proceed to the matter of fact. I will not trouble you with the relation of her former marriage with a *Canterbury Crispin* (a fit match for a Princess) nor with a second to an old superannuated Bricklayer; they are stories too well known: but only the third with Mr. *Carleton*, which is the proper subject of our intended Relation; and the rather, because she own'd that name from the day of her marriage to the last moment of her Life.

We have left her in *London*. How
she

she came thither, whether or no pickt up at *Billingsgate* by a Vintner, and so mann'd by him to the *Exchange*-Tavern, as some affirm, is not very material. But after that her Conductor, who ever he was, had complemented her with a Mornings draught of her supposed own Country Liquor, she betook her self to her repose, it being about five a clock in the morning; and there refreshed her Princely Carkass till eleven.

Then she rose equipt and splendidly accoutred, shining with a borrowed and counterfeit lustre. Her Landlord immediately accosts her with as much address and ceremony as could be expected from a person of his poor parts and mean Education; perswades her to make his house her residence, and to command there as freely as if it were her own more noble and princely Apartment. But this extraordinary kindness was the effect of his Lucrative and Mercenary designs,

signs, not of his Civility, becauſe ſhe was rather profuſe than parſimonious in her expences, which were correſpondent to the quality of the perſon, that ſhe perſonated her ſelf to be.

And by this time at the modeſt requeſt of her Landlord, ſhe had acquainted him with her Country, Religion, Eſtate and Quality, and withal diſcovered the great charge of Jewels and other Riches that ſhe had with her, which made him the more urgent to importune her to a ſtay with him, till ſhe could diſpoſe of her ſelf otherways, and appear in the world publickly furniſhed with all ornaments ſuitable to a perſon of her quality. In order hereunto, ſhe told her Landlord that ſhe would ſend to her Steward for a great ſumm of Money, and did accordingly write to him, and to a Prince by the name of Brother, ſubſcribing her ſelf *Henrietta Maria de Wolway*, Princeſs.

Theſe

These Letters were perus'd by the Vintner (who took care to see them delivered safely at the Post-house) and was not a little swell'd in conceit to think that he should be the Guardian of such a Princess.

Now the Vintner and his Wife were big with contrivances how to bring it about by some Intrigue or Artifice, that this Illustrious Lady might be matcht to some of their Relations; that so they might lay a sure Basis for their future fortune, and leave the Superstructure to event.

At length old Mr. *Carleton*, Father-in-law to *King* the Vintner, her Landlord, became acquainted with her; and they together with Mrs. *King*, entred into a private Cabal, and consulted how to model their designs so, as that they might answer their heightned expectation. And here it was first agreed by this petty Synod, that *George* the Eldest Son of Mr. *Carleton* should first make his address;
but

but he prov'd of too groveling and poor a spirit to make his Amours to so High-born a Princess. The imparity of their conditions put a stop to the vigorous Courtship of the modest Gentleman; so upon second thoughts, it was concluded that *John* the youngest Son should be encouraged to attempt the Lady.

The bold Britain enters the Lists, and bids defiance to all opposition, resolving like a noble Heroe to arrive at that comble of felicity, that he expected from so advantageous a Marriage, or to dye in the enterprise. And beyond all controversie that which buoy'd up his spirits in this daring attempt, was the hope that he had of immortalising his name, (if he should fall or fail in the engagement) like a second *Phaeton*, and having his Tomb adorn'd with the same Epitaph,

Mag-

―― *Magnis tamen excidit aufis.*

The young man's Courtship and Careſſes had an indifferent reception by the crafty Dame, who was not ſo ſupercilious and moroſe as to deſpiſe and ſlight his viſits; nor yet ſo open and free as to indulge him a wanton thought, or move him to a freedom that might offend her either in word or action. But however theſe neither cold nor warm entertainments put him on the ſpur, and inſpir'd the youth with more than ordinary flame. The Conſummation of the Match was the accompliſhment of his deſires, but how to effect it there's the queſtion――

Hic labor, hoc opus eſt――

Therefore in the firſt place 'tis contriv'd and ordered that ſhe ſhould be confin'd, ſo that her Chamber was a kind

kind of Prison; but it was not so cunningly plotted by them, but it was as craftily discover'd by her, tho' prudently dissembled (Collusion being a known qualification of that Sex) for she pretended as great an aversion to society as they could possibly perswade her to by all their Rhetorick: secluding her self from all company, but only her Inamorato. And the reason of this was that the noise of the Match of so great a Princess to a pitiful *scribere cum dasho* should not reach the Court, for fear that some Courtier should force Mr. *Carleton* to disgorge and disembogue her Estate and Honour, which he had already swallowed in his own conceit.

By this time she had receiv'd an answer to her former Epistles sent by the Post, the Contents whereof did import that they were come to hand, and that no less than thousands of (God knows what) pounds should be
im-

immediately return'd up to *London*, with a stately Carofs, and generous Steeds to grace her at the the Rounds in *Hide-park* the next *May-day*, with many other Bagatelles and Gallantries that she had sent for expresly. Now the amorous fever of Mr. *Carleton* increased, insomuch that the next paroxysm was so violent, that his friends did acquaint her in plain terms, unless she granted his suit, he was resolv'd to turn *Iphis* or *Leander*, he would either hang or drown himself for Love, or at least be confin'd into some lonely Desart in the remotest parts of the World, never more to return to his own Native Country; and there experiment what time and absence could contribute to the cure of his Malady, rather than consume here and dwindle away to nothing by an amorous Calenture. And now methinks I hear him rave and cry out;

O Love thy mighty power is not to be withstood! Thou forcest me to cry, come turn about Robin Hood.   Poor

Poor *Carleton*! Is it come to this? Is *England* of late grown so barren of Beauties, that thou must sail to *Germany* for a Mistriss? And thou hard-hearted, Inexorable Princess! Canst thou without internal regret and remorse perceive an English Gentleman pine and languish, when a little compassion would recover his former health, and reduce him to a state of happiness? Cruel she! Hast thou devested thy self of all pitty, that downy vertue of thy Sex, and art thou resolv'd to triumph and tyrannize over a submissive suppliant, that lies prostrate at thy Altar! 'Tis ignoble to give a dying man a blow. Clemencie is the most sparkling Diamond in a Prince's Diadem; and pardon obligeth the offender more than punishment.

But waving digression, we'l return to the business in hand. She continued still very reserv'd and demur'd to their demands, which put them upon another design.

The Landlady invites this Princess to a noble Treat, where there was nothing wanting that Art or Nature could afford, or a wanton appetite desire. The guests were several persons of Quality forsooth, among which was the never to be forgotten Mr. *John Carleton*; who the day after bestow'd a visit on her, being Lacquey'd by two Foot-men in a gentile Livery, who gave him the Title of my Lord; and so did Mrs. *King* likewise. The Princess knew him to be the person that she had formerly seen, and therefore wonder'd at this strange and sudden alteration; she inquir'd into the reason of it, and was answer'd, that it was his peculiar humour so to do, still maintaining that he was a person of honour.

This new Intitulado possibly somewhat puft up with his imaginary dignity, ty, began to be more warm, clofe and conftant in his applications, and to exert himfelf more freely than formerly, prefenting his Princefs (which all this while was only confident *Moll*) with a rare Box of Sweet-meats (little fenfible God knows of the fowre fauce that would follow) and it was kindly accepted. And now matters were arriv'd at that heigth, that not a day paffed without a vifit, and his Lordfhip daily coacht my Lady to *Iflington* and *Holloway* (little dreaming that at laft fhe fhould be carted to *Tiburn*) and there entertain'd her like a Lord, with coftly and chargeable entertainments. Afterwards his Lordfhip invited her to a fumptuous Banquet, which was graced with his Mother's company, a reverend Matron in a ftarcht City-drefs; and there he did openly declare that he would marry the Princefs, which fo incenfed the offended Lady, that fhe forbid him her prefence for the future; but

this Exorcism was so cruel and insupportable, that it mov'd the very Cockles of his heart, and drew whole rivulets of tears from his eyes; and after that a complemental Letter from his Pen, stuft with nothing but Love and Honour. She having thus proscrib'd him, went abroad about her own affairs; and one day returning home, finds this mock-Lord in a very disconsolate and melancholick condition; but spying his Lady, he suddenly clasped her in his arms, and bore the pretty burthen his Lady (the very statue of actual sin) to her Chamber *vi & armis.* She being inquisitive, desir'd to know the reason of this so passionate an action. He replyed; Madam, you have banisht me from your sight, the very life of my life, and this prohibition hath so ruffled and discompos'd me, that I am but an inch on this side of an Ideot, and shall turn absolute lunatick, unless you revoke that fatal sentence;

and

and once more readmit me to look Babies in your eyes, which is the fole Complement of my defire.

Now here you are to underftand that this obdurate Lady began to relent, and to confider withal, that repeated denials might make the young man turn Defperado; therefore in compaffion fhe demanded what his Lordfhip meant? What was his defign? What he intended by thefe ftrange kind of actions? The poor Pigfnie in a whining tone (like a howling Irifhman) with a trembling gefture, and a pale countenance replyed, I defign to marry you; backing his difcourfe with a million of affeverations, that he did entertain no other thought, notwithftanding the amplitude of his Fortune, and the largenefs of his Revenues, but to be linkt to her infeparably by the facred Tye of Matrimony, and that upon the fole confideration of her perfonal merit and defert, not fo much as looking a-
                    fquint

squint upon her Eſtate, or caſting an eye upon her Poſſeſſions.

Now it was that the wily Wench began to ſmell a rat; and underſtanding that opportunity is bald behind, was reſolv'd to tugg her by the forelock. Now ſhe craftily lets fall ſome favourable expreſſions that her enamour'd Captive might with ſome grounded confidence perſwade himſelf there was a poſſibility of enjoying her.

The young Lord being puft up with imaginary ſucceſs, and the hope of a prodigious Fortune, began to be very laviſh in his promiſes, provided ſhe would condeſcend to his deſires; and among many other Gallantries in the gayety of his now briſk humour told me, that he had beſpoke a large Glaſs-Coach à-la-mode, ſo capacious as to contain a Jury of perſons at once with convenience, which ſhould be followed by a retinue of Lacqueys and Pages in modiſh and faſhionable Liveries

veries agreeable to the State and Quality of the perſon deſign'd to be his Wife. Nay farther; that there might be nothing wanting, his troubleſome Silver muſt be changed into portable Gold, (the former being too ignoble a metal for the uſe of his Princeſs; but I ſuppoſe by this time the Common ſide in the Kings-bench hath made him change his opinion.) Then what follows? Why, the next thing is, his Lady muſt be Coacht to *White-hall,* and preſented to the King and Queen, his farther deſign herein being to purchaſe a Knighthood, that he might have ſome honour of his own to rely upon as a private perſon, and not altogether depend upon the Dignity and Eſtate of a Forreign Princeſs.

And now my new made Engliſh Lord is turn'd perfect Don, and all his diſcourſe is interlarded with Rodomontadoes. The only ſubject whereof is, the nobleneſs of his Family, the vaftnefs of his Revenue, the prodigious number of his Acres, the fruitfulnefs of his Soyl, the ftatelinefs of his Apartments, the delightfulnefs of his Walks and Gardens, the pleafantnefs of his Aquæducts and Fountains, the greatnefs of his Hofpitality, the fplendidnefs of his Retinue, and what not? But notwithftanding all this boafting, remember the Spanifh Curate. A word to the wife is enough.

And here you may be pleas'd to take notice of the tricks and fineffes on both fides to deceive themfelves, whenas the iffue will confirm you in this opinion that they were both colluded. Thus their full-fraighted expectations were equally fhipwrackt upon one another; and the matter is not great; for, to deceive the deceiver is no deceit.

On *Eafter-Eve* the German Princefs appear'd very gorgeoufly attir'd in her new Robes befpangled with Jewels,

Jewels, the luftre whereof did fo dazle the eyes of her young Lord, that he renewed his fuit with greater vigour and importunity than formerly; which made the kind Mother turn Sollicitrefs on the behalf of her Son; nor can I blame her; for certrinly her bowels muft needs yearn to fee her Child in fuch a heavy plight. The young Lord before he took his leave of her promifed to wait upon her the morrow morning, which was Sunday, *April* the 19. and to attend on her to St. *Paul*'s Church to hear the Organs and certain excellent Hymns and Anthems performed by rare Voyces. The hot Gallant was fo eager in his purfuit that he outftript the morning, and was up before *Aurora* or his Lady. He like a paffionate Lover waited at the Chamber-door till the Princefs was pleafed to give him admittance; which being granted, he very fubmiffively defired her to make all poffible fpeed to attire her

her self; for his Coach waited at the door, in which he carried her to his Mother's house in *Grey-Fryars*, *London*; where she was no sooner arrived than freshly charged with a volley of tears by her tender Lover, and his weeping Friends, pressing her with many brisk and fresh Assaults to consent to marry; a Parson and License being already provided, the two necessary Appurtenances of Matrimony, though it proved but a fallacy and cheat like the rest and best of all their future Transactions. Thus on *Easter* day the *English* Lord and the *German* Princess, with their Relations, went to Great St. *Bartholomew*'s Church, and there were joyned together in marriage by one Mr. *Smith*, who received an extraordinary reward for this his ordinary piece of service. And here I cannot forget the Old Proverb, Marriage and Hanging goes by Destiny; and in this case it is undeniably true; for the one was the
con-

consequent of the other, and both very ominous and fatal. Now it was that the young Lord and his Relations thought themselves as safe as a Theif in a Mill; their Designs, as they imagined, being succesfully accomplished, and that it was not in the power of wit or malice to put any *remora* in the way to their intended happiness and good Fortune. But to avoid all offence, and the better to secure this new Purchase, that she might not be ravished from this young Lord by some person of greater Quality, they furiously post it away to *Barnet*, and there after a noble Treat, they bedded one another, and lay together Sunday and Monday night. On Tuesday a Licenſe was produced, and then her consent to a second Marriage was desired, and obtained. O brave *Carleton*! Fast bind, fast find. 'Tis good to have two strings to ones Bow. The Marriage-knot was made indissoluble, and had continued

tinued so still, but that the Executioner untied it.

The Bird being thus taken, they were resolved to make her as trim and gay as she could possibly be in borrowed feathers. The Princess must now appear like a Princess; for they were so infatuated that they did all by an implicit Faith believe she was Mistris of 80000 *l. per Annum*, besides other additional hereditaments which in modesty were concealed, yet not so closely kept but that it came to be the publick Discourse in Coffeehouses (those smoaky Seminaries of idle Stories) and was there confirm'd by her credulous Husband. Her new Garments being now finished and sent home to her at the cost and charges of her Friends with all necessary and suitable Ornaments (they being grown proud of their new and noble Alliance) besides Necklaces, Bracelets, Pendents and Jewels of her own, with which she was sufficiently stor'd; she

she appeared in this stately and prince-like Attire on *May*-day next; and her Relations to accommodate her nobly, had procured a Lady's Coach, to convey her to *Hide-Parke*, whither she came accompanied with her Ladyship, attended by Footmen, and rid the round with that famous *Calvalcade*; the Lady giving her precedence, which she took (being as yet unacquainted with her Husbands condition) and treating her nobly, when she came home from the pleasant Divertisement of the Tour *a-la-mode*.

Thus they were as yet driven on with a prosperous gale. Fortune still smiled upon them and their proceedings. There appear'd not hitherto so much as one furrow on her brow. The same distance and respect was shown as formerly. And Lodgings were provided at a house in *Durham-Yard*, fit for the Reception of this new wedded and bedded Princess. All the Caresses and Endearments that could pass between

tween a young married Couple were mutually interchanged between them, and accepted with an equal Delight and Complacency. But see the fickle state of humane affairs (which indeed is no certain state at all) the Scene must now be altered. She that was formerly admired (I had almost said ador'd) for her Endowments and Qualifications both Natural and Acquisititious, must now on a suddain be contumeliously and opprobriously used, and as an infamous Criminal hurried away by Ruffians to a Justice, and be exposed to the severe Scoffs and bitter Taunts of the rude and headless Rabble.

The occasion was this. The return of her Moneys out of *Germany* failing at the day appointed, and their blooming hopes being hereby nipt in the very bud; old *Carleton* bestirs his stumps, thinks himself abused, and resolves to be revenged on that young Girl that had to the disparagement

ragement of his Gravity, Experience and Years so notoriously and palpably circumvented and baffled him. But yet like a subtle Fox, to avoyd all censure, and to clear himself from being the Authour of those Calumnies wherewith the poor Princess was so filthily bespattered; a Letter is produced directed to old *Carleton*, the Contents whereof were as followeth.

SIR,

I Am unknown to you; but hearing that your Son Mr. John Carleton *hath married a Woman of a pretended great Fortune and high Birth; I thought fit to give you timely notice of what I know and have heard concerning her; that she is an absolute Cheat, hath married several men in our County of* Kent,

Kent, *and then run away from them with what they had.* If it be the same Woman I mean, she speaks several Languages fluently, and hath very high Breasts, &c.

It was the misfortune of this *German* Princess to be at the Exchange-Tavern, when this Letter was delivered; upon perusal whereof there was a strange and suddain alteration in the Countenances of the whole Family. Not a face to be seen but what did bode ill luck, not an aspect or look but what was mixed with fear and anger. Immediately without any farther delay the Princess is summoned to appear before the Domestick Inquisition, and interrogated, concerning the purport of this Letter: She, like a true *Virago*, retaining still her Courage, though deceived in her Fortune, denied it absolutely,

imperi-

imperiously and with much contempt and disdain (Lord bless me! what an age do we live in that innocents should be so foully accus'd!) which did in some measure pacifie them, and abate the heat of their fury. Thus the Princess and her Lord took their leaves of them, and returned to their Lodgings, but they continued not long there without disturbance: for that very evening they were alarm'd by the whole gang, accompanied with a Gentlewoman a Neighbour, who came very rudely to them, and beat up their quarters. At their first entrance they meet with the Princess, and salute her by the name of cheating Whore (vile language indeed to upbraid a Princess with in her own apartment, tho' true, that's most certain) with many other *Billingsgate* terms; and from words they fell to blows, threw the poor Lady down (O horrid indignity but what can be expected from ill-bred mechanick peo-
D ple

ple?) disrob'd her, depriv'd her of all Ornamental Dresses and Embellishments, and stript her so bare and naked, that she had not so much as a Fig-leaf left to cover her shame. 'Twas an action, I confess, altogether misbecoming the modesty of the Female Sex, equalling (I had almost said exceeding) the impudence of a common Brow.

Nor was this all; this was but the bad Prologue of a worse Tragedie: for she was afterward haled and torn by the Ruffians and Officers to go before a Justice of Peace. The Prosecutor was her own dear Father-in-Law, whose accusation was, that she had two Husbands, and both of them alive at that time: Whereupon the Justice demanded of her, whether she had two Husbands; to which she replyed like a Princess with a very acute accent, If I have, you are one of them. This possibly might somewhat incense his Worship; but it was excufable in her, becaufe ignorant of the Dignity of his place, and the refpect that is due to one of his Authority; fhe being an Englifh-Forreignner. But in fhort, he made her *Mittimus*, and fhe was committed to the *Gatehoufe*; and the old reverend Gentleman *Carleton* was bound over by Recognizance to profecute her for Bigamy.

Nor was this the only crime that fhe was taxed with, there were feveral other Peccadillio's laid to her charge, *viz.* That fhe, meaning *Carleton*'s Lady, had pickt a Kentifh Lord's pocket; that indeed was unkindly done to abufe her own Countryman; That fhe had cheated a French Merchant of feveral Jewels, Rings, and other rich Commodities, and wheadled a Vintner out of fixty pounds. (fure fhe had a prejudice for thofe of that Trade, that fhe fo often cullied them) and was clapt in *Newgate* for it: but thefe ftories upon farther inquiry soon vanished; for her name was not then recorded there; so that *Carleton* was the only Prosecutor of his Daughter-in-Law; and all the other accusations were lookt upon as malicious & vindicative. Thus is it with this *quondam* German Princess, that was rever'd, admir'd and courted by all; not a supple ham, but bowed to her; all things were too little to gratifie her humour and please her fancie, and now she hath nothing at all; a poor disconsolate Woman, confin'd to a loathsome Gaol, destitute of all Friends, and which is worse, of Money too.

The very day of her commitment, her loving Husband came to visit her in prison, and there most passionately and tenderly bewailed her misfortune, complaining of his Father's usage as barbarous, renewing his former protestations of Love and Tenderness, maugre all the contrivances of his friends, and the disappointment
of

of their satisfactions. Poor thing! How soon the case is alter'd? Whenas a little before, this now fond man could suffer his Wife to be rifled of all she had, his dear Wife, and tamely condescend to the gross abuses put upon her, notwithstanding all her crys and complaints to him for Redress; and now his passion is grown so strong again, that he can live with her, love her and dye for her. These are his kind sentiments of her, after the unkind dealings of his friends with her. How to reconcile them together, I know not; but this serves to verifie that known saying; *Love covers a multitude of faults.*

Mrs. *Carleton* continued in prison the space of six weeks, and notwithstanding this injurious restraint, she had this comfort still in the very heigth of her misery to be civilly treated by the Keeper (O strange! a Keeper and civil? that's news indeed) besides the weight of her affliction

fliction was somewhat lightned by the compassion of some persons of Quality that at first out of curiosity came to visit her, who did contribute to her assistance and relief in this necessitous and calamitous condition.

But now to add affliction to affliction, some bold, shameless mercenary fellow, published a Pamphlet in Mr. *Carleton*'s name, wherein he complains of his imbecillity and weakness, exclaims against his misfortune, and blames his Stars for their unpropitious influence. The abstract of this abusive Scribble, as to some particulars (for it would be too tedious to relate it at large) you will find to be in these, or in words to this effect.

READER,

I Shall not give my self the trouble to recollect and declare the several Motives and Inducements that deceitful, but wise enough, woman used to deceive me with, &c. Her Wit did more and more engage and charm me : her qualities depriv'd me of my own : her courteous Behaviour, her Majestick Humility to all persons; her emphatical Speeches, her kind and loving Expressions; and, amongst other things, her high detestation of Vice, as Lying, &c. Her great pretence to zeal in her Religion; her modest confidence and grace in all

all companies, fearing the knowledge of none. Her demeanor was such, that she left no room for suspicion, not only in my opinion, but also in others both grave and wise.

How true the Contents hereof are, I leave it to the Reader to judge; she her self gave her Husband the lye for it when she was living, and I am sorry I cannot do the same for her now she is dead.

After that *Carleton* had visited his dear *Molly* in the Gatehouse, and promised to pay the Keeper for any thing that she desired, provided it did not exceed the summ of 40 s. He puts pen to paper and

and sends her a Letter to kiss her hands by proxie, because he would not come thither to do it in person. And this, it seems, was all the Amorous paper that she could preserve, the rest being hurried away, with her more pretious Utensils, that night that she was deprived of them at her Lodgings by her Husbands friends a little before her Commitment. And when you peruse it you may safely swear that Love is a perfect Ague, and hath it's hot and cold fits successively.

My

My Dear Heart,

*A*Lthough *the manner of your usage may very well call the sincerity of my Affection and Expressions to you in question; yet when I consider that you are not ignorant of the Compulsion of my Father, and the Animosity of my whole Relations, both against you and my self for your sake; I am very confident your goodness will pardon and pass by those things which at present I am no way able to help: And be you confident, that notwithstanding my friends aversion, there shall be nothing wanting within the reach of my power, that may conduce both to your Liberty, Maintenance and*

and Vindication. **I** *shall very speedily be in a condition to furnish you with Mony to supply you according to your desire.* **I** *hope Mr. B. will be very civil to you; and let him be assured he shall in a most exact measure be satisfied, and have a Requital for his Obligation. My Dearest, always praying for our happy meeting,*

May 11th.   I rest your most affe-
1663.   ctionate Husband,

John Carleton.

After this, several of her Husbands friends would needs give themselves the trouble to go and see her in the Gate-house: And one, among the rest of that great multitude of her friendly Visitants, accosts her in this manner.

Madam,

Madam, I have had a longing desire to wait upon you and enjoy your society, being one of your Husbands intimate Acquaintance, because I have heard much of your Breeding and Education. To which she replied smartly. Alas Sir! I have left that in the City amongst my Kindred, because they want it.

Another thinking to shew his wit and raillery throws out this Maxime; Marriage and Hanging goes by Destiny. She soon returned this answer, I have received Marriage, and you in probability may Hanging. She was very nimble in such kind of Reparties, and bestowed them very liberally on those that came with a design to disturb her, as most of *Carleton*'s Relations did.

Now the time of the Sessions of Peace for *London* and *Middlesex* approaching, she was sent from the Gatehouse to Newgate, but lodged in the Master of the Prison's house; and a great

great concourse of people did dayly resort thither to take a view of the so much famed *German* Princess. From thence on Wednesday the Third of *June*, towards Night, she was brought to the Bar at Justice-Hall in the Old Bayly, being the first day of the Court's sitting; and was there immediately Arraigned, and on the morrow being Thursday *June* the fourth was Indicted for marrying of young *Carleton*; *Thomas Stedman*, a Shooemaker in *Kent*, her former Husband, being then alive, as they alledged.

After a full Examination of the Business, and Evidence heard on both sides, the Jury went out, and in a short time after some Debate returned, bringing her in Not guilty: whereat the people there present at the Trial made a great shout, and gave a Plaudite with their hands for joy.

The *German* Princess being thus acquitted was carried back to Prison with the same equanimity, the same even

even and unbiassed temper as when she first came thither.

On Saturday *June* the Sixth, she was discharged of her Imprisonment and set at liberty; a very proper Expression; for now she had all the World to ramble in, no certain place of abode to resort to. All this while she heard nothing of her Husband, which made her suspect that he had more Irons in the fire and Engines at work to do her some farther prejudice; and therefore she took private Lodgings in *Fuller*'s Rents, hoping that her Lord would in process of time, when the edge of his malice was turned, be reduced to that duty and obligation that lay upon him. But in the interim she did not spare to spread abroad, in the hearing of all persons, very strange menaces and threats against old *Carleton*, that she would take as severe a course with him, for the regaining of her Goods and Jewels, as he had done with her, and that too at

the

the very same Barr where she was arraigned by him, that the World might be sensible of the Imposture.

Young *Carleton* understanding her resolves, and that she would proceed against his Father with all the rigor imaginable, came to her on *Sunday* in the Evening being the Seventh of *June*; where after some discourse past between them, she told him plainly, that she did persist in her former Resolution to prosecute his Father, seeming altogether inexorable, and absolutely deaf to any contrary motion. But he in a very submissive and humble posture on his knees, did beg and supplicate her not to deal with his Father so roughly. And what if she should? Why then the pusillanimous *Bravo* would destroy himself. Surely had she not had a peculiar love for him, since he said so very often before, she would have tried him now, and see whether he had so much courage as to be his own Executioner. But

But the distressed Lordling fell a-again to his accustomed Caresses and Embraces; thinking thereby to bring her to a more calm frame of spirit, and perswade her to renounce and vacate her former Decree of suing the old man, his Father.

Next day, being *Monday*, *June* the Eighth, she sent a Letter to her Husband, but received no answer, which did more than a little incense the abused Gentlewoman: in so much that on *Friday* Night, being the Nineteenth of *June*, she went to Mr. *Carleton*'s house in *Gray-Fryers*, knock'd at the Door, and the old man ask'd who was there? She made answer, your Daughter, when a Princess, but now your Son's Wife. He demanded what she desired? She replied, her Jewels, Goods, and her Husband, of all which he had wrongfully deprived her. His Rejoynder was short and sweet; As for your Goods your Husband is possessed of them; and he himself is is gone, nor for my part do I know where he is. Thus the poor *Titular* Princess went away with a flea in her ear, vilified and calumniated by the Father and Mother, scoft at and abused by their Relations, slighted, despised, nay which is worse, deserted by her Dear Lord and Master, and rob'd of her great Mass of Wealth by his unnatural Parents, having nothing left her but three Kingdoms to beg or steal in; both dangerous offences; for the first she must be whipt; for the last she may be hang'd, as she was.

Nay farther, poor soul! she hath nothing to sweeten all these calamities but the uncertain hope of revenge, whereby she may possibly bring these affianced offenders to a condign punishment, which may prove some abatement of her Affliction, and in some measure satisfactory, for the many injuries that she hath received from her Adversaries, by whose groundless malice and hatred she hath been publickly exposed to so much Contumely and Contempt.

Good lack! What a deal of do is here made about a *Westminster* Wedding? What a noise is heard in the World before the Consummation of these Nuptials? What a clutter is here before the Solemnising of this Marriage? What industry, art and care is used to bring, and how little to keep them together? Well! In civility I think we are obliged to give them joy, and so proceed to some other passages subsequent to the pompous Ceremony of their Matrimonical Conjunction.

A Princess hath not her full Retinue, unless she be attended by a Fool and a Poet. The first 'tis well known she had upon record, and lest she should want the last, a Gentleman (the Gentry of *England* being always prodigal of their Civilities to Forreign Ladies) did take upon him to be her Dramatick. Who examining the particula ticular Tranſactions between this Lord *Carleton* and his Lady, digeſted the matter into Play, and Intituled it, The *German* Princeſs. In the year 1664. this Play was repreſented at the King's Houſe, and the *German* Princeſs admitted among them as an Actreſs, who did Act her own part; but with no great Applauſe; for it was the opinion of ſome of the Critical Wits, that ſhe came ſhort of that excellency when ſhe perſonated upon the Stage, which ſhe was Miſtriſs of, when ſhe acted to the Life in the World. And of this ſhe was not inſenſible, which was the reaſon ſhe ſoon deſerted that Employment, and returned to her former Slights and Pranks, which ſhe managed with greater dexterity; and no wonder, for ſhe was as old in ſuch kind of Experience as in Actual Sin, and could filch from her very Cradle.

Now ſhe is mannumitted from her former Vaſſalage, and is no way ſubject to the Edicts and Laws of a Husband. She is a perfect Gentlewoman at large, an absolute Ubiquitarian, and may rome where she pleases; for she is turn'd into the wide World to shift for her self: Let her go; and withall have a care of her hits.

Hitherto she may boast that what Crime soever she committed was *prosperum & felix scelus*, a fortunate and successful sin as to punishment inflicted on her person, but yet there is a sting in the tail of such Actions that may possibly do her business. Well, what is the next News we hear of her? Why, she still sings the second Part to the same Tune; and where ever she is admitted, not a Tankerd or a Piece of Plate but sticks to her lime-twig'd fingers. At length she is taken napping, and for this kind of sport, her only Recreation & Employment too, committed to *Newgate*, and there is Indicted, receives a fair & legal Tryal, & upon the hearing of the whole matter

of

of Fact by very substantial Witness, is found guilty, and so brought in by the Petty Jury, but afterwards she obtained a Reprieve, and by the favour of the Court had the benefit of Transportation; and accordingly in *February* 1671. was sent over to *Jamaica* in the *West-Indies*. In her passage thither there was, it seems, a Design against the Captain's Life by the Ship's Crew, and she (being one of the number) timely discovered it (but of that more hereafter;) for which signal piece of service she was set at liberty as soon as she came a shore in those Parts, and left at her own disposal.

And here she also lives splendidly, maintains her antient Titular Dignity and State by her insinuating Tricks and Devices; verifying that saying, as if it had been calculated for her own *Genius*;

Terram non animum mutant qui trans mare currunt.

Which I English thus,

That which is bred in the bone, will n'er out of the flesh.

That warm Climate wrought no more upon her Constitution than our cold Country. Change of Aire works no change on the Affections of the Mind. Her Morals are as corrupt, her Life is as scandalous, her Demeanor as haughty and her Actions as sordid now, as ever. During her abode in these Parts, like a true friend, to shew that all the water between her and her Acquaintance cannot wash away their Remembrance; She, in a pretty kind of drolling way, with more than ordinary Confidence, sends a Letter from *Port Royal* in *Jamaica*, to all her fellow-sufferers in *Newgate*; which begins thus:

My

My Friends and once Fellow-Priſoners.:

INgratitude is the blackeſt of Crimes, and forgetfulneſs in a friend is more than a venial ſin. To avoid both (though our noble Extraction and the eximiouſneſs of our Birth and State might apologize for either) I ſend this Miſſive to inform you of my condition, ſince I was exiled the Britiſh ſhore, which is this; Health and ſucceſs ſtill waits upon me, and I cordially wiſh you the ſame Attendance.

Death pronounced with the mildeſt accent, is a word that Ague-ſhakes the whole frame of Nature, and ſtrikes the Microcoſm with an Univerſal Paraly-ſis.

sis. It breaths nothing but Terrour, and affects all that is Man with the horrid apprehenfion of Annihilation. Yet methought the Sentence of my Proscription was as dreadful to me as that of my Diffolution. To be banifh'd from the fweets of a Native Country, to which all perfons are born with a natural love and tendency, was fo harfh at firft, that it did afflict me with an internal regret beyond expreffion. But that which did in fome meafure dulcifie this bitter potion was the confideration and example of many perfons who have undergone the fame banifhment with matchlefs patience and undaunted courage, and thereby fignalifed themfelves to all pofterity.

rity. And is not this far better than to whine away one's dayes, as the witty, though weak Roman did, or waste them in scribling his de Tristibus? Certainly 'tis a more generous act and deserves greater commendation.

As to my Voyage at Sea; you must understand, that I came to the desired Haven with a prosperous Gale. Where I no sooner arrived, but I was, contrary to expectation, treated en Princesse, and accommodated like my self. But one thing I have omitted; When I first set sail from England I was lookt upon but strangely, and despised as the base brat of a Country Fidler. Yet this did not so much deject me but that I fled to my old
Asylum,

Afylum, the never failing Refuge of a Charming Tongue and Ready Wit, and fo had both my Lodging better'd and my Commons amended. For then I was furnifhed with a fpatious and commodious Cabbin fit for the reception of my felf and friend. And my food (which was before fo falt that there was no venturing upon it without running the risk and danger of an eternal Thirft) was foon changed, and frefh provifion was my dayly Diet.

At my Landing, inftead of a barbarous flavery accompanied with rudenefs the conftant Attendant thereof, I was immediately environed with a Crowd of Admirers. And no fooner was my name

name heard there, but it eccho'd into the remotest parts of the *Island*, and drew a wonderful confluence of the more vile and dissolute people to my Habitation.

I was astonished at first when I met so many of my former Acquaintance, as I did there; but that fit was soon over when I considered the cause, and found my self also among them. I must needs bestow a little advice upon you all in general, from the highest degree to the lowest, that ever had the happiness to be educated in your so famous Academy, 'Tis convenient that you all receive timely notice of what I am going to say, whether *Bulkers*, *Pads*, *Files*, &c. and others by what names

names or titles soever they are distinguished by the Canting Crew: for, I am resolved to tell you a piece of my mind, which I hope you will lay up in your heart and take into your more serious consideration, when the weighty affairs of your Employment will afford you a Retirement.

Do not in the least flatter your selves with an opinion that your Villanies will be connived at by the eye of Justice, any more than those of our Predecessors. For you cannot but be sensible that you are festered and gangrened limbs of the body politick; and therefore the experienced and grave Physicians of the Commonwealth, the Judges, will in time cut you off

off to prevent the absolute destruction of the whole Compositum.

I must confess you are not all to be so severely dealt with; if I may declare my thoughts: Some of you may be compared to ulcerated parts, or prodigious wens, and those must be absolutely cut off, or the whole body be endangered. Some to dead flesh, which must be burnt out with cauterizing irons; and others to noxious and filthy humours, that must be purged away, as I my self have been, into another Climate. But no more of this: Comparisons are odious; and I hope my fellow-Collegiats will excuse me, and not take it as an offence, because I make my self one of the number.

I live here beloved by all, dayly loaded with kindneſſes, which I know not how to retaliate. My freedom is greater here in my Confinement, than when I was among you free. My pleaſures are ſweet and uninterrupted: My perſon inſulted o're by none, nor chekt by any Lordly controle or prohibition: My phanſie unconfined and at liberty: My affections fettered to no particular perſon: My recreation is as diverting as my food is nouriſhing; and my fare as changeable as my appetite. In brief, I am left ſolely to my own conduct, and that is the conſummation of all my felicitie.

I am ſo taken up with multiplicitie

plicitie of businefs that I can trifle away no more minutes in my farther enlargement. You may, if you think it convenient, prefent my dutie to my Lord, and inform him that a Princefs is more acceptable in a forreign, than in her own Countrie, and I live now more like a Ladie than I did when I was his. So much for that; one word more and I have done.

If the Inhabitants of the Iflet do not furfeit me with Courtefie, and kill me with kindnefs, and you do not precipitately hurrie your felves to the Noofing-Cheat, you may, when I have no other divertifement, expect to hear again of my welfare. In the interim remember

member me to the Old Gang, the roguiſh Crew of all our former Acquaintance, of what Age, Qualitie, or Sex ſoever. I would deſire you to reclaim, but that I fear will be like waſhing the Blackamoor's head, and ſo conſequentlie labour loſt. But I will ſpend no more time, nor loſe farther labour than in ſubſcribing my ſelf,

Your real Friend in Exile,

M. C.

An Epiſtle is the only expedient that abſent friends have to communicate their mutual Sentiments at a diſtance. 'Tis a great and ſurpriſing ſatisfaction no doubt to underſtand by Letter, that a Friend in Forreign Parts is healthful and proſperous. And do you

you think that these *Newgate*-Birds were not ravish'd at the relation of the health and success of their own and only Princess? Surely yes: It must needs afford them matter of great joy and content. But wee'l leave them to their extasie, and return to the Authress and occasion of it.

You may well imagine without putting your phancy upon the rack, that she did live in no very mean condition; because whilst she continued there she cheated several persons, Merchants and others, and could not want till their Stocks were exhausted; nor would she desert them upon any terms so long as there was any mony stirring. She was the ruine of two or three substantial persons in a small time; destroyed both them and their Families; and at length came to be as well known, and grew as infamous there, as ever she was here. This possibly might be
one

one cause of her returning so speedily. Well; having play'd her pranks there sufficiently, so that she had gained a name among them, she began to watch for an opportunity of shipping, in order to her transportation; which soon offer'd it self, and she as soon embraced it. To sea she goes, but whips into *Holland* before she came into *England*, and there put a scurvy Trick upon a Herring-fed Dutch-man, and then resolv'd for *England*; which you shall find at large in this ensuing Story, as it was related by the party that was also defrauded by her, upon her arrival here.

The German Princess, as I told you, went into *Holland*, and there skrew'd her self into a credulous Family, by her specious pretences and fair Language. Where she was no sooner hous'd, but she began to be in a Romantick humour, and tell strange Stories of her prodigious Estate, Birth and Quality. And first, she

inform'd

inform'd them that she was a person of very considerable Parentage, but was compel'd, by their severity and hard usage, to fly thither; for they would force her to marry with a Papist, which she would by no means give ear to; she her self being a Protestant, and was resolv'd to lay down her Life rather than her Religion: Pious *Divota!* and yet she died a Roman Catholick. What a piebal'd Creature was this? As to her Country she was an English-German, as to her Religion (if any) a Protestant-Papist.

But to proceed. Besides, she lamented her Condition as very deplorable, being a stranger in a foreign Countrey, unfurnished of all necessaries, and absolutely destitute of friends, only she had still reserv'd one small sum of money, but was forced to leave it behind her. The credulous Man and his Wife began to commiserate her condition, and seriously

seriously considered what was to be done in the Case. They believ'd what she with so much dissimulation aver'd to be true; and therefore did accommodate her with all things convenient for her passage, that she might bring over her Wealth; for she promised to board with them, and live altogether in *Holland*. And for the better security of the Money, they sent their own Pleasure-boat and Servants to wait upon her over, with Letters of Recommendation on her behalf, to their Brother and Sister that liv'd then at St. *James*'s. As soon as she was Landed here in *England*, she steers her course directly to S. *James*'s, and as soon as she came to the place appointed, was as kindly entertain'd as could be expected. She was not long there before she began to complain that she wanted a faithful and trusty friend to go into the Country to receive the sum of mony for her above-mentioned, which was as she pretended

tended 6000. *l.* the place where it was to be received being eighty miles diftant from *London.* The Gentleman of the Houfe, being as credulous as his Relations in *Holland*, profer'd her his fervice, which fhe, without any farther Ceremony, kindly accepted: and withal gave him a Letter of Atturney, with full power to receive the faid fum, upon demand, for her ufe, and to give an Acquittance or any other Difcharge for the fame. Nor was this all; for fhe had the confidence to intreat him to lend her tend pounds to fupply her prefent occafions, and furnifh her with fome Neceffaries that fhe had occafion for, which he was to be reimburs'd upon his return. This created a kind of fufpicion in him that what fhe faid was not real, but merely fallacious, as it prov'd by the fequel of the ftory. Hereupon he difcovers the bufinefs to his Wife, who appear'd very much difcontented at his intended refufal fusal, because she came from her friends. This wrought so much upon the Gentleman, that he lent her ten pounds, and immediately undertook his journey to receive the money according to her former order and agreement.

The next day she resolv'd with her ten pound stock to visit the City, and to lay out part of it in Commodities that she at present wanted; but being destitute of Company, she very kindly invites her new Landlady to go a long with her and assist her, she being a stranger (as she pretended) and altogether unacquainted with the humours of the Town. Her Landlady accepted of her invitation, and accompanies her in a Coach to the Pye-Tavern at *Aldgate*; where she made the Coachman stop, pretending she had some urgent business there to dispatch. And so begging a minutes patience of her Landlady, enters the Tavern; passes clear through

through it into the *Minories*, and so gives her the slip, and never return'd more; leaving the Gentlewoman all this while in the Coach at the door, who never heard of her from that time till she was taken by *Lowman*, and secur'd in the *Marshalsea*.

After this she play'd another prank in *Lothbury* which was this, according to the relation of the party that knew it experimentally to be true to his own loss. This worthy woman coming by chance into *Lothbury*, spies a Bill upon a door, intimating that there were Lodgings to be let: She boldly knocks, and immediately has admittance. Desires the Man of the house to shew her a Room, pretending that she was newly come from *Norwich*, and was to continue here some time to dispatch her affairs. She view'd the Chamber, lik'd it well and took it, agreeing to pay for it four shillings and six pence *per* week. Being thus provided of a Lodging, she told

told her Landlord that she must needs go to the other end of the Town to see a Councellor at Law, and to require his advice in a business of great importance. Away marches my Lady, and returns towards the evening, keeping very good hours, and so retires to her Chamber, sends for her Landlady, and desires her to make her a good Sack-posset to settle her stomach, which was somewhat qualmish and troubled with Opilations, being tir'd with that days travel. Her Landlady according to her request provided her the best she could; being very unwilling to displease a person of her pretended quality; she promising great satisfaction, and a large recompensation for all civilities, besides her bargain, and beyond her former Agreement, tho' resolv'd to perform neither the one nor the other.

The costly drench is prepar'd for the Brute, and for the greater state brought

brought up by her Landlady in a Silver Tankerd valued at four pound ten shillings, she takes it, and begins to fall to; but here by the bie take notice she was so civil as to desire her Landlady to sip with her; but the modest Matron refus'd it, and so the remainder was set up for her Breakfast or Mornings draught (which you please, or both) the next day. When she had done, her Landlady takes her leave, wishing her a good nights rest in her new Lodging, and leaves her to her repose. But alas! she was mistaken; for her Tenant delighted in deeds of darkness, and was altogether for night-work, that her tricks might be undiscover'd. As soon as her Landlady had taken her leave, to work she goes; ransacks a Chest of Drawers that stood in the Room, and finds there a silver Cup of thirty shillings price, takes away a new laced Whisk and Ruffle, two large Cambrick Handkerchiefs, and a White Sarce-

Sarcenet Hood; and having so done in the Morning by five of the Clock, she packs up her bag and baggage, and gives them the slip; they hearing no more of her till she was a Prisoner in *Newgate*. Her Landlady, notwithstanding that she was so rude to leave her without taking her leave, like a good woman that can forget injuries, comes to visit her in the Gaol, and is admitted to see her. As soon as she came to her, she askt her whether or no she knew her; to which, impudence it self in the very abstract returns this answer, That she never saw her face before, days of her breath: She farther said, Did you not cheat me at such a time of several things which are before particularis'd. She replyed, she was then out of sorts, and not in a good mood to chat (which was a wonder, being a woman) but if she would come when she was in humour, she would talk with her: However she should
be

be very welcome then, if she would sit down with her, and drink a bottle of Ale (which was all the satisfaction she was like to have for her goods) and enter upon some other civil discourse, for that did not at all please her at that time; and this was all she could extort from her. Alas, alas! poor Gentlewoman!

The Tenant was too cunning to be courted into a confession by a modest Landlady. Besides it would have been a grand disparagement to a Princess to be perswaded by a private Subject. Thus her Landlady was forced to depart unknown and unsatisfied: tho' in my opinion 'tis great pity that so good a nature should be abus'd by a damnable *Prævaricatrix*.

But this is not all; This active Woman, when at liberty; this Machiavilianess, whose restless spirit was always plotting new mischiefs; her wits were always at work to find out new

new adventures; and having her Emiffaries abroad who did pry into the Eftates and Tempers of perfons fit to be wrought upon, fhe was inform'd of an Apothecary that liv'd fomewhere towards *Weftminfter*, he being a very young man, well ftockt, and newly fet up. And him fhe pitcht upon. He muft be the next Novice that fhe intends to Cully, and make the defrauded object of her fport and laughter. To effect which, fhe employs an old fuperannuated Beldam in this Embaffie between the Turk and the Divel. An aged finner, no doubt, that had formerly been good at the Trade; but being worn out with years and overgrown, was unfit for action as formerly; but yet continued a well-wifher to all of the prigging profeffion, and thought it no difparagement, but rather an honour in her decrepit age to be the Meffenger of a Princefs. Well, fhe is the perfon that muft go of her

Er-

Errands; and is often sent by her to the Shop for Pomatum, Treacle and Mithridate, and such kind of old Wive's Physick, which she had often occasion for: She being now a constant Customer, and grown somewhat acquainted, watcheth her opportunity, and one day when she thought it most convenient, asks him why he did not Marry, being a young man as he was, and having a good Trade in his belly. To which he readily answers; So indeed Mother I would, if I could match with a Virtuous Wife, and one that had something of a Fortune. Whereunto she replyed, that she was very intimately acquainted with a Gentlewoman, the Niece of an eminent Citizen, under whose tuition she was at that time, who had two thousand pound of hers in his hands as a portion, payable at the day of her Marriage; and withal told him the names of the persons and place of their abode, that he

might

might make inquiry, and be satisfied of the truth of her Relation: Nay farther, that she did not question but to prevail with her to appear in his company, if he did approve of it; and that she having an influence upon the Gentlewoman would perswade her to it, and make up the match between them. The young man return'd her thanks, and the very next day made diligent inquiry of the truth of the premises among his Neighbors, and found all that the old Woman had related to be certainly true, which made him very eager in his pursuit and earnest in his desire to see his design'd Mistriss. But hold young man, not so hasty; a soft pace goeth far: you must not think to catch old Birds with chaff, there must be some corn. There is the Matchmaker first to be considered before the interview of this couple be permitted. In short (for I am in as much haste

haste as he, and long to come to a conclusion) he enters into a hundred pound bond for the payment of fifty pound to the old Woman upon the day of their Marriage; which being seal'd and deliver'd, she then appoints a day of meeting; but yet to inflame him the more, she disappoints him twice or thrice, & at length produceth our Princess to personate the Citizens Niece. Several meetings they had, and several chargeable Treats; where he had the opportunity to caress and court her, which he did so effectually in a small time, that he soon understood her amorous inclination, which it seems was so violent, that she confest it to him; upon this the overjoy'd Gentleman immediately presseth a Marriage forthwith; his thoughts being now wholly taken up with that Solemnity, the Prelude to his future felicity. She puts him off with this excuse, that she was destitute of Apparel, and withal alledged that
she

she could not possibly procure any from her Uncle, without discovering the plot, and laying open their present design. But he being resolv'd to marry her before her return to her supposed Uncle, in a loving humour throws an hundred Pieces into her lap, to be dispos'd of as she thought fit in order thereunto.

To dispatch the business with all speed, he thirsting after the fruition of the sweets of a Marriage-bed, their Nuptials were celebrated the next morning; and when he had bedded her two nights together, she desir'd to return to her Uncle, and intreated him to come thither the next day to demand both her and her portion. This advice did no way displease him: for accordingly he went the next day to the Grave Gentleman her Uncle, who crav'd his name and his business, being an absolute stranger to him. He told him that he came thither to demand his Wife, who was there with him,

him, and hoped he would not rudely and by force detain her from him. The aged Citizen, being somewhat surpriz'd with the strangeness of his unexpected demand, askt him who was his Wife? he made answer, Your Niece, Sir, and I presume you are not ignorant of this too; that there is a certain summ of two thousand pound allotted for her portion, which I expect to be deliver'd up to me with her person. The old man being netled with this story, and really perswaded that it was true, being so seriously and confidently related; runs up in a fury to his Niece, and at her first rencounter salutes her very roughly. You disobedient baggage (saith he) there's your beloved Husband below that is come to demand you, e'en get you to him; go, for I'l have no more to do with you. I thought indeed you would serve me thus some time or other; now I find it too true to my sorrow. The Maid was so startled at her Uncles ſtrange carriage, and the novelty of his intelligence, that ſhe lookt upon him as an abſolute madman in a raving condition; but hoped when the fit was over, and he had recover'd his *Lucida intervalla*, ſhe ſhould be better inform'd; however, ſhe proteſted that ſhe did not underſtand his meaning, and was altogether ignorant of the buſineſs. Nay, ſaid he, never go about to deny it, and ſtand in a lye, and with that he pulls her by the arm down ſtairs, and ſhoves her towards the Apothecary; There take her, ſays he, and let me hear no more of you, for you ſhall never come within my doors again: and for the portion you mention, excuſe me in that particular; for I intend to preſerve that for the maintenance of her Children, if ever ſhe have any. The Apothecary ſurveying this his ſuppoſed Wife, was more aſtoniſhed than they, and ſays, Pray, Sir, what do you mean?

Do

Do you intend to put a trick upon me, and fob me off in this manner? This is none of my Wife, nor did I ever set eye of this Gentlewoman before now. Here they were all in a Labyrinth, and knew not how to extricate themselves; but at laſt the Apothecary giving them an account of the whole ſtory of his Amours in every particular ſoon undeceiv'd them, and found that he was moſt craftily depriv'd of his Miſtreſs, as well as his money. And ſo took his leave of them with a heavy heart, accompanied only with their pitty, and his own diſtracted thoughts to his own houſe, where we will leave him to conſult the Diſpenſatory for a Medicine to cure him of this *London*-trick put upon him by the Princeſs of *Colen*.

And now kind Reader, if you will have the patience to ſee one trick more of hers, we will put no more tricks upon you; and that is the

Rob-

Robbing of one of the King's Watchmakers, who lodged in the Hay-market by St. *Jameses*; which was acted in this ensuing manner.

This Gentleman, when this Fact was committed (as he himself related the Story) lived then in the Hay-Market, and had taken a Shop and a Lodging at the House of Mrs. *Williams*; and during his abode there, this Cheating *Carletonian* Princess came thither to take a view of a chamber over against him, which she soon liked at the first sight, and took it, (and here she made use of the Emperours *Motto*, though in a worse sence. *Veni. Vidi. Vici.*) and lay there but three nights before she began to play her Tricks. And the better to palliate her Designs, she very lovingly invites the Watch-maker being a Bachelor, and their Landlady, to go to a Play, at the Duke's House, which she intended to bestow upon them, and after that a Treat at the

the Tavern. They returned her thanks and accepted her Invitation. So together they march, and in their abſence a Gentlewoman came to her Landlady's Houſe and inquired for the new Lodger; her Maid being there anſwered, that her Miſtriſs was not at home; but if ſhe pleaſed to go up to her Miſtriſſes Chamber and repoſe her ſelf there a ſmall time, ſhe might ſpeak with her; for ſhe was confident it would not be long before her return; ſo ſhe went up ſtairs alone, and the Landladies ſervant askt her how ſhe durſt truſt her above being a ſtranger; ſhe replied it was her Miſtriſſes Siſter, and ſent for or procured a bottle of Wine to drink with the Maid below, while the Gentlewoman was employed above; who goes by the name of *Kate Hern*, *alias Keeling*, ſometimes by the one, & ſometimes by the other. And whilſt the two ſervants were carouſing their Miſtriſſes healths, ſhe brake open a Cham-

Chamber, and a Trunk that was there, wherein were thirty Watches, some of them Gold of 22 *l*. price; 60 Guinneys, and 160 *l*. or 180 *l*. in Silver, all which she stole and carried clear away with her, having been above about half an hour, and no longer. When she had got this rich Prize, she came down, and told the Maid that she came to visit her Mistriss, but she being abroad, and her time calling her away, could not possibly stay any longer, but would take another more convenient opportunity to wait upon her. By this time the Play was done, and they all went from the Theater to the Green Dragon Tavern in *Fleetstreet*, where they called for a bottle of Wine, which was not as yet touch'd; when Mrs. *Carleton* makes an excuse to step aside, and so going down stairs hastens immediately to her Lodging, and understood by her Mayd that the Business was done, and the Bird flown; and then she and her Mayd

Mayd followed after, and never returned to the Tavern, where she left the Watchmaker, and another Gentleman with his Landlady. They tarried above an hour in expectation of her coming; but finding the contrary, the Gentleman took his leave of them and departed, and soon after Mr. *Aspinal* and his Landlady went away likewise. As soon as they came home they ask'd if all were well, and the Mayd answered, Yes. Then they inquired where the Lodger's Mayd was; she told them that her Mistrifs came and fetch'd her out, and said she was going to such a place, but would not make any long stay. At this the Watch-maker grew somewhat jealous of what was too true to his Cost, and presently went up and found that he was rob'd, whose loss as he himself declared was about 600 *l.* Nor could he ever hear of her afterwards till he found her this last bout in the *Marshalsea*.

Thus I have given you a fhort or compendious Narrative of her Life, and fome of the moſt remarkable paſſages and Tranſactions therein. Many more might have been here inſerted, but that they would ſwell this intended Epitome to too prodigious a bulk, and make this ſmall Tract a a large Volume, which is contrary to the Nature and firſt Deſign of the Thing it ſelf, and therefore to be cautiouſly and prudently avoyded.

All theſe her prementioned Actions were but the Adventures of leſs than a brace of years ſince ſhe bid adieu to *Jamaica*. Alas! That ſmall ſpot of ground was too narrow for her ſpacious ſoul to act in. And it may very well be ſaid of her now, as it was of old of the *Pellæan* Youth in the Satyriſt.

Æſtuat infelix anguſto limite mundi.

And not to intermeddle with what
immediately

immediately follows, becaufe it is not for our purpofe; we will only take up the conclufion, and by changing the Sex as well as the Gender, make it both good Latine and good Verfe, and fo clofe all upon her account, as the Poet did on his,

Sarcophago contenta fuit. Mors fola fatetur
Quantula fint hominum Corpufcula—

To be juft to you, fhe had but a narrow (or to fpeak truly no) fortune of her own, and could not live in that petty Iflet according to the extent of her mind. And 'twas to be feared, that if fhe had continued there a little longer, fhe would have monopolifed all the wealth of that Ifland to her felf, and fo confequently have beggered all the Inhabitants. She muft have a more large Kingdom to wander in, that fhe may the better perform her Atchievements of Lady-Errantry

Errantry Incognita. Brave, Bold *Virago!* Fit to be Queen of the *Amazons*. Had your pregnant wit been well employ'd, so had all pens too in your deserved Eulogies. But it fell out otherways: And at last it was your sad fate to be unmask'd and discover'd by a Keeper, who committed you to one Gaol, from whence by order you were transfer'd to another, there sentenced to dy, and from thence carted to the Gibbet to receive the last and merited reward of your vitious Life and Actions.

The manner of her taking was as followeth.

ONe Mr. *Freeman* a Brewer in *Southwark* being rob'd, and having lost in Goods the value of 200 *l.* or thereabouts, he desired Mr. *Lowman* the Keeper of the *Marshalsea* to make diligent search in all suspicious places

places to the end that he might, if possible, make a discovery of some of the Thieves; which accordingly Mr. *Lowman* did; and at a House near New Spring-Garden in S. *George's* Fields, where he was upon the search for *Lancaster*, who was suspected to be one of the persons that robbed the said *Freeman*, he spied a Gentlewoman walking in one of the Rooms two pair of stairs high in her Night-Gown, with her Mayd waiting upon her (not in the least imagining her to be the *German Princess*) he presently enters the Room, and spies three Letters lying upon the Table, casts his eye upon the Superscription of one of them, which he found directed thus: For her Loving Friend Mr. *Hyde*, who was then a Prisoner in the *Marshalsea*, under his custody. The Gentlewoman being offended with him, told him it was a great piece of rudeness and incivility to look upon her Letters, whereat being somewhat moved,

and

and surveying her face more seriously he remembred her Physiogmony, and then replied as tartly; Mrs. *Carleton*, I will have both you and your Letters away together, and so presently secured her. She was taken in *December* 1672. was examined before a Justice the 17. of that Month upon the Watchmaker's account, and kept a Prisoner there till the 16. of *January* following (where she trifled away her time with as much gayety of spirit and briskness of humour, as if she had been at large and altogether unconcern'd.) And on that very day, that she was brought by Writ of *Habeas Corpus*, to the *Old Bayly*, to her Tryal; As soon as she appeared before the Court; the Judge ask'd her if she were the same Woman that went usually by the name of *Mary Carleton*, and was not long since Transported. To which she made answer, I am the same Person. Then the Court askt her what was the reason of her so suddain

suddain and speedy return. She replied; I have something to discover which troubled my Conscience, nor can I be at rest or quiet till I have disclosed it to a Magistrate of this Kingdom, and this made me presume to transgress the Law of Transportation.

Then the Judge moved her to declare those things to the Court that did so much disturb and discompose her. To this she answered. It is not convenient to unvail my thoughts about this Concern in so publick a Place, and therefore I humbly desire farther time till the next morning, which the Court readily granted.

And that day being the 17. of *January*, she was brought from *Newgate* to the Sessions House in the *Old Bayly* (but they found this Grand Discovery of hers to be a meer pretence, and absolutely fallacious.) And here I must not omit one pleasant passage of hers whilst she was in the Bail-dock, a little

tle before her Tryal. Some Ladies that were then at the Sessions House, who came thither only to satisfie their Curiosity, discours'd the *German* Princess, and among other Expressions, did attack her with these words, or words to this effect. Madam, 'tis very strange that a person guifted with that vivacity of spirit and pregnancy of wit, as you are, should be guilty of such base, beggerly and sordid Shifts to promote your Designs. To whom she made this Repartie. Ladies, your failings consist in *falling*, and mine in *filching*, there's the difference: Yet if you will be so charitable as to forgive me, I will freely forgive you. After this she was called to the Barr, and upon her appearance Arraigned and Indicted for stealing a piece of Plate from a Person in *Chancery-Lane*, and upon hearing of the whole matter of fact, was found guilty by the Jury. She being now in a desperate condition had recourse to her last refuge

fuge (a perfect *Newgate*-Trick) and pleaded her belly: Whereupon a Jury of Women was Impannel'd and sworn, and when they had all taken their Oath, and heard the Instructions of the Court, they went forth to consult in private about this weighty matter; and after an hours Debate, or thereabout, they came again into Court, and brought her in Not quick with Child; so that Sentence of Death was pass'd upon her according to the known and established Laws of the Land in such Cases provided; hereupon she was presently committed to *Newgate* to the end that she might prepare for another World, reconcile her self to an offended Deity, and to confirm and settle her mind as to a future and eternal state.

The

The Deportment and Carriage of Mary Carleton, aliàs *the German Princeß, immediately before and at her Execution, with her laſt Speech at* Tyburn, *being the* 22. *of* January, 167$\frac{2}{3}$. *And her Epitaph.*

THough we have left *Mary Carleton* in Priſon, yet we muſt not leave her ſo, but ſpeedily reviſit her. She is now a confined, condemned perſon, without hope of Reprieve, or poſſibility of Pardon. Now the Scene is changed, ſo muſt our Style be too. Here is no room for Raillery, though never ſo piquant; that gay humour, *non eſt conveniens luctibus,* ſuits not with our ſad condition. Smiles and Jollity are not the Dreſs of Sorrow and Mourning. Our Pen muſt be as grave and ſerious in the

Concluſive,

Conclusive, as it was lusory and wanton in the Precedent Part of this Discourse. And here Reader you are to prepare your self for Tragical Expectations. Entertain your thoughts with nothing but Death, Graves, Tombs and Epitaphs, that you may be a welcome Guest; for now you are entring the House of Mourning; where you may find an infamous and formerly lewd Woman as to her Life and Conversation, embrace Death with more seeming satisfaction and content than could be expected from her frail Sex; and so we leave you to judge whether she died a Penitent, or Presumptuous.

After she was sentenced to dy, she was not with the rest of the condemned persons committed to the Dungeon, but had a private Chamber provided for her, where she was dayly exposed to the view and Discourse of several Visitants.

H *And*

And now I must needs take notice of a conference between the German Princess, and a Gentleman that came with two or three friends to visit her, the Sunday evening before her execution, which for the solidity and rationality of the discourse deserves to be here inserted, and is worth your perusal.

Gent. MAdam, I hope you will not take it ill that we come to visit you upon a more worthy design than to gratifie our curiosity.

Pris. No, Sir, I do not.

Gent. I hope you consider how great a change you are shortly to be exposed to, from a Temporal to an Eternal State of Woe or Bliss; a dreadful state for you that have but one cast for Eternity.

Pris. Sir, I consider I am near death; and were it only to dye, I should not be much troubled: But oh that which follows upon, and is at deaths back, that's the thing. *Gent.*

Gent. Madam, it's to help you about that, that we come.

Pris. *I thank you for your good will; truely I have been of late much discomposed between the hopes of life and the fear of death, and therefore unsetled in respect of my religious concerns, yet I hope I am now setled in the way of Religion.*

Gent. It is a great happiness to be well setled about the way to Happiness; I hope you will look to it that it be upon sure grounds.

Here another of the Gentlemen spake to him that was discoursing her [Sir, I suppose the Gentlewoman is turn'd Roman Catholick] which she did not deny.

Gent. I discourse her as one that owns the Christian Religion, and shall not take notice of Parties, or Sects in this case. And then proceeding, said, Madam, you are a person of a pregnant Wit (however misimploy'd) and therefore cannot but know no
per-

persons in their wits (unless stupified and blinded by the Divel, and their own deceitful hearts) could dye with composedness of mind, so long as they were but in suspence or doubt as to their Eternal State: the Stake being so many millions beyond the hazard of our temporal lives, that it cannot be rationally supposed, any that have the use of reason, are able to indure the least sense of hazard of Salvation without horror at death.

Pris. That's very true.

Gent. Then it's your business now to inquire what rational ground of perswasion you have (that you, who have so grievously provoked God, and see how his wrath already is broken out upon you to the destruction of your outward man) that now God is reconciled to you; or else to consider what is the properest expedient to make peace with him; and also if you have put such means into practice

ctice as the nature of the thing calls for.

Prif. Sir, all this is but reasonable, and I cannot blame this discourse: but truely I have so many diversions, by reason of companies coming in to see me, and some not contented with their coming in, but will pluck up my hood to see my face, that I cannot get things considered of. [And here she fetcht a deep sigh, and said in French, *Oh bon Dieu.*

Gent. All crimes committed against God are capital, according to the dignity of him against whom they are committed: And God is essentially just as well as merciful, which makes the redemption of the soul so precious, that the Gospel it self is so far from admitting of gold, silver, or the bloud of Bulls & Goats, that it will not accept of the Children of a Womans body for the sin of her soul; God will have an infinite satisfaction from the sinner, or his surety: And there is but one Mediator between God and man, that is the Man Chrift Jefus, who only was capable of giving God an infinite fatisfaction.

Prif. But he dyed as he was man.

Gent. True, but yet the blood that came from him is called *the blood of God*, as 'tis faid in the *Acts* ; fo that although his Divine Nature could not fuffer, yet by reafon of its Union with the humane Nature, it became intitled to it: If any therefore fhall go to perfwade you, that the meritorious works you can do, or any Saint or Angel, will be effectual for the expiation of your fins and reconciling you to God, you cannot but in reafon fee it bears no proportion to an infinite fatisfaction.

Prif. Thefe things be true, and I hope all will be well with me as to that.

Gent. The knowledge of this is neceffary: But the bare knowing of it will not fave your foul, no more than it will the Divels, who know all this

this to be true, and yet are never the better.

Prif. *What do you understand will do.*

Gent. Repentance towards God, and Faith towards our Lord Jesus. These are expedients propounded in the Gospel, whereby we are made freely and heartily willing to receive him, as the Father hath tendered him in the Gospel, not only as our Priest to save us from wrath and hell; but also as a King to rule and govern us, our Prophet to teach and instruct us: are you willing to be taught by him? as he himself is the way to Life, so is he able to bring you into it.

Prif. *Oh that I had my days to live over again.* *But*——Here she made a pause, and then proceeded. *But I don't desire it.*

Gent. Madam, the circumstances wherein to God, for your sins hath brought you, will not admit you longer life; and seeing the forsaking of all

all other Lords is not now so obvious in your choice, becauſe thoſe (to wit your luſts) have left you firſt, and are no more in your power to gratifie. Therefore it will be hard to take true meaſures of the purpoſe of your heart, by that of deſiring life to ballance that ; you muſt now judge of the truth of your Repentance and Faith, by what apprehenſions you have of your former *Ignorance*, *Guiltineſs*, *Filthineſs* and *Slavery* to the *Divel* and *Sin*, and ſee how your heart (I mean your mind, your will and affections) are *ſhapen* out to accept of Jeſus Chriſt, as he is propounded for Wiſdom, Righteouſneſs, Sanctification and Redemption. Sure I am, if you are ſincere in this matter, your ſorrow will be very great, and you will have ſuch dreadful apprehenſions of the ſins of your nature and life, that you will ſoon abhor your ſelf; and be ſo wonderfully affected with the condeſcenſion of the great

great God and your Saviour, that those few days and nights you have yet to live, will be breathed out in the contemplation of sins vileness, and Chrifts willingness to appear thus a friend at midnight to you. What a wonder of mercy will it be, if he accept you, now all your other lovers have forsaken you?

Prif. *O those Women that were my Jury could not be certain I was not with child, and yet would not favour me with more time.*

Gent. God is to be reverenced in all his providences, and is to be observed in ordering both Judge and Jury: that was no small evidence of his anger: women are naturally more tender than men. But you see what apprehensions they had of you. The world knows a great deal by you, for you have not injured one but many: But if you don't know more of the plagues of your own heart, than they have declared of your life, it will
be

be a sign you have not yet come to true repentance. [Here the Keeper interrupted, and company thronging in, he desir'd them to forbear any farther discourse.

On *Monday*, being the next day following, *Mary Carleton* was shackled, having fetters put upon both legs, for some reasons best known to those that order'd it, and therefore it does not become me to pry into the cause.

On *Tuesday* night being still expos'd to a croud of Visitants, she appear'd to be the most disconsolate and dejected person that ever eye beheld. Her face was cover'd with her hood, and so shrowded from the sight of the spectators that were present. Her speech languid, and very faint, being broken and interrupted with deep and frequent repeated sighs; the seeming prognosticks and symptoms of remorse and

con-

contrition, which some judged to proceed from the dismal apprehensions of the terrors of approaching death, and the dissatisfaction of her mind as to her condition in the other world, upon the account of her misspent days in this. So overcast and clouded with melancholy and discontent, that she appear'd to be a woman only in effigie. And in this pensive, heavy humour she continued all that Evening, having her Sister, and another person supposed to be a Popish Priest, constantly at her elbow.

On *Wednesday*, which was the 22*th.* of *January*, and the day of her Execution, there was such a strange alteration in her temper, as would exceed the faith of a serious man to believe it. She appear'd very brisk, as if she had not been then to act her last part upon the Stage of this World. She was now found in a more quiet and calm temper of mind than the night before, and more willing to dye
in

in the opinion of those that were present; earnestly desiring and wishing for her expected and deserv'd Dissolution. She voluntarily without any instigation from a second person confest the hainousness of her sins; and being told by one of the company, that she had been very notorious, and that the world had strange apprehensions of her: she replyed, The world cannot say more of me than I deserve; but I hope you are so much a friend to Justice, that you will not believe all vain reports to be true without farther examination: to which the Gentleman made answer, God forbid I should; and withal added, I have heard it discourst that you have had twenty Husbands. Sir, I have been told my self I had fifty; but 'tis all false. He said farther, that it was a sad thing for a person in health to hear his passing-Bell. She replyed, It is not so to me, for I am us'd to it, having heard it once before.

A

A Pardon she did declare neither to expect, nor desire. Death she had merited, and was willing to undergo that hard task, was fully satisfied in all particulars, and fit to drink off that bitter cup. When she heard the Bell at St. *Sepulchre*'s first toll, she us'd these expressions. This is my Passing-bell. Lord Jesus! I am coming to thee. There is no person knows what it is to be under the terrors of the Almighty, but those that feel them. O my Saviour! I am coming. Lord strengthen me! Lord step between me and poor weak nature! O how doth nature cling to me, and is unwilling to leave me! It was a great trouble to me at first to dye; but now I have overcome it, and am satisfied. After this, she suddenly brake out into this passionate exclamation. O if I were to live my life over again! and as suddenly and abruptly interrupted the sequel of her discourse with these words, But I don't don't defire it now. And thereupon defired more than once that her Fetters might be taken off in order to her going to Execution, the expected Recompence of her Inglorious and Infamous Life.

One remarque fhe made of her own accord, acquainting the Company therewith, and told them it was worthy Obfervation, *viz.* This day (being the day of her Death) was the day of my Baptifm. I was born on the 11th. of *January*, and Baptized on the 22th. Pray take notice of it. This very day I was Baptized, and before night I expect to be fprinkled with the blood of the Lamb, which will be a fecond Baptifm. Her Sifter was conftantly with her before her Execution, and another Relation of hers came in that Morning who was a Kinfman, to whom fhe committed the care of her decent Burial, and the defraying of all Charges in fuch Cafes required, and delivered them mony

for

for that purpose. But the one bursting into tears, and the other lamenting her sad and deplorable condition; She desired them to rest satisfied and content, as she her self did, intreating them to abstain from mourning in her sight, saying, the tears of her Relations did but increase her grief and aggravate her affliction; and therefore beg'd of her Sister to forbear.

All this while I should have acquainted you that there were two persons with her judg'd by the Spectators to be *Romish* Priests; one of them did often approach her like *Mahomet*'s Pigeon still prompting her in the ear, or as if they had been at Auricular Confession, and after that such kind of Actions had often pass'd between them, she at last lifted up her hands on high crossing her self in the Elevation, & then the supposed Priest made a very low obeisance to her, and so took his leave of her and departed.

parted. The other made up to her & accosted her with great reverence & gravity, presenting her with a Guinny, as it was very probably conjectured by the Standers by, and afterwards saluted her, and so withdrew to one side of the room, making way for other friends that came in to speak with her, and take their last farewel; where he stood in a leaning posture, with all the visible marks of a dejected person that was disconsolate and crest-faln; and after he had there ruminated some time, the persons that did interpose before, quitted; and the passage being open between the *German* Princess and the Gentleman; She chanced to cast her eye upon him again; whereat she bowed to him, and said in *French*, *Mon ami le bon Dieu vous benisse*, and so after they had mutually resaluted one another at a distance, he without any farther Discourse or Ceremony took his leave.

After this the Master of the Prison ordered

ordered her Irons to be taken off, she having twice or thrice requested it before; which being now done, she took out of her pocket Mr. *Carleton*'s Picture; and said to her Sister and Kinsman then present; This Picture hath been my Companion in all my Afflictions and Miseries, and I earnestly beg of you that it may be buried with me; and so she delivered it to them.

Then the Company was desired to avoid the room, which accordingly they did; she being left with her Sister to change her Apparel, as it was thought, and in a short time she came down stairs in order to her going into the great Hall on the Common-side to have the Halter tied about her, before she went into the Cart. But before she went up into the place appointed for that purpose; A Gentleman told her that it would be a great satisfaction to the World to understand of what Religion she was,

and

and she returned him this answer, I am a *Roman Catholick*. So without any farther delay she was conveyed by one of the Under-Keepers into the upper Hall in *Newgate*, and was the first that was Halter'd of the six that were executed; there being five young men besides who all suffered with her at *Tyburn*; where it was observed that those 5 could not among them all complete the number of 120 years, and that they had all a spice of her humour, being so unconcerned as they were. For she her self as to outward appearance, was so unaltered, that during all this time not one drop did distil from her eyes, nor did she bedew her cheek with a single Tear. But what was the reason of that, I leave the World to judge.

And here though I told you before that she had delivered her Husband's Picture to her Relations to be disposed of as is formerly mentioned; she it seems had changed her mind, and

and for some reasons best known to her self, had pinned it on her left side, and wore it so to *Tyburn*. Whether she thought this would be an Argument of her Conjugal Love, or that it would redound to the honour of her pretendedly beloved Spouse, or prove a credit to her self, I will not here dispute. She had also in her hands two Popish Books, the one Entituled the *Key of Paradise*, and the other the *Manual of Dayly Devotion*; and when she came to the Gallows she delivered them both to a Friend in the Cart, who pocketted them up (no doubt) as a Sacred Relique, being the last Guift of a departing Friend.

When she came to *Tyburn* she was soon tied up, and was observed to take the Picture from her Side and put it into her Bosome. Then came the Subordinary into the Cart, and asked them all in general, whether they had any thing to say before they

they departed this World; which words he repeated twice, and receiving no anfwer from any of them, he betook himfelf to his Devotion, and prayed with them a confiderable time, and having finifhed his Oraifons, another Perfon ftept up and beg'd leave to lift up his heart in Prayer with them likewife, which being granted, he accordingly proceeded: and immediately after his conclufion, *Mary Carleton* defired to know whether fhe might have liberty to fpeak to the People? And it was anfwered, Mrs. your Voice is low and the noife, of the People great, fo that you cannot well be heard by the multitude here prefent; but if you pleafe to acquaint me with your defire, I will difcourfe it to them afterwards. Then fhe began a fhort Speech in thefe enfuing words.

You

You will make me a President for Sin. I confess I have been a vain Woman. I have had in the World the Heighth of Glory, and Misery in abundance, and let all people beware of ill Company. The World hath condemned me, and I have much to answer. Pray God forgive me and my Husband likewise. I beseech God lay nothing to his charge for my fault.

Thereupon a Person that was there present proposed this Question to her; Have you any thing to your Husband? to which she return'd this Answer, Only my Recommendations, and that he would serve God and repent: for I fear he wants sober Admonition; and I beseech God lay
nothing

nothing to his charge upon my account. Upon which a Person interposed and said, Then so in perfect Charity you dy with all the World? And she replied very seriously, Yes, I do. And so with many pious Ejaculations, such as, *Lord Jesus receive my Soul! Lord have mercy upon me! Christ have mercy upon me!* frequently reiterated and repeated, she departed this Life.

About an hour after she was hanged, or thereabouts, she was cut down and by her Friends conveyed in a Coach to her Coffin, which waited for her at a place appointed, they having paid all due Fees for her Body and Clothes, and from thence she was carried to St. —— and there buried in the Church-Yard. Thus *Exit German* Princess, in the 38th year of her age, and the same Moneth she was born in.

Now the Play is done, we'l make an end too, in the same humour as we began;

began; only we are firſt bound in Civility to draw the Curtain, bid her good night, and ſo leave her to her repoſe; cloſing all with her ſad *Epicedium* in the mournful accent of the Poet,

Per varios caſus, per tot diſcrimina rerum,
Tenditur in Furcam ———

Thus we have attended her from her Cradle to her Coffin, diſcovered and diverted our ſelves with the Adventures of her Life and the Circumſtances at her Death, followed her from the Cart to the Church-Yard, and performed her laſt Funeral Rites and Obſequies. And now there is but one thing wanting to complete our intended Deſign, and 'tis pitty a Perſon of her Titular Dignity and Quality ſhould be deprived of ſo modiſh an Ornament, *viz.* an Epitaph; which may fore-
warn

warn all Paſſengers from trampling upon or rudely diſturbing the Aſhes of a Deceaſed Princeſs.

THE

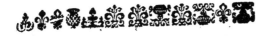

THE
EPITAPH
Of the supposed
German Princess.

Here lies one much against her will,
 Who did lye living; and dead, lies
But to be plain I'l tell you, that (still.
It is I know not whom, nor what.
She has more names, says the Relater,
Than Goldman, or a Nomenclator,
She's icleap't Moders, Stedman, nay,
Carleton, and Moll et cætera.
A long hard name indeed, 'tmay be
Compar'd to a Welch Pedigree,
And us'd to scare Babes that do harm,
Or serve Agrippa for a Charm.
She is a false Religionist,
A Lutheran, a Calvinist,
And neither; (this is strange tho' true)
What a Di'el is she then? Guess you.

K Her

Her Birth-place, like a baggage sullen,
She'd ne'er tell; but 'twas Kent or Colen:
Survey her strictly, and you'l swear,
She is all over motley-ware.
Subject and Princess too, no less;
She's th' Anglo-German Gusmaness.
And tho' now coffin'd up in Chest,
Ne'er think that she'l there tamely rest.
Assure your self alive, or dead,
She can't keep constant to her bed.
Therefore look to't, lest out she steal,
And cheat the worms of a set meal.

FINIS.

THere is published this Term, The *Mercury-Gallant*, containing many true and pleasant Transactions of the Court of *Paris*, and of the Camp, this last year of 1672. newly Translated out of French. In *octavo*: price bound 1 *s.* 6 *d.*